Islam in the Political Process

Islam in
the Political Process

EDITED BY

JAMES P. PISCATORI

Published in association with
The Royal Institute of International Affairs

Cambridge University Press

CAMBRIDGE

LONDON   NEW YORK   NEW ROCHELLE

MELBOURNE   SYDNEY

Published by the Press Syndicate of the University of Cambridge
The Pitt Building, Trumpington Street, Cambridge CB2 1RP
32 East 57th Street, New York, NY 10022, USA
296 Beaconsfield Parade, Middle Park, Melbourne 3206, Australia

First published 1983

Printed in Great Britain at the University Press, Cambridge

Library of Congress catalogue card number: 82–9745

British Library Cataloguing in Publication Data
Islam in the political process.
  1. Islam and politics
  I. Piscatori, James P.
  297'.1977   BP173.7
    ISBN 0 521 24941 4 hard covers
    ISBN 0 521 27434 6 paperback

Contents

Contents

Contributors

FOUAD AJAMI, *School of Advanced International Studies, The Johns Hopkins University*

DONAL B. CRUISE O'BRIEN, *School of Oriental and African Studies, University of London*

ALEXANDER S. CUDSI, *Hellenic Mediterranean Centre for Arabic and Islamic Studies, Athens*

HAMID ENAYAT, *late of St Antony's College, University of Oxford*

ALBERT HOURANI, *St Antony's College, University of Oxford*

MICHAEL C. HUDSON, *Center for Contemporary Arab Studies, Georgetown University*

ŞERIF MARDIN, *Faculty of Administrative Sciences, Bogaziçi University*

RUTH McVEY, *School of Oriental and African Studies, University of London*

JAMES P. PISCATORI, *The Royal Institute of International Affairs, London*

DAVID TAYLOR, *School of Oriental and African Studies, University of London*

JEAN-CLAUDE VATIN, *Centre de Recherches et d'Etudes sur les Sociétés Méditerranéennes, Aix-en-Provence*

Preface

This book is the result of a conference held by the Royal Institute of International Affairs at Chatham House and is funded by the Ford Foundation. The Institute and its Research Committee are grateful for the comments and suggestions made by C. F. Beckingham and Edward Mortimer, who were asked to review the manuscript of this book. From conference to book, several people have been of great help to me as editor: Albert Hourani gave generous and prudent advice; Adeed Dawisha provided encouragement; Elizabeth Watson brought common sense and efficiency to the organization and typing; and Pauline Wickham improved the manuscript with her shrewd and careful editing. I am grateful to them for making my job easier.

Finding a consistent and comprehensible system of transliterating Arabic words was a problem, however. I have decided to indicate the 'ayn (') and the medial hamza ('), but to omit the hamza when it occurs at the beginning or end of a word and to delete all diacriticals. In the case of Arabs mentioned in the text who themselves have written in European languages, I have tried to use their own spelling of their names. I have followed the standard English spelling for most place names, except when the French spelling is more common.

J.P.P.

September 1982

1 Introduction

JAMES P. PISCATORI

This book is an attempt to analyse the roles that Islam plays in the political process of several countries. It is a topic that has gained a great deal of attention in the media, particularly since 1979, when the revolutionary government in Iran was established, Afghanistan invaded, and Sa'udi Arabia's Great Mosque seized. The assassination of President Sadat in 1981 and the fighting in Syria in 1982 have heightened the interest and have probably confirmed the stereotype of 'militant Islam'. The picture that seems to come naturally to mind is of noisy Muslims, moved by righteous indignation, seeking to overthrow impious governments. Islam seems to have become the centre of political opposition, and its adherents, somewhat unexpectedly, real contenders for power. Like V. S. Naipaul, most outsiders have been fascinated, and not a little frightened, by this 'rage about the faith' and its apparent interchangeability with 'political rage'.[1]

Although Naipaul argues that the turbulence is a feature of the late twentieth century, the image that he and others present of the rifle-toting *mulla* evokes the old vision of the scimitar-wielding Muhammadan. Such accounts play on a strong, even if unformulated, set of notions that Westerners have of Muslims becoming politically active out of an excess of zeal rather than with clearly defined goals. 'Islam' conjures up ideas of fanatical opposition and aimless revolution, of anti-Westernism and anti-modernism. The political calculations of Muslims are of course infinitely more complex.

Yet to date there have been only a few empirical studies that try to go beyond the impressionistic and general, and take the measure of Islam's current political activity. One work puts special emphasis on the ability of Islam to keep pace with, and sometimes to facilitate, social change; another considers the impact of the 'revival' throughout the Islamic world; and a third examines the nature of the revival among one section of the believers, the Arabs.[2] This book covers much the same ground, but focuses on the broad question, how is Islam politically significant?

In attempting to answer the question, we have restricted ourselves to a few countries, and have had to leave out many interesting examples; there is no claim to comprehensiveness. Furthermore, in order to emphasize domestic politics, we have given little attention to international issues. Finally, there is no single model of explanation or even a standard terminology; the contributors have brought their own approaches and styles to their studies. For example, some authors refer to 'traditionalism', while others prefer to speak of 'fundamentalism' or 'conservatism', but we believe that the meanings are clear from the context. In general, we hope that the presence of alternative ways of looking at the subject will have its advantages when dealing with so fascinating a chameleon as political Islam.

The study of Islamic politics

There is no doubt that Islamic politics is an elusive and contentious subject to study. The usual starting-point of discussion is the unique inseparability of sacred and secular, of religion and politics. The reality is somewhat different: throughout Islamic history temporal authorities have wielded a weightier sword than that of the spiritual authorities; moreover, an examination of European history confirms that the lively interjection of religion into politics and of politics into religion is not an exclusively Islamic phenomenon. Nevertheless, the comprehensiveness and self-sufficiency that Islam proclaims for itself do set it apart, at least from Christianity, which encourages a distinction not only in theory but in practice between God's and Caesar's due. Unlike Christians, who are pilgrims *en route* to the true world, Muslims do not have the luxury of presuming that the validity of their beliefs lies beyond practical – and political – demonstration.

Yet, the Muslims' belief that their faith fully covers life here and now, gives rise to sharply different views as to Islam's exact political relevance. The Iranian revolution has given new life, ironically, to two such competing views. Some observers speak with renewed respect of Islam as the guiding force of the revolution, as if it were somehow above the fray and giving concrete direction to political and cultural liberation.[3] Others see in the dominance of the *mullas* further evidence that religious obscurantism is the servant of political and cultural tyranny.[4]

Rather than two general approaches to Islamic politics, there are of course several, and a brief survey of some of them, and of their variations, will help to explain the assumptions that underpin them. Although the categories that follow imply a greater degree of similarity of thinking than in fact exists among the many contemporary observers of Islam, I believe that they are suggestive of the different and distinctive ways that both Muslims and non-Muslims view Islamic politics. In discussing these categories, I shall focus, first, on how Islam is viewed; second, on how politics is viewed; and, third, on how the future is viewed.

A conservative Muslim approach make politics religious.

A common approach among Muslims themselves stresses the imperative of returning to an unadulterated version of Islam in order to overcome the debased politics of our age. Typically, they lament the fact that the world has become degenerate, with men enslaved by dictatorship, technology, and sex, and with nations subservient to alien ideologies and the superpowers. Rather than protecting the life, property, and dignity of their citizens, political rulers have become 'corrupters of the earth', stealing the issue of honest labour and holding on to power by deceit and force. These oppressors will stop at nothing, even manipulating popular religious sentiment to cloak their motives and legitimate their authority.

The typical remedy is to educate people that their freedom lies in religion: the 'liberation from their tyranny lies in the attribution of all authority to God'.[5] They must understand also that Islam is the best religion; it is their immanent as well as transcendent salvation because it is a practical religion, offering guidance in political, social, economic, and international affairs. Within this comprehensiveness politics is merely one, relatively indistinct, part; politics will find its proper place when the whole of Islam is free, and this will occur only with faith and sacrifices. If Muslims today recapture the zeal of the early believers, they will, in some vague but predestined way, unshackle Islam and allow it, according to its own logic, to transform their politics as well as other dimensions of their lives.

Those who argue along these lines share basic assumptions about Islam, politics, and the future. First, they assume that Islam is best thought of in civilizational terms, and as a mystical whole which somehow maintains its integrity. This preference for dealing at the broadest level accounts for their seeing the West as a grand – and hostile

3

— – monolith. Second, because they stress the unity of *din* (religion) and
— *dawla* (state), they assume that it is futile to try to identify the boundaries
— of politics. Third, they are not concerned with the details of the future
– that is, how the regeneration of politics is to be tied to the regeneration of Islam. These both are to take place, simply, with a leap of faith.
A widespread Muslim opinion, therefore, is that politics needs, above all,
to be 'spiritualized'.

Other Muslim approaches *make religion more political!*

There are others, however, Muslim and non-Muslim, who have given
considerable thought to the subject and do not hold this conservative
view. If in the first approach there is an imperative to make politics
more religious, in the specific sense of Islamic, there is another approach
which calls for religion to become more political. It centres on the
urgency of tailoring religious doctrine to radical, usually leftist, political
ends, and takes as its point of departure the debilitating effects that
staid and institutionalized religion can have. It argues, for example, that
theologians subtly indoctrinate us with a conservative political message:
that God in His omnipotence is above us and remote, little concerned
with the injustices and inequalities that afflict most of mankind. By thus
focusing on His transcendence, His celestial passivity, these theologians
give aid and comfort to members of the feudal and aristocratic class,
who are happy to have the rest of us think of passivity as part of the
natural order of things. It becomes urgent for Muslims, then, to turn
religion into an ideology that emphasizes the immanent over the trans-
cendental, and the linear over the hierarchical: 'God becomes history,
religion and ideology, revelation an analysis of the real, the cult a
revolutionary act.'[6] Theology and religion generally need to provide the
'inner logic' – not of capitalism, as in the past,[7] but of revolutionary
socialism.

We can compare the assumptions of this approach with those of the
others. First, Islam is here seen as an ideology, a righteous programme
of principle and activity, which can galvanize Muslims by the passion
→ of its commitment to social justice and the clarity of its challenge to
→ the *status quo*. Second, politics is not merely an indiscriminate part of
Islam but, in many ways, its *raison d'être*. Indeed, Islam needs to be
judged by whether political rulers use it as the opiate of the people,
or whether the masses invoke it as 'the cry of the oppressed'. Third,
with regard to the future, reassertion or even reinterpretation of faith
is not enough, though each is necessary. Particularly in its current form

of fundamentalism, Islam needs to be more than 'pure messianism': the 'Muslim masses are waiting for radical change' in their economic, social, and civic lives, and Islamic groups must meet the people's expectations and lead the revolution.[8] In short, this view holds that Islam must be politicized.

Another general way of looking at Islamic politics differs from the preceding approaches by stressing the necessity, or at least the desirability, of minimizing the intrusion of religion in political life. In the last three decades, adherents of this approach have multiplied, although their precise arguments do not always coincide.

One variation, Marxist in inspiration, views religion *per se* in public life as debilitating, and thus believes Islam's elimination is essential and inevitable. It argues that groups like the Muslim Brotherhood are now resurgent because the contradictions of feudal and comprador economies force petty-bourgeois nationalists to sell out to the imperialists and so cause a backlash, particularly among the urban proletariat and students. But this cannot last, and it is certain that a future of 'materialism and nationalism' will replace that of 'idealism and metaphysics'. The historical destiny is clearly exhilarating: 'Islam itself will be forced to cede its place.'[9]

Others support the idea of separating religion from politics, but differ in two ways. Instead of referring to the harmful qualities of religion generally, they point to the peculiarly unhelpful qualities of Islam itself. Also, rather than speaking of the imperative, or even the inevitability, of separation, they prefer to speak of its desirability or prudence.

Some, for example, find in Arab politics an unholy alliance between reactionary political forces and reactionary religious authorities. It was not always so, but the original vigour of Islam dissipated as folk Islam grew more popular. This Islam makes the unity of religion and state dangerous because it allows the *'ulama*, or religious authorities, to become a hereditary class claiming a monopoly of knowledge and of income from the pious endowments (*waqfs*). Moreover, the values they preach, such as submission to Allah and predestination, only compound the peasant's sense of fatalism and make his domination all the easier. The conclusion is clear that it would not be such a bad development if 'the tie between religion and state' were to become undone.[10]

Despite the variations, the proponents of separation share several assumptions. First, they do not think of Islam as a civilization or an ideology, as in the other two approaches, but as a problem that is intractable and needs to be overcome. Second, they see politics as the main sphere of activity, in which everything important is decided; in this regard, there is a similarity with those who want to politicize Islam. Third, whereas the 'politicizers' advocate a future that is religious in a revitalized way, this group of 'separaters' differs from them, and from the more conservative writers, in that they see the modern age as essentially secular and therefore prescribe a separation of religion and politics.

Social scientific approaches

Social scientists also have a variety of ways of looking at Islamic politics. Because very few are Muslims themselves, they generally assume, sometimes almost automatically, that the separation of Islam and politics is desirable. Many, in fact, would subscribe to the views of the last group considered: that Islam is stagnant or rigid and, in any case, a problem; that politics is the main centre of activity; and that a future of modernization hinges on the creation of a secular order.[11] But others perceive the subject differently.

One group, for example, thinks of politics in developing countries as influenced more by family, ethnic, and bazaar identifications than by bureaucratic policy and institution-building. In contrast with the West, the formal sources of authority in these countries are rarely the only effective sources of loyalty and power. In countries with large numbers of Muslims, moreover, Islamic authorities and traditions often have an importance disproportionate to their officially recognized social role; they are often political in an informal sense. Some argue that this has been the case in Iran. Although there were constant rivalries and balances of power in the clergy's ranks which the government was able to exploit, all the while that the *'ulama* were ceding place to the government they were retaining the loyalty of the people. Khumayni's success, then, lay in the viability of a religious opposition whose power the best designs of the Shah failed to circumscribe: 'It seems to be the informality of the structure of clergy relations with the masses and the state that provides the context for [the *'ulama*'s] regained autonomy.'[12]

By way of contrast, others suggest that the informality of Islamic politics might not be so much of an advantage. The argument here is that politics in Islamic countries lags in institutional development because Islam lacks an organized priesthood. This has had two consequences. One is that there was no need in Islamic history for a Reformation. Because there was no movement to root out abuses in the power of the clergy, the kind of organizational skills that would have developed did not appear in Islam. The second consequence is that the *'ulama* were never established sufficiently to wield real power and, fearing to display their impotence, they simply acquiesced in the *status quo*: 'They lacked the ideology and organization characteristic of Puritans in the West.'[13] The combined heritage for modern Muslims is a political culture that feels no need for 'practical ideology' to legitimate particular political policies or organizational strategies. In countries like Egypt, therefore, where there have been no real corporate institutions to mediate between the state and its citizens, it is 'natural' by default for politics to be authoritarian.[14]

Despite their differences, these students of informal politics generally agree on how they view Islam, politics, and the future. First, they look upon Islam as simply 'there', a fact of life which they must take into account. The normative tendencies evident in the other approaches are absent. Also, the Islam they see has some vitality of its own, but is checked by the environment in which it operates; it is only partly independent. Second, because of their concern to trace the interaction of formal and informal factors, they give to their politics a greater analytical attention than is the case in the other approaches. Politics is something complex to be observed; it is not automatically subsumed under Islam, or regarded as a field of action for it or even as the main arena of activity. Third, they see the future as an extension of the past. Short of revolution, the Islamic network will neither direct political change nor retreat as secularism advances; it will persist in its characteristically nebulous way to influence how the people react to the formal sources of power.

There are still other writers who emphasize what some imply – that Islam is important for its utility in a complicated political environment. These writers are intent on gauging how instrumental Islam is, and they conclude that it generally has an indirect connection to political action. We can compare their assumptions with those of the preceding writers.

First, Islam in this view is seen as an ideology, a set of beliefs that may influence behaviour but that provides little opportunity for independent action. It is, rather, a 'dependent variable', the manoeuvrability of which is subject to the political context – a different view from that of the 'politicizers'. Second, more like the informal politics approach, this utilitarian approach holds that politics is a rich network of social relationships based on age, family lineage, official position, and knowledge; yet here these are thought of as the moulders of politics itself. As one writer observed of Indonesian politics between 1948 and 1962, 'Traditional loyalty bonds structure politics, and the modern political process is merely an ephemeral organism that adapts itself to the traditional social mechanisms of Sundanese political culture.'[15] If Islam is a dependent variable of sorts, then so too is politics. Third, regarding the future, it is likely that, with the progress of modernization, the content and configuration of social forces will change. When this occurs, there will also be changes in who holds power and how they exercise it, and it is only in the context of these interrelated changes that we can evaluate the specific political importance of Islam.

The difficulties of studying Islamic politics

As we can readily see, there are disconcerting differences of approach among contemporary writers of Islam as to how to view Islam, politics, and the future. First, in viewing Islam itself, many Muslims refer to Islam in broad and convenient terms: that is, as a civilization. The writers who want to make politics dependent on Islam do this the most frequently, but I think this leads to a serious problem. Dealing with Islam at this level seems to invite a preoccupying comparison with the West and to distort both civilizations by pitting 'us' against 'them'. It probably also obscures the dissimilarities among Muslims and, by concentrating on a cultural whole, it makes short work of underlying economic and social realities.[16]

Perhaps those who think in cultural terms fall most easily into this trap, but we are all guilty at times of speaking of Islam as if it means the same to everybody. Jacques Waardenburg, in a review of Muslim views of world religion, warns us against assuming too much: 'Our sources allow us to say only what Muslims thought other religions and their own religion to be, not what Islam itself and Islam's views of other religions are.'[17] To be so precise, however, is easier said than done, and it is certain that everybody will continue to use 'Islam' as a shorthand expression. The task is to avoid generalization, and thus the important thing is always to ask: whose Islam? and when?[18]

Historians and literary experts are rather better at answering these questions than political scientists, but we too can avoid the dangers of simplification if we focus on the specifics of Islam as an historical phenomenon, as the record of how divine commandment translates into practice in specific nation-states. Islam, then, becomes a 'given'; it is facts to be observed in their particular contexts, much as the writers on informal politics and on utilitarian politics presume. Still, the raw material will be distorted if the observer ignores the spirit that suffuses it, and makes 'Islam observed' simply an historical, human construct. That Islam is also 'the inner aspiration of [the Muslim] heart'[19] sometimes accounts for the vibrancy and the course of its historical behaviour, and suggests that the social scientist should be wary of concluding that it is inevitably a dependent variable.

Second, in viewing politics, several writers do in fact think of Islam as dependent. But I believe that trying to decide which is dependent or independent is often futile, and that it is more helpful to think of something called Islamic politics. Because it is a specific variety of politics generally, it involves contention over the uses and ends of power, with social and economic factors, such as the strength of the middle classes, the rate of urbanization, and the distribution of income, directly affecting the configuration of power.

But Islamic politics is distinctive as well. If Muslims practise the politics of informality in common with other inhabitants of the Third World, they also engage in ritualized politics in which men of religious learning and scriptural ideas have influence. There is no doubt that the rituals often seem incongruous and the symbols murky, as the curiosities of non-usurious banking and Islamic Marxism testify. But Muslims have neither completely abandoned old ideas nor uncritically adopted new ones, and it is this durable framework which gives Islamic politics its colouring. In addition, precisely because they hold some values in common, Muslims find in Islam a particularly potent instrument for their designs. They invoke 'Islam' to advance their causes, and in using it they generate not only lively debate on its nature but charges and counter-charges that political competitors subject it to base political expediency. The reality is that everybody finds a use for it.

Moreover, even though certain values are held in common and probably because Islam is so important as a political instrument, Muslims within one state and from state to state continue to disagree on the ends and uses of power. They disagree because of the different historical and cultural conditions they encounter and because of their different social and economic positions. The political process within one society is complex enough; given that to a large extent Islam has been nationalized and differs from country to country, that complexity is infinitely magnified. Adherents of the Muslim Brotherhood in Syria differ from their counterparts in Egypt, and both view politics differently from the members of the Nahdatul Ulama in Indonesia. The title of this book is thus another of those convenient shorthands.

Edward Said raises the question, 'Is there such a thing as Islamic behaviour?'[20] The answer, in so far as it concerns Islamic political behaviour, is both yes and no. There is no reason why Muslims cannot act politically like anyone else or join non-Islamic political movements. But there are times when 'Islam', because of its high symbolic content and emotional appeal, rouses Muslims into political activity. Nevertheless, there is nothing preordained about that way of acting, and the exact shape such action will take depends on the broader politics of the country under study. It is important, if one succeeds in identifying an Islamic political component in a society, not to generalize. After all, to paraphrase Said, how really useful is 'Islamic politics' as a concept for understanding Algeria *and* Sa'udi Arabia *and* Syria *and* Indonesia? The answer is that however much it might help in the understanding of individual countries, when talking of the Islamic world generally, it will probably lead to crude stereotypes of the kind that this book seeks to avoid. 'Islamic politics' generally, therefore, cannot be said to be revolutionary or anti-Western, although there may be specific instances when these descriptions apply.

Third, in viewing the future, writers on Islam disagree vigorously. It seems to me that the only safe response to 'What does the future hold?' is, once again, 'It depends,' for almost everyone (except the most conservative devout) thinks the days ahead are uncertain. The assumption of some writers, however, that secularism is inevitable, or at least prudent, should be questioned. The activity of *da'wa*, or missionary, organizations in most parts of the Third World and elsewhere indicates that Islam's appeal is not diminishing in the modern age; and the way in which many modernizing reforms are legitimated by reference to Islam shows that its content has not ossified.

Part of the trouble with assumptions to the contrary is that they give undue weight to one section of Muslim opinion – those who argue that the only desirable change is to re-create the long-gone Prophetic community and who pretend that no legislative innovations are possible in Islamic law. Muslim opinion is, of course, richer and more flexible than this: it incorporates many formerly alien ideas that came in with the Western invaders. Islamic politics, like Islam itself, is both adaptable and tough; its viability in any given area rests finally on the possibilities that the national context affords, but its vitality is undeniable. This book seeks to document instances of that vitality.

Notes

1. V. S. Naipaul, *Among the Believers: An Islamic Journey* (London, Deutsch, 1981), p. 360.
2. John L. Esposito (ed.), *Islam and Development: Religion and Sociopolitical Change* (Syracuse, Syracuse University Press, 1980); Mohammed Ayoob (ed.), *The Politics of Islamic Reassertion* (London, Croom Helm, 1981); and Ali E. Hillal Dessouki (ed.), *Islamic Resurgence in the Arab World* (New York, Praeger, 1982).
3. See Hamid Algar's lectures delivered to the Muslim Institute in London: Kalim

Siddiqui (ed.), *The Islamic Revolution in Iran* (London, Open Press, 1980), esp. pp. 62–3.

4. See Mangol Bayat, 'Islam in Pahlavi and Post-Pahlavi Iran: A Cultural Revolution', in Esposito (ed.), *Islam and Development*, esp. pp. 104–6.

5. Muhammad Qutb, *Shubahat hawl al-islam* (Baghdad, Maktabat al-Mathna, 5th edn, 1962), p. 16. For similar arguments, see Sa'id Ramadan, *al-Mushkilat al-kubra al-thalath fi 'alamna al-islami al-mu'asir*, No. 1 (Geneva, Islamic Centre, n.d.); and his *Qu'est-ce qu'un Etat Islamique?*, No. 4 (Geneva, Islamic Centre, September 1961).

6. Hassan Hanafi, 'Théologie ou Anthropologie?' in A. Abdel-Malek, A. A. Balal, and H. Hanafi, *Renaissance du monde Arabe* (Gembloux, Duculot, 1972), p. 261.

7. Hassan Hanafi, 'al-Din wa'l-ra'samaliyya', *al-Kitab*, 9 (December 1969), 116.

8. Hassan Hanafi, 'Origin of Modern Conservatism and Islamic Fundamentalism', unpublished paper prepared for the Conference on Religion and Religious Movements in the Mediterranean Area, Amsterdam, 18–20 Dec. 1979, pp. 6, 16, 18. The Iranian writer 'Ali Shari'ati is another, though less cogent, advocate of politicizing Islam. See Hamid Algar's translation of some of his lectures: *On the Sociology of Islam* (Berkeley, Mizan Press, 1979).

9. Sadok Mahdi, 'Le Mouvement des Frères Musulmans en Tunisie', *Oriente Moderno*, 59 (1979), 706. For a variation of the criticism of religion generally, see Nadim al-Baytar's 'al-Takhalluf al-siyasi wa ib'adahu al-hadariyya', *Dirasat 'arabiyya*, 10 (July 1974), 26–45; and his 'Ba'd al-asbab al-ba'ida li-zahira al-takhalluf al-siyasi al-'arabi', *Dirasat 'arabiyya*, 10 (August 1974), 31–41.

10. Shakir Mustafa, 'al-Ib'ad al-tarikhiyya: azma li-tatawwur al-hadari al-'arabi', *al-Adab*, 22 (May 1974), 19. Mustafa says that he does not intend to criticize that tie, but the critical implication is manifest.

11. See, for example, Manfred Halpern, *The Politics of Social Change in the Middle East and North Africa* (Princeton, Princeton University Press, 1963), *passim*; and Morroe Berger, 'Economic and Social Change', in P. M. Holt, Ann K. S. Lambton, and Bernard Lewis (eds.), *The Cambridge History of Islam*, vol. 1 (Cambridge, Cambridge University Press, 1970), pp. 698–730.

12. Shahrough Akhavi, *Religion and Politics in Contemporary Iran* (Albany, State University of New York Press, 1980), p. xv.

13. Clement Henry Moore, 'On Theory and Practice Among Arabs', *World Politics*, 24 (1971), 114.

14. Clement Henry Moore, 'Authoritarian Politics in Unincorporated Society: The Case of Nasser's Egypt', *Comparative Politics*, 6 (1974), 216.

15. Karl D. Jackson, *Traditional Authority, Islam and Rebellion; A Study of Indonesian Political Behavior* (Berkeley, University of California Press, 1980), p. 276. For a critical evaluation of Jackson's study, see Ruth McVey, 'Islam Explained', *Pacific Affairs*, 54 (1981), 260–77.

16. See Roger Owen, 'Studying Islamic History', *Journal of Interdisciplinary History*, 4 (1973), 287–98.

17. Jacques Waardenburg, 'World Religions as Seen in Light of Islam', in Alfred T. Welch and Peter Cachia (eds.), *Islam: Past Influence and Present Challenge* (Edinburgh, Edinburgh University Press, 1979), p. 268.

18. Edward W. Said, 'Whose Islam?' *The New York Times*, 29 January 1979.

19. Wilfred Cantwell Smith, 'The Historical Development in Islam of the Concept of Islam as an Historical Development', in Bernard Lewis and P. M. Holt (eds.), *Historians of the Middle East* (London, Oxford University Press, 1962), p. 497. Note Albert Hourani's warning that we must not carry Smith's argument too far: *ibid.*, p. 455.

20. Edward W. Said, *Covering Islam* (London, Routledge & Kegan Paul, 1981), p. xv.

2   In the Pharaoh's Shadow: Religion and Authority in Egypt

FOUAD AJAMI

There is a scene in one of the historical novels of Egypt's celebrated writer Najib Mahfuz in which the pharaoh is told by his lovely mistress Radubis of rumours of pending rebellions, of popular disaffection. 'And they say that the priests are a powerful group with control over the hearts and minds of the people.' But he smiles and answers: 'But I am the stronger.' 'And the anger of the people, my lord?' 'It will calm down when they see me on my chariot.'[1]

Since then, Egypt's 'priests' have changed: they belong to a different religion; the chariot has been 'modernized'. But the primacy of the ruler remains, and so does the subjugation of the priests. Durable also is the dimension of politics as theatre: the ruler goes out there, and sufficient numbers of people are either taken in by the act or cowed by the might at his disposal.

I do not wish to argue for the persistence of all things. Mine is not another restatement of the 'hydraulic society' hypothesis, according to which life, as the caricature of Karl Wittfogel would have it, is 'total terror, total submission, total loneliness'.[2] For in the scheme of things, in comparison with the terror of other societies, rule in Egypt is mild indeed. Submission is common, but men still take the state and its president to court; lawyers, journalists, and engineers try to protect the autonomy and integrity of their professions against the encroachment of the state. Men do not 'disappear' as they do in Argentina; they are not executed or 'liquidated' as they are in Iraq and Syria. In its own way, Egypt continues to resist the tyranny of the state. Loneliness is not a word one would use to describe a society as crowded, as 'chatty' as Egypt.

But, admittedly, there is in this inquiry scepticism about religion as a revolutionary force in Egypt. Iran treated the world to the fury of religion; Egypt is another case. There, as shall be argued, either religion is emasculated by the state, or it turns (in the language of E. J. Hobsbawm) into primitive rebellion.[3] The first situation buttresses the power of the state and fortifies its banalities by giving them religious sanction; the second burns out as fury and wrath. In a curious way, the second, too, serves as a pillar of political power, not so much because it collaborates with the state (though there are rumours and evidence of the Muslim Brotherhood's collaboration with the dominant political order), as because it allows the state to hold up before the society an image of the chaos that would threaten everyone if the state were to falter. Authority is vindicated because the alternative is depicted to be a reign of 'virtue and terror' that has few, if any, takers.

An inquiry into religion in Egypt is really, and has to be, an inquiry into the nature of authority in that country. It is with religion that I begin. But my ultimate destination – and the thread running through the analysis – is authority in the Egyptian political culture. If there is a sense that religion cannot do much to change the distribution of power or to make the system more democratic, it does not grow out of a despair about religion as such. It reflects a broader judgement about authority in the Egyptian polity: it recognizes the essentially 'stalled', or jammed, nature of Egyptian political culture. To say that there is no Islamic way out for Egypt is not to suggest that a liberal or a Marxist alternative would be any more viable. 'There is a crisis of the regime,' I was told by an upper-class Egyptian Marxist whose derision of Sadat alternated between aristocratic scorn and Marxist conviction. But he added, with compelling candour, 'There is a crisis of the opposition as well.' Authority hangs on, rides so many storms, survives so many 'violations', either because the metaphors put up by the rivals are so remarkably similar to the reigning ones as to be dismissed as no alternatives at all, or because they are so remarkably alien to popular sensibility, to the sense of the familiar and the possible, as to be judged irrelevant.

Three voices of Egyptian Islam

Two books and a set of court proceedings will be used to outline the range of Islamic alternatives and world-views in Egypt. I shall use them as convenient pegs on which to hang my own argument. Texts are not as important as those who use textual analysis would like to believe. The texts used here will serve as points of entry to the varieties of Egyptian Islam. The first book is by Shaykh 'Abd al-Halim Mahmud and is entitled *Fatawa 'an al-shuyu'iyya* (*Fatwas on Communism*); when it was written, in the early 1970s, its author occupied the position of Shaykh al-Azhar, which is the oldest Islamic university. The second book, *al-Din wa'l-ishtirakiyya* (*Religion and Socialism*), written at roughly the same time, is the work of Khalid Muhyi al-Din, President Sadat's most prominent opponent on the left. The court proceedings are from 1966, and in the main they are a set of illuminating exchanges between the prosecutor representing the Egyptian state and Sayyid Qutb, a brilliant thinker of the Muslim Brotherhood.[4]

Shaykh 'Abd al-Halim Mahmud and al-Azhar

Fatwas on Communism, which is a compilation of legal opinions issued by the *'ulama*, or religious authorities, was published in 1976. It is highlighted here less for its intellectual quality – for, alas, it is a very shallow book – as for the identity of the man who wrote it, and for the 'hegemonic discourse' of which it is part. Right from the start in the book, the Shaykh lays claim (and a legitimate one as far as it goes) to a body of authority and to a heritage. His views on communism are not merely the views of an ordinary writer. Those could be right or wrong, sound or not; one could refute them, be moved by them, argue with them. The Shaykh's utterances are of a different order: they are *fatwas*, binding religious opinions. Behind them is the authority not only of the dominant tradition, but – given the close connection between al-Azhar and the state – of the state as well. What a reader encounters in this text, then, is the burden of an established tradition: religious interpretation in the service of the custodians of political power. But, like all orthodox and officially sanctioned texts, this piece of writing does not face up to its own assumptions, or try to be self-critical or honest. It takes its own assumptions as givens. Because of its author and idiom, it claims for itself prerogatives that are denied to less socially established discourse, in which text and author stand on their own.

The Shaykh's conclusions on communism are all 'unavoidable, inescapable': he who subscribes to communism is a *kafir*, an unbeliever. If a communist dies, prayer for him is prohibited; he is not to be buried in the cemeteries of Muslims; Muslims cannot inherit his property and he cannot inherit from them.[5] In the Shaykh's opinion, communism is heresy, for, among other things, it attacks private property, whereas Islam sanctions property and opens before the individual the path to wealth and prosperity. Islam gives every *mujtahid* (every man who 'struggles': notice here the equation of seeking wealth with *ijtihad*, or independent exertion) the fruits of his own labour in this world. It clears the way for competition and incentives and, thus, it corresponds to the true bases of human nature. Islam not only accepts and facilitates private property; it also surrounds it with 'mighty protection and imposes penalty on those who transgress on this property, whatever the forms of their violations'.

In the context of the time in which they were made, Shaykh 'Abd al-Halim's opinions were neither accidental nor irrelevant. The 'open-door' economy was in full force, and the debate about inequalities was an intense one. Both in this book and elsewhere the Shaykh had joined that debate as an important participant and a highly committed one at that: he who tampers with the right of ownership, particularly owner-ship of land, he argued, will sooner or later meet with the wrath of God. The owner of property has every right to protect his property, even if he kills the 'aggressor'. In such an eventuality, he is not to be punished. But if he dies defending his property, he dies a martyr, 'for the Prophet said, "He who dies without his property is a martyr."'[6]

The *fatwas* of Shaykh 'Abd al-Halim are partly his, and partly the *ijtihad* of other 'prominent authorities', men of religion, and those in politics who had 'reached the summits of power and for whom the men of religion have a great deal of respect'. His political authorities are three: the late King Faysal, the late King Khalid, and King Fahd of Sa'udi Arabia. All three agree with him that communism is evil, that it aims to subvert and dominate the world, that it alienates man from his property and liberty. All agree that wherever communism rules, man is in chains, that his dignity and possessions are taken away. Fellow men of religion, too, agree with him and with the political authorities that communism is a form of *jahiliyya* (infidelity and ignorance), that communism and Islam 'cannot meet on the same soil'.[7] The testimonies of the men of religion and those of the political authorities close the circle: communism is heresy and disorder. There is a correct path, *al-sirat al mustaqim*, in both politics and religion. It is elaborated in the texts of the *'ulama* and the pronouncements of the men of religion.

From its founding by the Fatimids in 972 to its sanctioning of President Sadat's trip to Jerusalem in 1977, al-Azhar has been willing to repeat the utterances of the state and to give the deeds of rulers religious sanction and cover.[8] The men of al-Azhar have always been ready to quote scripture and use it against rebels or Marxists, for or against socialism or war. As always, the opinions of the *'ulama* of al-Azhar are the opinions of Islam itself. Islam is what they will it and pronounce it to be. The manner in which al-Azhar gave its approval to Sadat's journey to Jerusalem is illustrative: 'The *'ulama* of al-Azhar', we are told in a *fatwa* issued in May of 1979, 'believe that the Egyptian–Israeli treaty is in harmony with Islamic law. It was concluded from a position of strength after the battle of the *jihad* [holy struggle] and the victory realized by Egypt on the tenth of Ramadan of the year 1393 (6 October 1973).'⁹ And to show how traditions can be stretched and manipulated, al-Azhar's *'ulama* managed to find a precedent for the Egyptian–Israeli treaty in the Prophet's diplomacy and conduct of war and peace – the Hudaybiyya Treaty of 628 with the clan that then controlled the city of Mecca. This *fatwa* might have been a tough one to ponder and to arrive at – after all, it was issued a good eighteen months after Sadat's deed. But the balance of power between the state and the *'ulama* had been established long ago. Thus it was inevitable that in this, as in so many other painful situations, al-Azhar would capitulate and say that Sadat was *wali al-amr*, the man who disposes of things, and that to him and him alone belonged the right to make such decisions of national import.

Throughout its long history, al-Azhar has conveyed the message that political power is a capricious thing, that rulers ought to be obeyed, that the best that ordinary men can do is to duck and stay out of the way. Otherwise blood will be shed, property will be lost, and rulers will become vindictive. That which exists might not be particularly just, but it is dangerous to play with fire and take on such hopeless odds. The troops of the ruler – Fatimids, Mamluks, French, British, monarchical, or revolutionary – are always destined to win: what good is it to incur their wrath? Rarely did al-Azhar seek to contest the primacy of the rulers or to give men the sense of individual importance or shared fellowship that men need for that terrifying encounter with the mighty state. On the contrary, it has traditionally urged quietism and with-drawal. Humble men, so it would seem to suggest, ought not to entertain delusions of importance. Politics is the domain of a different breed of men who might not be virtuous, but who are powerful, and whose will must for the time being be obeyed. The *'ulama* ask: in the absence of an established social contract, what else holds men together? What keeps the order from falling apart? In time, the rulers might pass from the scene or their power might slip away. Then the mob could tear them from limb to limb, but, for now, ordinary men must accept those who rule them.

This was the way the *'ulama* spoke to their flock in 1798, urging obedience to the French occupiers:

We seek refuge in God from *fitan* [plural of *fitna*, sedition], overt and covert, and we ask Him to disown those who spread evil in the world ... and who caused trouble between the people and the French soldiers after they all had been beloved friends. As a result, some Muslims were killed and some homes were plundered. But thanks to the mercy of God, the *fitna* has subsided because of our intervention with the prince of the army, Bonaparte. The trouble has been lifted because he is a man of reason, with pity and mercy towards all Muslims and love for all the oppressed and humble people. Had it not been for him the soldiers would have burned the whole city, plundered all your wealth, and killed all the people of Egypt. It is incumbent on you not to provoke *fitan*, not to obey trouble-makers, or listen to hypocrites or pursue evil. Do not be among the losers and fools who don't appreciate the consequences of things ... God, praise be to Him, awards rule to whomever He wishes. Thus our advice to you: busy yourselves with your livelihood and your worship, pay the taxes you owe . . .[10]

The same themes recur in another important call issued by the *'ulama*. This time it was 1914, on the occasion of the declaration of martial law by the British occupiers. Prime Minister Husayn Rushdi sought a statement from al-Azhar condoning martial law and, after some quibbling by the *'ulama*, he got what he wanted:

Praise be to God who cautioned those who worship to avoid all *fitan* . . . O Muslims, you know that this war is afoot, that its sparks are flying to all countries, that its destruction has befallen all countries . . . God has decreed that you Egyptians be spared its evil and catastrophes without costing you *nafsan wa la nafisan* [life or treasure]. Thus it is your duty to remain tranquil and silent and to advise others to do so, to avoid interfering in things which do not concern you.[11]

In a culture in which men have been spectators at their own destiny, the *'ulama* have generally upheld the dominant political viewpoint. This tells us something about the comparative strength of the state. But there is something here about the evolution of the *'ulama* as a class, and the institutional base of official religion, that needs to be emphasized in order to understand the emasculation of official religion in the Egyptian polity.

During the age of the Mamluks, the *'ulama* were guardians of tradition and served as channels of communication between ruler and ruled. In the traditional balance of power that obtained then, a division of labour was respected. The Mamluks needed the intellectual, administrative, and educational services of the *'ulama*, and they were able to count on them. As a result, the *'ulama* prospered. As Afaf Lutfi al-Sayyid Marsot says, summarizing their position in the eighteenth and nineteenth centuries, to join the ranks of the *'ulama* was a promising avenue of social mobility for gifted boys from rural Egypt. The *'ulama* were able to acquire property, to become *multazims* (tax farmers), to accumulate respectable fortunes, to develop 'links with the *suq* [market], the country-side, and of course the ruling class who were the main source of wealth.'[12] This was not the stuff from which rebels and rebellions are made, 'for as *multazims* the *'ulama* were often rapacious and abusive toward their *fallahin* [peasants] as were the Mamluks.'[13] Bonaparte caught the essence of the social and political position of the *'ulama* when he decided to work with them on the grounds that they 'have gentle manners, love justice, and are rich and animated by good moral principles . . . they are not addicted to any sort of military maneuvering and they are ill adapted to the leadership of an armed movement.'[14]

Largely disconnected from the populace, the *'ulama* were and remain dependent on the patronage of the state. Power came their way when the state faltered, but their power declined again when the state re-asserted itself. What one observer called the 'Golden Age' of the *'ulama* occurred during the period 1798–1809, a period of civil chaos.[15] Then Muhammad 'Ali subjugated the polity as a whole, and the *'ulama* were no match for him. Muhammad 'Ali purged those who opposed him, confiscated the property of others, and drove home the lesson of the modern state system: states devour what stands in their way and expand their domain over time. According to Muhammad 'Ali's plan, the *'ulama* were to become obsolete. They would remain to sanction things and to display the rituals of religion, but their power was to be irretrievably shattered.

Muhammad 'Ali's successors came in the same mould and continued to control al-Azhar in the name of modernization and reform. Al-Azhar had to adjust to the modern world, they said; it needed bigger and bigger budgets. The successive reforms of 1895, 1908, 1911, 1936, and 1961 eroded what little autonomy al-Azhar had possessed. For example, the appointment of Shaykh al-Azhar, the paramount Egyptian religious leader, became the sole prerogative of the ruler. In 1911 the Supreme Council of al-Azhar brought it under still greater state control; in particular, unlike the Iranian *'ulama* whose financial independence was preserved, the Egyptian *'ulama* became salaried employees of the state. Also according to the 1911 legislation, an *'alim* (singular of *'ulama*) could be dismissed 'if he behaved in any manner unworthy of the *'alimiyya* [dignity of the learned]. His name shall be stricken from the records of al-Azhar and he shall be expelled from all positions; his salary shall be terminated whatever source it came from; he shall no longer be eligible for any governmental employment, religious or non-religious.'[16]

Brave indeed would any man be who ran afoul of this legislation.[17] This is another area in which men are told to acquiesce and mind their own affairs. Religion is to retain an honoured position in the society, but it is to be shackled and quarantined, paid homage to but kept on the margins of power. The religious authorities are given access to the air-waves, but they are to spread the good word that all is well, and that the pollution of the world is partly illusion and does not matter anyway. The *'ulama* have acquiesced because of the logic of survival. At a certain point they must have come to realize that the world had passed them by, that there was no use bucking mighty trends. But opportunism does not explain everything, for their own ideology has also been at work: the fear of chaos, the desire to be on solid ground. This attitude is illuminated by a writer from a different culture in a passage that applies here very well: 'Better that thousands should suffer than that a people should become a disintegrated mass, helpless like dust in the wind. Obscurantism is better than the light of incendiary torches. The seed germinates in the night. Out of the dark soil springs the perfect plant. But a volcanic eruption is sterile, the ruin of the fertile ground.'[18]

Khalid Muhyi al-Din

It is against the background of this kind of official Islam that Khalid Muhyi al-Din, a member of the Revolutionary Command Council of the Free Officers, labours in his book *Religion and Socialism*. His is a defensive effort: an attempt to make sure that his readers do not regard him as being out of the political mainstream, or use his Marxism to question his Islamic faith and devotion and, hence, his claim to political leadership.

Khalid Muhyi al-Din had been the only Marxist among the members of the Revolutionary Command Council. He now heads al-Tajammu' al-Watani al-Qawmi al-Wahdawi – a fairly loose party of Marxists, pan-Arabists, professors, and intellectuals who are at odds with the orientation of the Sadatist regime. They oppose the dismantlement of the public sector, the country's alignment with the United States, and the exercise of authority that reduces their political influence and that of other opposition groups. They continue to honour the memory and achievements of 'Abd al-Nasir, even though some of them – men like the journalist Lutfi al-Khuli and the prolific writer Rif'at al-Sa'id – did time in prison during the Nasir years. They try to do their best within the confines established by the regime. They benefit from the legitimacy conferred upon Muhyi al-Din himself as one of the 'historic' leaders of the 23 July Revolution.

Religion and Socialism is a collection of essays written between 1968 and 1975. They reiterate one central theme: Muhyi al-Din is a Marxist and a Muslim and he sees no contradiction between the two. In his view, his work and his assumptions are thoroughly Islamic, for social justice lies at the core of his quest and, as he sees it, at the core of Islam. For him, as for many other commentators before him, Islamic history went awry with the Umayyads. They turned rule into what it is today: capricious will, plunder, the state as an extension of the will of the ruler, wealth as something to be appropriated by a narrow class. The dominant theme in Muhyi al-Din's Islam is socialist and collectivist. The earth and what it has are the common heritage of all. The early Muslims were social rebels who clashed with the Meccan aristocracy; the early caliphs, particularly 'Umar, were men who were moved by the plight of the poor. Muhyi al-Din's Islam is a revolutionary enterprise: it not only preaches a doctrine of social justice; it also gives men the right to challenge inequality and injustice.

Because Muhyi al-Din's political work – under both 'Abd al-Nasir and Sadat – has been conducted against an exalted and mighty presidency, he devotes some attention to the question of political authority in Islam. The source of political power in the modern state, he insists, is not religion but popular will: Islam is not a political order but a religious one. The tendency to claim political power by invoking divine sanction or claiming infallibility is alien to Islam. Like 'Ali 'Abd al-Raziq, the Azhar-educated judge who more than a half century ago called for separation of religion and state, Muhyi al-Din wants the state to stand on its own without the cover and mystification of religion. For authority in a Muslim society is a civil and not a religious matter. Authority is also democratic: the ruler is to be chosen by consensus; the community is to define for him the limits of his power.

In his capacity as a leading member of the opposition, Muhyi al-Din has to dwell, as he does, on matters of foreign policy, on the open-door economy, on the rights of labour unions, on the contracts awarded by the state to the tycoon 'Uthman Ahmad 'Uthman. That he has to venture into an enterprise of this kind, citing scripture, recounting the deeds of the Prophet and his companions, tells us a good deal about the obstacles that religious orthodoxy connected to the state puts in the way of those who wish to challenge and change the distribution of wealth and power. His is, as I said, a defensive attempt to make sure that his belief is not questioned. Because the state brandishes Islam as one of its weapons, he finds that he, too, has to insinuate his views into Islam, to find roots there for what he believes in. At one point he calls upon those who attack his Marxism as heresy to put aside that easy (but effective) tactic of declaring men like him to be *kuffar* (unbelievers): 'Let us put that aside,' he says. 'The core of my position is that I call for the intensification of the struggle against the Zionists and imperialist enemies of our nation; that I am one of those who want a serious attempt at economic development, a just distribution of the fruits of development to the workers who made it possible . . . that I call for the establishment of a political authority led by workers, peasants, and progressive intellectuals.'[19]

Muhyi al-Din does, however, leave us with a sense that he understands the difficulty of his own position. He realizes that Islam neither speaks nor governs, and he cites the Caliph 'Ali to that effect. 'The Qur'an,' 'Ali had said, 'is but words between two covers. It does not speak; men do.' Muhyi al-Din knows that Islam, like any other system of beliefs, has been manipulated to suit the needs of the more powerful, that the Sultan in the Muslim world has always claimed God on his side.

So long as those in the saddle continue to profess their devotion to Islam, consciously and unconsciously to manipulate its symbols and claim its mantle, their opponents on the left can be expected to affirm their own devotion and to argue the compatibility of their own views with Islam. But the so-called *al-yasar al-islami*, the Islamic left, is but a minority, and the attempt to blend Marxism and Islam has not been particularly successful. Marxism, too, turns out to have its own obscurantists: its categories have a way of missing the reality of many Muslim countries, and its proponents seem hopelessly disconnected from the political ground on which they stand. The texts they read seem to have a tyranny of their own, and those texts and categories (very much like the incantations of Muslim fundamentalism) are not relevant to the lands and social system of Muslims, whose ailments the Marxists have yet to understand, let alone to cure.

The cult of authenticity (*al-asala* or purity of origin, Islam, and the strictures against *al-mabadi al-mustawrada* or imported doctrines) may strike us as unfair and cynical. But it does seem to work. The weight of established tradition in the Arab-Muslim order has more or less succeeded in declaring that Marxists and Marxism are something for which there is no room in the world men know, the world of the elders and the ancestors; that Marxism would tear asunder that world; that Marxists would deliver it to alien powers and alien social systems. Even that aside, the record of what passes for Marxism elsewhere has not been very inspiring of late. Few, if any, Egyptians or Arabs today could confidently state that the solution is to be found in some Marxist technology of power. Some years ago, the Algerians (in a passage recounted by Muhyi al-Din) vowed to redeem Algeria's future with the Qur'an in the right hand and *Das Kapital* in the left. Today the Algerian experiment itself is on the ropes. Vulnerable, too, is the belief that some large ideology could remake the world of a nation – particularly one as old, as scarred, as sceptical, as Egypt. The authority which men know – with its sycophantic men of religion, its exalted presidency, its own categories and discourse, its own limitations – defeats its 'alien' rival not only because of its preponderant material force but also because the ordinary triumphs over the exceptional, because currents borne by the wind confer upon familiar things great power and legitimacy.

Sayyid Qutb and the Brothers

Of the three points of entry chosen at the outset, Sayyid Qutb's is the most compelling. There is in this story a prosecutor and a defendant. The prosecutor takes the classic role of inquisitor displaying his wit and knowledge, the serenity of the state. The defendant is already doomed; what matters is the words he will leave to posterity, the dignity of his death.

Sayyid Qutb's fate recalls the fate of others before and after him. Since its founding in 1928, the Muslim Brotherhood started fires that claimed its own members as their prime casualties. From the assassination of the Brotherhood's Supreme Guide, Hasan al-Banna, in 1949, through the execution of some of its leading members in 1954 for an attempted assassination of 'Abd al-Nasir, to the execution of Sayyid Qutb in 1966, to the attack by Shabab Muhammad ('Muhammad's Youth') on the military academy in 1974, and finally to the drama of the Brotherhood's latest offshoot, al-Takfir wa'l-Hijra ('Repentance and Holy Flight') in 1977, the logic has inexorably led towards violence and self-destruction. Each time frustration and millennial despair led the movement to do something dramatic, to take on the state, to try to cleanse the world through plots and assassinations. Each time the state struck back: al-Azhar denounced the activists as dangerous and misguided zealots; highly publicized court proceedings dramatized the futility of daring to challenge the might of the state. In each case, there were dramatic executions serving in ways subliminal and conscious to remind all that authority is here to stay, and that there comes a time when men have to pay for the thoughts they entertain and the conspiracies they hatch.

Sayyid Qutb occupies an honoured place in the memory of the Muslim

Brotherhood. His book *Ma'alim fi'l-tariq* (*Signposts on the Road*) is probably the Brotherhood's most sustained and inspiring book. Scores of young people were and remain deeply influenced by it – so much so that when Sayyid Qutb was released from prison in 1964, after an imprisonment of nearly ten years, he was 'drafted' into leadership by devoted young followers. In late 1965, then sixty years of age, he was arrested on charges of leading a terrorist apparatus that was reportedly plotting to assassinate President 'Abd al-Nasir, to destroy public installations, even to assassinate the popular movie stars and idols Um Kulthum, Muhammad 'Abd al-Wahhab, 'Abd al-Halim Hafiz, Najat al-Saghira, and Shadia. The prosecutor's case was offered replete with signed confessions, confiscated weapons and cash, and evidence of connection with Sa'udi Arabia. He was executed in August 1966.

Sayyid Qutb left us with two principal documents: first, *Ma'alim fi'l-tariq*, a vibrant book in which he divided social systems into either *al-nizam al-jahili*, a decadent, ignorant order of the kind that existed in pre-Islamic Arabia, or *al-nizam al-islami* (Islamic rule), a society in which Islam not only reigns in name but also governs; and, second, the record of his trial in 1966. Throughout his ordeal he faced the court with courage and integrity; he faced up to the things he did. The court proceedings are largely taken up with displaying the impasse of the confrontation between a millenarian group with its own beliefs and a dominant political order that the group rejects.

An encounter with the record of the trial (we can only sample it here) shows that Sayyid Qutb understood the futility of his own position. He knew that the deeds proposed by his followers – military training, the putting together of bombs and molotov cocktails, the proposed assassinations of President 'Abd al-Nasir and his Chief of Staff 'Abd al-Hakim 'Amir and other officials – were doomed. But he also understood the impatience of his own disciples. His advice that premature action was dangerous fell on deaf ears, for his disciples had their own fears and frustrations: what good is it to try to 'educate' people? how many people would you have to educate? how can you save such a thoroughly compromised society by words, by sermons about the brotherhood of all Muslims, about the corruption of the rulers? is not a total war warranted on *al-nizam al-jahili*, which betrays the essence of Islam and compromises all those who acquiesce in it? On one side was the pit of terror ending in self-destruction; on the other, the fear that one's work can degenerate into words. In one way, the vision dies in a cataclysmic deed; in another, it turns into suppressed chatter. But, they asked, might not the risk of action pay off and bring about the millennium? Out there, enough people might be galvanized and might opt for something other than safety: assassinate the men at the helm, avenge what they had done to the Brotherhood in 1954–5, and enough people sitting on the fence might join.

Sayyid Qutb chose death by fire, as it were. He knew that small cadres armed with a few weapons, and some funds sent by exiled Brothers in Sa'udi Arabia, were likely to be defeated. He understood that arrest meant torture and sure death. Over and over again in the proceedings, he recalled the haunting memories of the 1950s: the interrogators, the prison cells, the attempt to break the spirit of the survivors, the loneliness of not knowing whether your 'brothers' betrayed or caved under, the forced confessions, and then, of course, the executions. Sayyid Qutb understood the risks of premature action; he knew that the security apparatus was not far away. He dreaded the responsibility of leading others to their death: 'images of torture and death that befell the Brothers flashed before my eyes.'[20] As a man of ideas, he said, he was repelled by violence. But he shared the conviction of his disciples that something had to be done.

The state, too, must have had 'convictions' of a similar kind. By 1965–6, the Egyptian effort was stalled in Yemen. The experiment with state capitalism had fallen on hard times. There were many in the apparatus of the state zealous enough to show their dedication to the revolution and its leader, and to exaggerate the dangers that attended their work. Here was a way of sending a message to the reactionaries, of reminding ordinary men and women of the dangers beneath the surface, of fanatic plots to interrupt the routine of their lives, of sordid deeds that would even do away with their beloved movie idols and singers!

As seen in the following exchange, the prosecutor probed the financing of the operation. On one level, the question was a tangible one: where did the funds come from? But there was, obviously, a symbolic level as well, involving the clash between Sayyid Qutb's belief in the Islamic *umma* and the prosecutor's belief in the state:

The prosecutor: As their leader, was it not reasonable to try to ascertain the sources of the funds in their hands in order to know who might have instigated them?

Sayyid Qutb: I had a general impression from what 'Abd al-Fatah Isma'il [forty-one years of age, another member on trial] said that the money came from Brothers in Sa'udi Arabia whom he contacted when he was in the Hijaz.

– Does this mean that you understood that the financing of this operation came from abroad?

- Yes, from abroad. But it is our belief that any Muslim Brothers in any country are related to us on the basis of ideology and belief and not on a regional basis. When one mentions Brothers, one never asks about their nationality.
- And this bond among the Muslim Brotherhood, is it in accord with patriotism (*wataniyya*)?
- I believe that the bonds of ideology and belief are sturdier than those of patriotism based upon region, and that this false distinction among Muslims on a regional basis is but one consequence of crusading and Zionist imperialism which must be eradicated.
- But you have decided that the relation that matters, and that matters more than patriotism, is to belong to the Muslim Brotherhood and not to Islam!
- In my opinion Islam is the essence of the Muslim Brotherhood.[21]

The prosecutor, as we observed, was a man of the state. By his criteria, in his universe, things were very clear: one got money from outside the state; one professed loyalty to something larger and more elusive than the state. This constituted sedition and disobedience. Indeed, the organs of the regime had repeatedly pointed out that the Brotherhood denies the primacy of the *watan*, the homeland, that the state (and presumably Egypt as a whole) could not tolerate the Brotherhood's belief that the *watan* is not a piece of land but a community of believers.

The impasse between the totalism of the political authority and the universe of the Muslim Brotherhood is described more fully and clearly in the following exchange. Here we see the full logic of the Brothers' charge that they are living in a non-Islamic order, or *al-nizam al-jahili*:

- I believe it is non-Islamic.
- Do you believe that there are *jahiliyya* societies and non-Islamic societies?
- No, I don't believe that there are any such things as non-Islamic societies. I believe that the society is either Islamic or *jahiliyya*.
- And in light of this belief, how would you classify the current system?
- I see it as *al-nizam al-jahili*.
- Does this mean that you believe in the necessity of changing the current system?
- I believe that it will change when the bases for creating *al-nizam al-islami* are secured.[22]

For the small Islamic order, a nucleus of brothers and believers, to live in *al-nizam al-jahili* is sheer hell. Between it and *al-nizam al-islami* there can be no cooperation: one is *dar al-harb*, the house of war; the other is *dar al-islam*, the house of peace. Theoretically, the believers cannot bid for power, run for elections, even perfect a method for the seizure of power, without terror – a messianic cleansing of the world. The state insisted on drawing out the full logic of this position: according to the Brotherhood, if someone is declared an infidel, a *jahil*, then his life and property are forfeited; terror against him is permitted. To die while trying to obliterate a *nizam jahili* is not sedition and terrorism but martyrdom.

> *The prosecutor*: The leaders of your *tanzim* (apparatus) said that you led them to understand that they are a community of believers (*umma mu'mina*) in a *jahili* society, and that nothing binds them to the state or society or current government, and that as an Islamic *umma* they must consider themselves in a state of war with the state and with the society in which they live; that you designated the rest of the country as a *dar al-harb*, and thus any acts of murder and destruction are not crimes but pious acts for which there is religious sanction.[23]

The prosecutor's purpose was, at least as seen in the above passages, to show the seditious and potentially criminal import of Sayyid Qutb's position. But, as seen in the next passage, the prosecutor moved to the inevitable, as it were: he, too, established Islam on his side; he showed that Sayyid Qutb's position was not only an affront to the state but a heresy against Islam:

> *The prosecutor*: Don't you see that establishing an armed secret apparatus among Muslims leads to *fitna* (sedition), that it is rejected and prohibited by Islam?
> – It might lead to *fitna*, but those responsible for it are those who ban public organizations, and they force others to resort to secret activities.
> – Does not your Islamic religion oblige you to prevent any *fitna* before it happens, to avoid its eruption by not forming a secret apparatus, by not training your men in the use of explosives, by not importing weapons from abroad to resist *al-sultat* (the ruling authorities)?
> – It is imperative to do one's religious duty. Sedition is a possibility and, if that possibility materializes, its burden falls not on me but on those who forced me to resort to secrecy.[24]

If Sayyid Qutb was able to sustain his argument, other members of the Brotherhood had earlier faced the same kind of interrogation and they caved under. The following exchange took place in Mahkamat al-Sha'b (People's Court) in 1955, and the man on trial was a member of the Brotherhood, Muhammad 'Abd al-'Aziz 'Abdullah:

> *The prosecutor*: Killing Nuqrashi [Prime Minister Mahmud Nuqrashi, assassinated in December 1948], was it *halal* (permissible)?
> *'Abdullah*: A crime.
> – Killing Khazindar [a judge, Ahmad Bey Khazindar, another victim of the Brotherhood], was it *haram* (prohibited)?
> – Yes.
> – A deed of Islam or *kufr* (unbelief)?
> – *Kufr*.
> – And his killer?
> – Enters hell.

– Under whose rule and guidance was Khazindar killed?
– Under the rule of Hasan al-Banna.
– And al-Nuqrashi?
– Under the rule of Hasan al-Banna.
– And he who authorizes murder: is he a *kafir* (an unbeliever) or a Muslim?
– A *kafir*.[25]

Also on trial in the same court was Muhammad al-Hawatka.

The prosecutor: Was the murder of Khazindar amongst the mistakes?
Hawatka: Yes.
– And those who committed the mistakes: are they Muslims or non-Muslims?
– The attribute of belief is denied them.
– And those who sanction and approve such murders: are they Muslims or non-Muslims?
– Non-Muslims.[26]

In the prosecutor's exchange with Sayyid Qutb, and in the other two exchanges as well, is the classic encounter between the Islam of the state and the Islam of revolution. The Khawarij, an early sect of rebels who rose against the Caliph 'Ali and his Umayyad challengers, had confronted the dominant order with doctrinal and political challenges a mere three decades after the establishment of Islam. Others had done the same and, in the process, the doctrines of rebellion and authority had drawn sharp and usually irreconcilable cleavages. Blood was often shed: ideas served, as they always do, both as moving forces and as cover for the ambitions and fears of men. Authority thought that the world belonged to it, thought it proper only in the way in which it had built and structured it. Rebellion was moved by a sense of violation and injury and then by a vision of struggle. Sayyid Qutb's encounter with the state was one such clash, and he paid with his life.

A mere decade after Sayyid Qutb's death, Ahmad Shukri Mustafa, a charismatic young agronomist who founded and led al-Takfir wa'l-Hijra, faced the same logic and met the same fate. The roots of Ahmad Shukri Mustafa's cult (an appropriate term, I believe) are to be found in the Muslim Brotherhood. He himself had been arrested in 1965 as an activist of the Brotherhood when he was studying in Asyut.[27] In prison he reached the conclusion that the spirit of the older members of the Brotherhood had been broken, that they were burned out.[28] He formed his own group in 1971, which pursued its goals more relentlessly than the Brotherhood. Not only was Egyptian society as a whole indicted as a *mujtama' kafir* (an infidel society), but so too were the members of the Muslim Brotherhood. This time the search for purity was almost neurotic: members of his sect were not allowed to pray behind *imams* (prayer leaders) in mosques, for these *imams* were hypocrites and sycophants. Moreover, members were not to accept military service: one could not fight and die for so defiled a society. The dominant instinct of the group was one of escape – from a defiled world into the discipline of the movement. To avoid the pollution of society, the members thought it best (like the Prophet himself) to undertake a *hijra*, a migration, to an isolated plot of land. There they could create their own society and set their own laws. Like the Prophet, who came back from Medina to claim Mecca, they too would presumably return to claim Egypt. Meanwhile, they owed full obedience to their leader (*al-amir*); he was a man with a sense of destiny and a mission, a *mahdi*. Until the coming of that world, all would try to remain as pure as possible. They lived together; they kept their children away from schools taught by *kuffar*, or unbelievers; they recruited or forced their sisters to marry other members of the group. The ideal was self-sufficiency: a flight from the world around them, a declaration that others were *kuffar* – hence the name al-Takfir wa'l-Hijra.

As in Sayyid Qutb's drama, violence was not far away. On 3 July 1977, the group (which had long been under surveillance) kidnapped Shaykh Muhammad Husayn al-Dhahabi, former Minister of Awqaf and Azhar Affairs – symbol, that is, of official Islam. The Shaykh was chosen because he had been the principal author of an Awqaf and Azhar document (1975) that denounced al-Takfir wa'l-Hijra as a group of extremists 'sowing corruption in the land'. The group demanded a ransom in the form of some money and the release of some of their activists from prison. On 6 July the Shaykh was found murdered. The predictable cycle happened: arrest of the members on 8 July – the state works wonders when it wants – publicized trials, and finally executions. The final judgement of the court, it should be noted, took place in late November, early December 1977 – that is, in the immediate aftermath of Sadat's visit to Jerusalem. Here was a public reminder (yet another one just when needed) of all the follies of interfering with the work of the state.

In this case, as in previous clashes between the state and Muslim fundamentalists, the state defended both its secular and its religious prerogatives. The tribunal's final verdict condemned a group that wanted to be 'a state within a state', that rejected its obligations to the armed forces and that resorted to kidnapping and terror. But there was also a defence of religious orthodoxy. The judgement was reached in the name of the 'true community of Muslim believers'. These young men and women had dared entertain notions alien to Islam: they ought to have known, stated the tribunal, that there could be only one *hijra*, that of the Prophet; that *ifta* (the issuing of *fatwas*) is limited to those authorized to pursue it; that violence was antithetical to the spirit of Islam; and that one had no right to challenge the belief and piety of other Muslims. These young people, declared Shaykh 'Abd al-Halim Mahmud, whom we encountered earlier, had been 'seized by the devil'. It was up to the religious and political authorities to defend the world of Islam against such heresies.[29]

In condemning the band of young rebels, the society spoke of itself, of those solid and suggestive things that reveal themselves to us when men ridicule others, when they ponder the strange deeds of those who do not recognize agreed upon scruples and limits. Ahmad Shukri Mustafa, we were told, came from a 'broken family'; his deputy, the philosopher Mahir 'Abd al-'Aziz Bakri, had not gone beyond secondary school education. (How could the latter philosophize in a society of so many Ph.D.s and so many Azhar-educated authorities?) These young men and women lived together in close proximity and conducted their own wedding ceremonies – unimaginable deeds in a society with a straight-laced morality. The zealots could have done better with their lives, refrained from 'shaming' their loved ones.

The secret yearnings of other Egyptians were played out in the drama of al-Takfir wa'l Hijra, replete with acts of rebellion, insinuations of sexuality, a break with family and friends, and a challenge to the state. Rebellion was found helpless and absurd. The court did all it could to convey to the audience, and to the wider society that followed it through the press, the utter futility of the deed. The world of familiar things and scruples – loyalty to the state, loyalty to family and friends, respect for the official *'ulama* and *imams*, the difficulty of getting married in a place like Egypt – was once again vindicated as a better world. Five men were sentenced to life imprisonment; less severe punishments were handed out to others.

Clearly Ahmad Shukri Mustafa and his band of followers were not the first, nor are they likely to be the last, accomplices and victims of this vicious circle of total authority, on one side, met by total negation on the other. In the language of E. J. Hobsbawm, the members of the Brotherhood and its variations are millenarians. Of the typical millenarian movement he observes:

Its followers are not makers of revolution. They expect it to make itself, by divine revelation, by announcement from on high, by a miracle – they expect it to happen somehow. The part of the people is to gather together, to prepare itself, to watch for the signs of the coming doom, to listen to the prophets who predict the coming of the great day, and perhaps to undertake certain ritual measures against the movement of decision and change, or to purify themselves, shedding the dross of the bad world of the present so as to be able to enter the new world in shining purity.[30]

Since the 1920s, Muslim cults and the Brotherhood have looked at the defiled world around them – wild cities, shocking cultural trends, foreigners with alien ways, subjugation to outsiders, a world that seems to be perpetually in crisis, young men and women who have strayed from time-honoured ways – and have felt at one time or another the urge to destroy or the urge to withdraw and escape. But the system proved tenacious. Destruction did not accomplish much. In a cautious culture, the world stood still. The infidel society withstood the assassination plots, the attack on academies, the food riots. Each time the state came back; each time its custodians claimed for themselves enlightened rationality. And what must have been particularly painful, the custodians of the state claimed Islam on their side.

Withdrawal into the inner life of the movement and its ritual promises personal salvation. But in a crowded society, where there are so many bodies and so many men, the world could go on as usual. It could withstand, perhaps welcome, the withdrawal of some. Capitalists will go on to accumulate large wealth; army officers will be there to bail out the regime; sycophantic writers will be there to honour and praise the rulers, whoever they may be. And, as always, there is the man at the helm: the media record a barrage of his words; his photos are everywhere; he is all-knowing and all-seeing. Indeed, like all masters, he has a monopoly on sight. He saw the need for war; he saw the need for peace; he saw his way to Jerusalem. Faith sustained him: as a child he was saved from a certain death; he survived an era of Nasirist madness; he undertook the crossing of the Suez Canal in October 1973 and angels came down to fight on the side of his army. Men would have to be either saints or made of steel not to be demoralized by all this, not to begin to doubt the worth of their withdrawal or the efficacy of their wrath.

Stretching cultural limits

In ways more intuited than seen, cultures act to flash danger-points, to instil discipline when discipline breaks down, to strengthen cultural boundaries when these boundaries become dangerously permeable. At certain points, cultural systems will, as it were, 'scream' and draw limits. To the extent that Egypt's Islam forms the cultural system of the country, it will always matter. Rulers and opponents alike will phrase their concerns in Islamic categories. While there are some things which this cultural system will not tolerate, the point is that, beneath that 'cosmic' level, cultural limits in Egypt (and elsewhere) can be stretched to accommodate a wide range of things – high inequalities or socialism, war or peace, a break with the Arab world or a strident version of pan-Arabism.

In the twists and turns of Ahmad Husayn's political career, the quintessential chameleon who founded the Young Egypt Party, we may observe just how far these limits can be stretched, how meaningless the Islamic categories can become. In a dizzying political career that spanned the years 1930–53, Ahmad Husayn embraced at one time or another chauvinistic pharaonic doctrines and militant versions of pan-Arabism, fascist doctrines and socialist ones, and so forth. But all his shifts were draped in Islamic colours. When he supported the monarchy against the Wafd Party and the national movement, he did so on the ground that 'God is with the King' and that King Faruq ought to be the Caliph of all true Muslims. When he became infatuated with fascism, he declared upon his return from Italy in 1938 that 'fascism has plenty of Islam in it'. With the defeat of the fascist powers in World War II, he embraced socialism as a new cause, changed the name of his party, and declared to the faithful that the programme of his socialist party was not to be found in Karl Marx but instead derived from Islam![31] Ahman Husayn may have been more of an opportunist than others, but his example tells us something about the ease with which men can twist sacred symbols to serve any set of needs. His story also suggests that all-inclusive symbols (like Islam in Egypt) can smother and accommodate all things, and thus lose their effectiveness as concrete ways of organizing politics, of sorting out relations between contending classes and groups, rulers and dissidents.

For those who wish to prophesy the rise and fall of political orders and regimes (and I must disown that kind of pursuit), there is a way in which Islam, broadly conceived, can matter. As the open-door economy digs a deeper ditch than ever between the poor and the rich, between those living on fixed incomes and those with foreign connections who participate in the windfall economy of speculation, it also risks digging a culturally offensive ditch between the glamorous ways of the new economy and those of the traditional one that lives by its side. Nativism/Islam and class resentment (a classic combination in Egypt and other societies subjected to an intolerable degree of economic and cultural dualism) can come together to provide the basis for large-scale upheaval. Indeed, the schizophrenia between the new culture of Egypt's economy (foreign travel, deeper integration into the Western economic system) and the retreat into old pieties (the regime's encouragement of tales of saints and miracles) is a dangerous combination. A society's professed symbols cannot war with its realities for very long. Sooner or later the gap will turn into an intolerable chasm, which will be filled either by terror or by an appalling slide into mediocrity and cynicism.

Shortly before his assassination in October 1981, it will be recalled, President Sadat imprisoned some fifteen hundred of his critics and opponents. The list covered the entire range of the political spectrum: liberal professionals, *ancien régime* elements, Muslim fundamentalists – in fact almost anyone who thought that the world of politics was not the sole prerogative of the man at the helm. The only kinds of political men he left out of prison, so it seemed, were two: the sycophants and the conspirators. The former hid the world from him, and the latter came to speak in the only language they felt still mattered in Egypt. Sadat had, as it were, cornered his own country. Terror offered an illusory sense of a new beginning and a way out. The man at the helm had become bigger than his country. His repeated 'violations' had become an open challenge. The men who risked their lives in order to take away his in so open, so shocking, a manner must have believed they were serving an overdue warrant.

Where a large rebellion was not in the cards, the assassins did what the 'stalled society' could not do for itself. They expressed the society's distress and confusions. Whereas the instinctive Egyptian dread of sudden changes had usually worked for Sadat, his erratic habits had become a source of anxiety. He had ridden out great dangers many times by appealing to the country's desire for safety; now many came to feel that the public order would be safer without him. The electric shocks of what one Egyptian critic called a 'stream-of-consciousness presidency' had placed Copts and Muslim fundamentalists on a collision course, and had frightened off those in the country who wanted to place public order on something firmer than the will of the man at the helm.

No sooner had his death been announced than it was clear that anything was possible. Muslim fundamentalist frenzy had presumably eliminated him and it could, so it was argued, topple the whole order. It could, as had been its pattern, work through the army or the universities and destabilize a system whose corruption was openly acknowledged – every now and then even by President Sadat himself. True to form, the fundamentalists would presumably gain because they are willing to take the risks of political action, to take on the state when others would prefer to duck and stay out of the way.

All this is conjecture, however. For all the claims of political risk-analysis, there is no way of knowing when and how political regimes will change, under what condition men in power will no longer awe and intimidate others, or when those who sit on the fence will decide to throw caution to the wind and place their loyalties at the disposal of a dimly perceived new order. Far more likely than the dissolution of political authority in Egypt is the reassertion of the power of the state. The millenarian instinct would continue to live on, lurk beneath the surface, erupt every now and then whenever the world's confusion becomes intolerable. Its utopia and energy would live on. But so would the power of the state – threatening, promising, appealing to the fear of disorder, to the innate human desire for remote structures of power onto whom mortal, weak men can project illusions of order and omnipotence.

But even if the dominant political order in Egypt were to come un-stuck, it is not likely that Islamic fundamentalists would come to dominate the new world. Again in those subtle and mysterious ways in which societies (most of them, and particularly one like Egypt) under-stand their own dilemmas and refrain from playing with fire, the likely outcome would be a course dominated by secularists and nationalists. From roughly 1919 onwards, the national movement in Egypt has kept sectarianism in check. Deep down most Egyptians know that a political order led by true believers and fundamentalists has no way of accom-modating the 3–5 million Egyptians who happen to be Christian Copts, that the 'comparative advantage' of Egypt as a nation-state in its region – its relative unity and its stability – would be torn asunder.[32] This is a society which is used to 'harmonizing contending assertions'.[33] It may not be the cosmopolitan oasis that some have imagined it to be; nevertheless, the dominant national instinct understands that the quest for purity, for a 'tribal' kind of truth, is not only unworthy of Egypt but unattainable.

In a sympathetic and thoughtful analysis of Egypt's 'militant Islamic groups',[34] the Egyptian sociologist Saad Eddin Ibrahim writes that the vision of an Islamic order will continue to dazzle and inspire the imagina-tion of Muslim societies, and that we shall hear and see more of such groups in Egypt. Indeed we shall. But what of its significance? A society can live with such outbursts. 'Sufficiently studied,' we are told by David Apter in an essay on terrorism, 'nothing is shocking. Indeed, examining terrorism has become a growth industry. Psychologists, police chiefs, specialists on violence and deviant behavior, counterintelligence pro-fessionals – all are busy helping to repair the damage and restore "rationality" by determining causes. When terrorism becomes common-place it can be accepted.'[35] What begins as a challenge to the state ends up confirming its rationality, its monopoly on steering a reasonable course in a world that either is mad or is capable of becoming so at any moment. The state is said to be (by its custodians, by its many, many spokesmen) the only dike against great upheaval and disorder. This is a game that all states play; this also happens to be a game at which the Egyptian state is particularly skilled.

The discontents upon which revolutionaries feed are certainly to be found in Egypt. There are plenty who would want to topple the existing order, for, as Luwis 'Awad has noted, the social contract of the 23 July Revolution has eroded and the revolution has aged.[36] But the means and the will to bring down that order are not clear to me. The perseverance of revolutionaries and 'saints' we can admire. But we ought to be careful not to read our impatience into that old culture, not to look for revolutions around every corner. In Egypt the Hegelian pro-position about the inevitability of revolution may have found a sure graveyard.[37] There revolutions either do not happen or, when they do, they are turned into familiar and harmless things.

Notes

1. Najib Mahfuz, *Radubis* (Cairo, 1978), pp. 152, 212.
2. Karl Wittfogel, *Oriental Despotism* (New Haven and London, Yale University Press, 1957).
3. E. J. Hobsbawm, *Primitive Rebels* (New York, Norton, 1965).
4. Shaykh 'Abd al-Halim Mahmud, *Fatawa 'an al-shuyu'iyya* (Cairo, Dar al-Ma'arif, 1976); Khalid Muhyi al-Din, *al-Din wa'l-ishtirakiyya* (Cairo, 1976); the court proceedings of Sayyid Qutb are to be found in Sami Jawhar, *al-Mawta yatakallamun* (Cairo, al-Maktabat al-Misri al-Hadith, 1977).
5. Mahmud, *Fatawa*, pp. 93–4.
6. *Ibid.*, p. 57.
7. *Ibid.*, p. 54.
8. I have found particularly useful Sa'id Isma'il 'Ali's book *al-Azhar 'ala masrah al-siyasa al-misriyya* (Cairo, Dar al-Thaqafa, 1974).
9. *Al-Ahram*, 10 May 1979.
10. Isma'il 'Ali, *al-Azhar 'ala masrah*, pp. 103–4.
11. *Ibid.*, p. 299.
12. 'The Ulama of Cairo in the Eighteenth and Nineteenth Centuries' in Nikki R. Keddie (ed.), *Scholars, Saints, and Sufis: Muslim Institutions Since 1500* (Berkeley and London, University of California Press, 1972).
13. *Ibid.*, p. 159.
14. *Ibid.*, p. 161.
15. Daniel Crecelius, 'Nonideological Responses of the Egyptian Ulama to Moderniza-tion', in Keddie (ed.), *Scholars, Saints, and Sufis*, pp. 173–80.

16. See 'Asim al-Dasuqi's excellent study, *Mujtama' 'ulama al-Azhar, 1895–1961* (Cairo, 1980), p. 57.
17. This was the legislation on the basis of which 'Ali 'Abd al-Raziq, an Azhar-educated judge and author in 1925 of the controversial *al-Islam wa usul al-hukm* (*Islam and the Principles of Government*), was tried and stripped of his '*alimiyya*. 'Abd al-Raziq had called for separation of religion and state. The case against him was decided by twenty-four '*ulama* led by Shaykh al-Azhar. The '*ulama* offered an exhaustive refutation of 'Abd al-Raziq's view in an interesting document, *Radd hay'at kubar al-'ulama 'ala kitab al-islam wa usul al-hukm* (Cairo, 1925).
18. Joseph Conrad, *Under Western Eyes* (London and New York, Penguin, 1979), p. 36.
19. Muhyi al-Din, *al-Din wa'l-ishtirakiyya*, pp. 106–7.
20. Jawhar, *al-Mawta yatakallamun*, p. 122.
21. *Ibid.*, p 129.
22. *Ibid.*, pp. 133–4.
23. *Ibid.*, p. 138.
24. *Ibid.*, pp. 139–40.
25. *Mahkamat al-Sha'b*, vol. 2 (Cairo, 1955), p. 376.
26. *Ibid.*, p. 254.
27. My account of al-Takfir wa'l-Hijra relies principally on the reportage of *al-Ahram* covering the period of 3 July–1 Dec. 1977. I also benefited from reading Professor Saad Eddin Ibrahim's paper, 'Anatomy of Egypt's Militant Islamic Groups' (Cairo, 1980).
28. Ibrahim, 'Anatomy', p. 21.
29. For the tribunal's verdict, see *al-Ahram*, 1 Dec. 1977; for Shaykh Mahmud's statement, see *al-Ahram*, 16 July 1977.
30. Hobsbawm, *Primitive Rebels*, pp. 58–9.
31. See the excellent biography of Ahmad Husayn by Rif'at al-Sa'id, *Ahmad Husayn: kalamat wa mawaqif* (Cairo, 1979).
32. Milad Hanna, *Na'am aqbat wa lakin misriyyun* (Cairo, 1980).
33. E. M. Forster, *Pharos and Pharillon* (Berkeley, Creative Arts, 1980), p. 41.
34. Ibrahim, 'Anatomy', p. 46.
35. David Apter, 'Notes on the Underground', *Daedalus*, Fall 1979, p. 167.
36. Luwis 'Awad, *The Seven Masks of Nasserism* (Beirut, 1976).
37. This observation was made by one of my students, Bertrand Denieul, in a series of astute remarks on Egypt.

3 Islam and Politics in the Sudan

ALEXANDER S. CUDSI

In the summer of 1980, President Ja'far Numayri of the Sudan published a book on Islam.[1] It is basically an exposition of his views on the social and political role of Islam and is intended to explain his adoption of pro-Islamic policies in recent years. The purpose of this chapter is to trace the role of Islam in Sudanese politics, particularly since Numayri came to power, and to identify the evolution of a consensus calling for the establishment of an Islamic republic.

The socio-religious framework of Sudanese politics

Before proceeding with our analysis, we must review the two main characteristics of the Sudanese political framework. The first of these is the Sufi nature of the Sudan's Islamic heritage. The rise of Islam in the Sudan has been the result of seven centuries of continuous, and often imperceptible, penetration by Muslim settlers, so that by the middle of the fifteenth century the three Christian kingdoms of the Sudan had become completely Islamized.[2] With the establishment of the Funj Sultanate (1504–1820), Sudanese Islam began one of its most active phases. In terms of the growth of a religious tradition, the chief influence was that of Sufism, whose followers began to arrive at this time and who were to become the torch-bearers of Islam in the new state. Sufism had begun to evolve into institutionalized *tariqas* (orders) by the start of the eighteenth century, replacing to a large extent the Sufi role of the earlier *faki* (colloquial for *faqih*, jurisconsult). In this new form, the influence of many of these *tariqas* extended beyond their local areas, thereby rendering their leaders politically important as agents of support or opposition to existing regimes.[3]

Yet, in this role, the Sufi orders could exert at best an *indirect* political influence. The main objective of Sufism is to achieve holiness through contemplation of the deity and imitation of the Prophet's life. The pursuit of political power or direct involvement in temporal affairs is regarded as a distraction from the Sufi path and hence an obstacle to the achievement of holiness. It is mainly for this reason that established *tariqa* leaders rarely resorted to revolutionary activity. Instead, they contented themselves with offering or withdrawing their religious sanction for existing political regimes.

This indirect political influence could function least effectively in Western liberal party systems. The vacuum created by the reluctance of *tariqa* leaders to assume a direct political role was inevitably filled by secular liberal nationalists, who used the sectarian movements primarily to win away popular support from their rivals. On the contrary, this indirect political influence enabled Sufi orders to accommodate themselves more smoothly to, and play a more effective role in, subsequent non-democratic systems.

This was not the case with the Mahdist tradition in Sudanese Islam. The arrival of Turko-Egyptian rule in 1820 brought foreign impulses for modernization and cultural change. However, the economic dislocation and political inefficiency associated with this administration gradually generated political opposition which, under the leadership of a revivalist Sufi teacher (Muhammad Ahmad al-Mahdi), flared into a fundamentalist revolution.[4] Unlike Sufism, Mahdism is an activist movement; *direct* involvement in a political struggle to set up a reformed Islamic state is therefore consistent with its ideology. This type of movement functions least effectively in secular non-democratic systems, with which it cannot accommodate itself without compromising its ideology.

The second main characteristic of the Sudanese political framework is the close alliance between the religious sects and the secular nationalist parties.[5] The split in the nationalist movement into pro-independence and pro-unity factions inevitably drew the religious sects into supporting one or the other group. Thus emerged the political parties in the post-war period, the main ones being the Umma, which was pro-Mahdist and pro-British, and the Ashiqqa, which favoured the Khatmiyya Sufi Brotherhood and the Egyptians. The Umma drew most of its support from members of the Ansar, a Mahdist movement, and eventually incorporated other pro-independence, nationalist groups. The Ashiqqa Party, in turn, was subsequently enlarged to form the Nationalist Union Party (NUP), from which in 1956 the Khatmiyya forces defected to form their own People's Democratic Party (PDP).

The differences in sectarian organization and ideology were reflected in the respective party structures. On the one hand, the vacuum created by the reluctance of Sufi leaders, especially the Khatmiyya, to assume political roles inevitably gave the primacy to the secular nationalists within the NUP. These regarded themselves as the agents of modernization and sought, through a policy of gradual secularization, to eradicate sectarian influence. But the lack of a centralized party organization under their effective control meant that their policies could yield limited results at best, and even then mainly in urban areas. On the other hand, the activist political nature of the Mahdist movement, together with its centralized sectarian organization, retained the primacy for the sectarian leadership and robbed the movement's secular nationalist allies of an effective role in policy-making within the Umma Party. But, in the event, the secular nationalists did use some sectarian support to pursue their objectives, and the sectarian movement made use of secular support.

The 'Abbud military regime (1958–64)

The transitional constitution that the Sudan had implemented immediately following its independence in 1956 was, as would be expected under the governing Nationalist Union Party, secular and liberal. The task of drafting a permanent constitution inevitably raised the issue of secularism versus Islamization. As the struggle unfolded, the position of the secular nationalists increasingly weakened following the defection of Khatmiyya forces from the NUP. By early 1957, the Constitutional Committee had committed itself to the principle that Islam was the official religion of the state and that the *shari'a* (sacred law) was one of the basic sources of legislation. To eliminate any doubt about where they stood in this regard, the sectarian leaders Sayyid 'Abd al-Rahman al-Mahdi and Sayyid 'Ali al-Mirghani, both of whom had never really reconciled themselves to the secular-liberal model, issued a joint demand that the Sudan be declared an Islamic parliamentary republic, with the *shari'a* established as the main source of legislation. In this, they were strongly supported by the Muslim Brotherhood movement, which had campaigned since 1954 for the adoption of a permanent constitution based on the Qur'an and the Sunna (traditions of the Prophet).

This sectarian commitment, however, did not bear the desired fruit. The political process was again to be undermined by party factionalism (fuelled by a growing Nasirist influence), an unstable economy, and the lingering problem of the southern Sudan. In November 1958, General Ibrahim 'Abbud headed a coup which was the Sudan's first experiment with military rule. The officers of the coup came from the same liberal background as the nationalist leadership; as a result, no major socio-political changes were made and, although the political parties were dissolved, the political framework remained on the whole unaltered.

Certain important changes, however, did come about as by-products. In the first place, the dissolution of the political parties further weakened the bond between the secular nationalists and the sectarian leadership. The vacuum created by the imprisonment of party politicians was soon to be filled, particularly in the Umma-related Ansar movement, by a newly emerging sectarian leadership which was critical of its elders' unsatisfactory response to an increasingly unpopular military rule. In the second place, the failure of the 'Abbud regime to deal effectively with a worsening economic situation drove discontented urban and suburban elements to swell the ranks of both leftist and rightist organizations. These changes contributed greatly to the Islamization of politics in the Sudan.

The October regime (1964–9)

In October 1964, 'Abbud's military regime was unceremoniously overthrown by civilian action. Of all the established parties, only the Communist Party of the Sudan (CPS) was well enough organized to step into the vacuum.[6] Accordingly, the first transitional cabinet was heavily dominated by a new coalition of leftists, known as the United Front of Professionals. This body had been formed on 25 October 1964, and incorporated a group which initially consisted of Sudanese faculty members of Khartoum University and Khartoum Technical Institute, but which was promptly enlarged to include representatives of workers, peasants, and other professional organizations.[7]

Uneasy about this leftist domination, the traditional sectarian forces called for the immediate election of a new Constituent Assembly to draft a permanent Islamic constitution. The leftists responded by passing a motion in the Council of Ministers to enlarge the franchise to include all Sudanese over eighteen years of age. This measure had the far-reaching effect of radicalizing politics by drawing the younger generation into the political arena. Unlike their older counterparts, who were essentially established members of the then emerging middle class, most of the younger members of the intelligentsia were either unemployed or else dissatisfied with their jobs. They had little faith in the ability of the traditional political organizations and institutions to achieve the rapid social and political changes that were necessary. Accordingly, they turned increasingly to extremist organizations that espoused radical solutions for these complex problems. The scheduled elections, there-

fore, were no longer seen as offering a choice between parties of traditionally dominant personalities but with very similar political programmes;
rather, they offered an opportunity to choose between traditional and
radical movements advocating essentially opposing approaches to
national problems. The former sought to re-establish the situation
obtaining before the coup, and promised the usual gradual steps of
economic and social development. The latter demanded a complete over-
haul of political and social conditions, including the elimination of
conservative and sectarian organizations.[8]

Although the elections of April 1965 resulted in a victory for the traditional forces, leading eventually to the banning of the CPS in
December of the same year, the old party organizations, particularly
the Umma, were undergoing significant modifications. The Umma
leadership, for example, was now divided along functional lines. In late
1961, Sayyid Siddiq al-Mahdi had made a deed establishing a *shura*,
or consultative council, at his death, which would be headed by Sayyid
'Abdullahi al-Fadil and would include Sayyid al-Hadi al-Mahdi and
Sayyid Sadiq al-Mahdi. The day after he died, the council elected al-
Hadi as the new *imam*, or religious leader. By 1963, Sadiq al-Mahdi
had become critical of al-Hadi's attitude towards 'Abbud's regime, and
began a reform movement within the Umma Party. He denounced the
political role of the imamate and called for a more modern and democratic
party structure, better suited to current conditions and a more educated
electorate. After the 1965 elections, Sadiq took political control of the
party, while al-Hadi remained spiritual head of the Ansar, with the title
of *imam*. The *imam* was more conservative in outlook, while Sadiq
championed progressive ideas and sought to turn the Umma into a
political rather than a sectarian organization, committed to political,
economic, and social change.

Sadiq's measures to bring a modern element into Islamization made
him extremely popular, especially among the younger intellectuals. But,
at the same time, they alarmed the traditional secular and sectarian
leaders, who stubbornly refused to recognize the emergence of political
forces that could not be dismissed by mere appeals to the traditional
symbols of loyalty. Thus the very popularity that had brought Sadiq
to the premiership in July 1966 was instrumental in splitting the Umma
Party into traditionalist and modernizing factions – a split which led,
in May 1967, to his fall from office. He continued, however, to campaign
for the adoption of an Islamic constitution, and in January 1968 a
draft document, formally banning communism and its propagation in

the Sudan and establishing the *shari'a* as the basic source of legislation, was presented to the Assembly.

But political events now moved fast, preventing the Assembly from taking action on the draft constitution. Isma'il al-Azhari, who had foreseen the consequences of Sadiq's redrafting of the rules of the political game, resurrected the old secular–Khatmiyya alliance by merging the NUP and the PDP into one Democratic Unionist Party. He must have believed that, through this alliance, he would at least be in a position to influence the adoption of those articles in the proposed constitution that would have preserved the influence of the secular nationalists. Azhari's alliance won for him the next round of elections, but at the same time it provided the impetus for a reunification of the Umma Party.

In order to reverse the tide, Sadiq al-Mahdi planned a two-stage course of action. The first stage was to eliminate the divisive influence of the secular nationalists – represented by Muhammad Ahmad Mahjub – within the Umma Party. Therefore, in April 1969, he made an agreement accepting al-Hadi as both *imam* and president of the Umma Party, in return for which al-Hadi accepted Sadiq as successor to both posts. The second stage in Sadiq's programme was to deprive Azhari of his Khatmiyya sectarian support. Accordingly, in early May 1969, he made an agreement with the PDP on principal national policies, including the basis for a new constitution. On 23 May 1969, all the political parties in the Constituent Assembly accepted the principle that the Sudan should have an Islamic presidential constitution, and elections were scheduled for January 1970. Less than forty-eight hours later, the army was to assume power under Colonel Ja'far Muhammad Numayri.

The May revolution (1969)

The 'contradictory actions of coalition parties and their political manoeuvres', of which Muhammad Ahmad Mahjub complained when resigning as Prime Minister in April 1969,[9] had created an unsatisfactory political climate, prompting most Sudanese to call for drastic remedies. One such solution was, of course, the return of Sadiq al-Mahdi to power, a prospect that became more realizable after the reunification of the Umma Party and the agreement with the PDP.

It was precisely this prospect that motivated leftist nationalists to consider an alliance with a group of Free Officers who had been planning a coup to overthrow the government. They were moved by two important

41

considerations. First, they had everything to fear from a strong, unified Umma Party, led by the staunchly anti-leftist Sadiq al-Mahdi; second, they were convinced that, without military backing and the support of the socialist camp, no revolution could succeed in the Sudan.[10] Accordingly, on 25 May, they allied themselves with the Free Officers to topple the October regime, and to set up a government oriented towards secular socialism, with Babikr 'Awadallah as Prime Minister and Numayri as President of the new Revolutionary Command Council.[11]

The leftist orientation of the May regime was evident from the start. In his broadcast to the nation, 'Awadallah declared that the country would henceforth adopt the 'socialist, democratic' model and would promote closer relations with 'progressive Arab States'.[12] At the same time, his cabinet was heavily dominated by communists and those other 'socialist' forces that had been prominent in the first transitional government of the October regime.[13]

Within a few weeks, 'Awadallah moved from words to action, abolishing the native administrations in the central and northern provinces. In the eyes of the secular nationalists, particularly the more leftist of them, these institutions, formerly instruments of indirect rule for the colonial administration, had become equally reactionary instruments in the hands of conservative native forces. In order to free the people from exploitation by local autocrats, the leftists wanted the administrative structure to be reformed, and a programme of modernization and development to be put in hand. A proposal along these lines had already been submitted, during the October regime, by Shafi' Ahmad al-Shaykh, at that time Minister for Cabinet Affairs.[14] But his subsequent removal from the cabinet, and opposition by conservative forces to his scheme, prevented its implementation. As members of the newly established 'Awadallah government, the leftists discerned a second chance to set the reforms in motion.

The abolition of the native administrations was opposed in particular by those tribal leaders who had established themselves in positions of authority in the relatively modern world of commerce, farming, and party politics. The aspiration of this group to be 'patrons' inevitably involved the preservation of a political system in which their influence was well-established.[15] This was also the concern of the sectarian leaders. They saw in these measures a leftist conspiracy to eliminate religious influence in the political process. They voiced their opposition privately at first, but eventually they felt compelled to take a public stand. At the funeral of Isma'il al-Azhari in August 1969, Sayyid Muhammad 'Uthman al-Mirghani (the new head of the Khatmiyya order) declared that he rejected rule by the radical left and vowed to resist communism with every means at his disposal. At the same time, al-Hadi al-Mahdi had already embarked on a more militant course of action, a course that eventually led to military confrontation with the regime, as a result of which Mahdist influence was severely weakened.

With the most formidable opponent thus effectively removed from the field, the May regime proceeded to implement the other aspects of its 'socialist' programme. In May 1970, it confiscated major domestic and foreign business concerns, intending thereby to break the economic foundation of established parties and also to 'liberate' the economy from 'capitalist' control. At the same time, political and economic relations with the communist bloc were expanded, and Soviet advisers were called in to assist in drawing up a properly revised five-year economic development programme. These measures, and the mobilization of sectarian opposition to them, had the general effect of awakening the masses to the irreconcilable threat that communism posed to the political and economic foundations of Islam.

The July putsch (1971)

As popular opposition to the regime mounted, a split was developing within the ranks of the Free Officers, which was eventually to lead to a conflict with the Communist Party. A number of factors contributed to the growth of this split. A major one was the leftists' evaluation of the military's role in the coup. The Communist Party believed that the army, by its very nature, could not represent the working class, the peasants, or the revolutionary intelligentsia. As *petit bourgeois*, the Free Officers were not thought to be in a position to effect the desired proletarian revolution, which only the peasant and working classes, acting under the guidance of the CPS, could bring about. Accordingly, although the CPS supported the coup as a first step in the overthrow of 'reactionary' forces, it was none the less convinced that the new regime would have to be pressured into adopting fundamentally Marxist courses of action. The more the CPS organized mass demonstrations in support of these aims, the greater the split became within the ranks of the Free Officers.[16]

The second major bone of contention was Numayri's commitment in 1969 to join the Arab Federation proclaimed in the Tripoli Charter. Realizing that such a federation could work against a communist take-over in the country, the CPS opposed the Charter – at first secretly, through its members in government circles, but from October 1970 onwards publicly. Numayri responded by removing communist ministers from office and, as the CPS escalated the campaign against him, he launched an all-out war on the party and disbanded communist-controlled organizations.

This rupture with the CPS did not, however, prompt Numayri to turn for help to the conservative and sectarian forces. Instead, he chose to go it alone. And it was this complete political isolation that the CPS was able to exploit in a coup against him in July 1971. Initial popular reaction to the coup was neutral, rather than unfavourable, since most Sudanese, already alienated by the regime's measures, were willing to reserve judgement until more was known about the identity and policies of the insurgents. It seemed, therefore, that there would be no popular uprising to save Numayri's regime – until the insurgents committed a fatal mistake. In a radio broadcast, Hashim al-'Ata promised 'scientific' economic reforms, reactivated the disbanded communist organizations, and allowed Red-Flag-bearing demonstrations to parade in the streets. The people immediately identified the coup as communist-inspired, and their enormous anti-Marxist sentiment sprang to life, rescuing Numayri and his regime in the process.

The return of Islamization

The July coup made two things clear to Numayri: the first was the enormous popular opposition to movements of the left, the strength of which he had apparently underestimated; the second was the extent of his own popularity, which he interpreted as a sign that the masses were finally prepared to replace the old order with a new one.[17] A year before, in a political rally organized at the Khartoum race course, Sufi orders had offered him their popular support if he abandoned his communist allies. At that time, Numayri did not accept the offer; after July 1971, he decided to make use of it.

Following the purges of leftists from his government, Numayri offered ministerial and senior government posts to men of Sufi background or to those related to families closely connected with Sufi orders. Thus, men like Ja'far Bakhit (Minister of Local Government), Bashir 'Abbadi (Minister of Communications), Sharif al-Khatim and Rashid al-Tahir Bakr (subsequently Vice-President and Prime Minister) came to play a distinctive and decisive role in Sudanese politics.

At the same time, Numayri adopted public postures which conveyed the impression that he was essentially a devout man and a sincere friend of the *waliys*, or holy men. Every Thursday the President's Office would announce the village or town in which Numayri would perform that week's Friday prayers.[18] In addition, he greatly increased his personal visits to Sufi leaders and invited them to the presidential palace for Ramadan festivities. In more material terms, he provided them with state grants to subsidize their religious celebrations and to build mosques and *zawiyas*, or lodges.[19] By 1974, he publicly acknowledged that 'the role of religion should not be thought of as confined to the level of individuals and the sphere of ethics only, for religion is the cornerstone and basis of all social and political institutions in society as a whole.'[20] Following this, and despite objections from the newly created Ministry of Religious Affairs, he promoted the informal incorporation of Sufi orders into the structure of the Sudanese Socialist Union. By 1976, when this phase of the reconciliation process was completed, Sufi orders had become officially recognized and openly organized in support of Numayri and his regime.

All this inevitably enhanced his image in public eyes. The people's first impression had been that Numayri had faithfully adhered to his declared ideological position, and that accordingly he could ally himself only with those socialist forces that were represented by the United Front of Professionals. Since November 1970, when he dismissed the communist ministers from his government, this impression had begun to change. Numayri was now seen as a relatively unsophisticated but genuinely sincere and patriotic officer, who had not in fact forged a political coalition with leftist nationalists; rather, these forces had used him and his presumed military power-base in order to overthrow, and subsequently crush, conservative political organizations. He was duped, it was argued, into embracing an ideological position and specific policies that were contrived by outsiders, and it was not until a year and a half later that he began to realize how he had been manipulated.[21] His promise in May 1971 that a Sudanese Socialist Union (SSU) would be formed along the lines of Egypt's Arab Socialist Union,[22] and that elections for civilian leaders would be held within two years, had gone a long way to neutralize opposition to him personally. This factor, together with his devout and uncompromising response to the leftist challenge, turned him into the 'saviour' from the communist menace.

This change in public sentiment encouraged Numayri to proceed promptly with the political reorganization of the country.[23] For this, however, he needed a new political structure. The old multi-party system was ineffective and had contributed to the country's social and economic backwardness. Party politics in the Sudan, he argued, was a process through which sectarianism (*ta'infiyya*), as a mystical movement incapable of intellectual development,[24] perpetuated conditions that had prevailed since the Middle Ages.[25] By using political parties for their own selfish aims, the sects prevented not only the modernization of Islam but also the country's political development.[26] To achieve both, he felt, the country had to overcome the political divisions that were the product of sectarian strife. This could best be achieved by adopting a one-party system, in which political power would be concentrated in a Union of Popular Forces (*ittihad al-quwa al-'amma*) as the dominating instrument of change, not only in the political but also in the social and economic domains.

In this political reorganization of the country, Ja'far Bakhit was to make his most important contribution. As a specialist in public administration, he appreciated the subtleties of the 'politics of collaboration' that were associated with the system of native administration. He detested the extreme conservatism of the tribal authorities and he believed, like the leftists, that the existing system of native administration needed to be reformed. But, unlike them, he did not subscribe to the view that it should be abolished altogether. As a strong proponent of local government, he wanted to transform the native administrations into more responsive institutions. In 1968 he was seconded to a post as lecturer at Khartoum University, where, away from the drudgery of civil service work, he had the opportunity to develop his ideas in class debates with students. In 1970, under pressure from leftist students, he was returned to the Ministry of Local Government, and in February 1971 he was made minister. Bakhit thus ironically found himself, at the peak of the anti-communism campaign, in a unique position to effect the much-needed reforms. He crossed 'Abbud's model of the Central Council with Numayri's directives for popular participation in a one-party system and produced a model in which, while the principle of local government was preserved, women and professional organizations were substantially represented in the composition of People's Councils. With conservative and modernizing forces properly balancing each other, the ground was prepared for elections to a Provisional People's Assembly in September 1972.

Once again, the issue of drafting a permanent constitution was to re-emerge. This time, however, it came after an intensive anti-communist drive and a political reorganization that reflected the new realities. The final document, though essentially the handiwork of Ja'far Bakhit, reflected to a great extent the reformation of Numayri's own political beliefs. For him, the Sudan's backwardness was due primarily to the fact that people had long since ceased to behave as good

Muslims.[27] This was partly the result of the decadence that had crept into the Muslim social structure over the past centuries, and partly the result of the religious alienation that derived from the colonial experience. Regarding Islam as regressive and an obstacle to modernization, the colonial regime had introduced Western standards and values in government action, in education, and in economic relations – in fact, in most aspects of public life. Apart from the disastrous effects that it had had on political development under colonial rule, this form of Westernization continued to exert disruptive influences even after political independence had been achieved.[28] What was needed now was to achieve a cultural independence as well. Like the Muslim fundamentalists, Numayri believed that Sudanese society should be purified from all Western behavioural patterns and infused instead with Islamic standards of action. Islamic revelation, he reaffirmed, is valid for all times and places. It defines man's obligations to God and society, and provides him with the motive force necessary to achieve social and intellectual progress.[29] All that is needed is for the Muslim to restore his conviction in, and devotion to, the Islamic faith.

Thus, while he wanted to enforce a separation between sects and state, Numayri none the less sought to preserve a close relationship between religion and society. Such a relationship was imperative if a truly Islamic community was to be re-established, a community in which people are committed to ethical values and in which each person is, first and foremost, his own keeper and not his brother's keeper.[30] Accordingly, in the 'permanent constitution' which was adopted by the People's Assembly in May 1973, Islamic law and custom were established as 'the main sources of legislation'. This Islamization process was advanced one step further in April 1977, when Numayri set up a Committee for the Revision of Sudanese Laws, with a view to bringing them in line with Islamic principles.[31]

Numayri's genuine commitment to the process of Islamization facilitated his political reconciliation with the traditional forces. Since early 1972, he had begun to re-establish contacts with the progressive leaders of these parties, but it was not until July 1977 that the reconciliation process culminated in a formal agreement. According to the terms of that agreement, Numayri restored to them the right to participate in the political process, provided, of course, that they exercised this right within the existing political organization and constitutional framework of the country. In return, they undertook to dissolve the National Front which they had formed as an instrument of opposition to the regime in the early 1970s.

The Muslim Brotherhood movement was the first to cash in on the benefits of this reconciliation agreement. Since 1954, when it was formally organized in the Sudan, its objective has been to establish an Islamic order (*al-nizam al-islami*), run on the principles of the *shari'a*.[32] Although the organization's structure strongly resembled that of its Egyptian counterpart, the Muslim Brotherhood in the Sudan inevitably came to incorporate Sudanese social and religious values. Its leadership and membership came from that generation of nationalists who had grown up under the influence of Sudanese Sufism and had acquired, through modern education, an appreciation for, and a commitment to, economic and social development. As a result, the movement's programme came to be characterized by a high degree of political moderation. Moreover, lacking a popular power-base, the movement initially restricted its participation in national politics to supporting other party candidates who favoured the adoption of an Islamic constitution.

The growing influence of leftists under 'Abbud's regime, particularly their predominant role in the first transitional government after October 1964, necessitated a change in the Muslim Brotherhood's tactics. The stormy political rivalry between communists and Muslim Brothers in the university campus spilt over into the streets. Under the leadership of Hasan al-Turabi, who had been elected secretary-general in 1964, the movement was turned into a political party, calling itself the Islamic Charter Front and embracing a series of other Islam-oriented groups. Turabi's strategy was to form a political alliance with other sympathetic forces, with a view to achieving two aims: first, to isolate politically and then to ban the Communist Party in the Sudan; and second, by exploiting Islamic sentiments, to campaign for an Islamic constitution based on the Muslim Brotherhood's principles. The former was achieved by December 1965, but the latter was obstructed by the imposition of a pro-leftist regime in May 1969. Like other political parties, the Muslim Brotherhood quite understandably opposed that regime and spared no effort to overthrow it. It took an active part with the Ansar in organizing resistance on Aba Island and subsequently helped set up a National Front in exile.

Numayri's suppression of the CPS in 1971, and his subsequent pro-Islamic measures, brought to the surface the fact that in many respects his personal convictions resembled the views held by the Muslim Brotherhood. Like him, the Brothers believed that Western political models, based on a separation between Church and state, were not applicable to the Muslim world and, consequently, that Western ideologies (including Marxism) were politically destabilizing.[33] Islamic standards and social structure, both argued, are not impediments to economic and social development, but rather provide a framework within which such progress can combat social injustice and political oppression.[34] The Qur'an must be re-established, not only as the source of legislation, but also as the foundation of a national constitution that recognizes the *umma* (community of all believers) as the source of all authority, defines people's rights and the state's responsibilities, and is accepted as binding upon both ruler and ruled.[35] Although they disagreed with Numayri on certain details surrounding these general principles, Turabi and his colleagues were convinced that his genuine personal piety had rendered him more susceptible to popular demands for Islamization. By mobilizing this popular sentiment, and by influencing the proceedings of the Law Revision Committee, the movement hoped to introduce legislation that conformed to the *shari'a*, the implementation of which was fundamental to Muslim society, whatever the form of the political order. Accordingly, the influence of the Muslim Brotherhood was restored, and its leaders assumed ministerial and senior government posts in the Numayri regime.

This reconciliation (*musalaha*) was not achieved without a price. The Muslim Brotherhood eventually split into two factions – a moderate one led by Hasan al-Turabi, and a militant one led by Sadiq 'Abdullah 'Abd al-Majid. For Turabi, the conditions of the *musalaha* provided the Muslim Brothers with a valuable opportunity to participate in policy-making. The dissolution of the party organization, which was a *sine qua non* of this reconciliation, was not seen as an insurmountable obstacle. The old structure was irrelevant to the new conditions in any case: political parties were still banned and the only political organization in existence was the SSU. Admittedly, the SSU had retained its original form, but it had nevertheless undergone profound changes in its orientation and political role. Besides, the ideology of the Muslim Brotherhood advanced the establishment of a *shura* model of 'democracy', the details of which were still to be worked out, but in which political parties as such do not exist and legislation or policy-making is the product of consultation with *'ulama*. With Numayri's acquiescence, the People's Assembly had increasingly assumed the functions of just such a council on the *shura* model. Turabi therefore considered it expedient to build a new basis of organization for the Muslim Brotherhood, one that enabled its members to be integrated into the SSU and, at the same time, permitted the movement to mobilize or incorporate other Islamic revivalist groups. This policy of 'flexibility', he believed, would provide the movement with the opportunity to pull strings at two levels: first, by assuming senior government posts, members would be in a position to influence policy; and, second, by not being restricted to the old party structure, they would have greater freedom to propagate their ideology in their cultural centres – *ihya al-nashat al-islami* ('revival of Islamic activity'). Through its control of these centres, the mosques, and the student organizations, the Brotherhood could bring additional pressure to bear on decision-making.

A number of Brotherhood leaders, however, opposed Turabi's policy of integration within the SSU.[36] Since 1978, these militants increasingly denounced Turabi's tactics as essentially 'un-Islamic' and called for a stop to these 'unethical' activities. They were convinced that, despite the Brotherhood's participation, Numayri's regime would not ultimately be Islamized, and they feared that the mobilization of people who were still substantially influenced by Sufi practices could boomerang and lead instead to a dilution of the movement's orthodoxy. Rather than participating in SSU politics, these hardliners urged that the movement should concentrate its efforts on educating the population in regard to the Brotherhood's principles so that in due course the movement would have the required firm social roots.

The political benefits of Turabi's more pragmatic approach, however, were to become unmistakably evident as time passed. By autumn 1980, the movement was sufficiently well reorganized to enable it to gain a substantial number of seats in the elections for a new People's Assembly. As the majority of the Muslim Brotherhood's leadership followed him, Turabi decided to put an end to the political embarrassment caused by the opposition of the militants and formally terminated their leaders' membership in the movement.

Turabi's policy of integration within the SSU provoked opposition from other religious groups as well, albeit for different reasons. One of these groups was the Ansar movement led by Sadiq al-Mahdi. From the outset, the Ansar leadership was unequivocally opposed to the communists' predominance in the Numayri regime and, in a meeting held on Aba Island in late May 1969, it put forward two possible courses of action. The first was to persuade Numayri to terminate communist participation in the government; the second was to arm the Ansar so that, in the event of failure in the first course, it would be in a position to confront the leftist regime militarily. Accordingly, Sadiq al-Mahdi met Numayri in early June 1969 and demanded either the removal of the communists from the new cabinet or the participation of all other parties. In addition, Sadiq proposed a programme of action which contained most of the economic and agrarian policies that were subsequently to be implemented by Numayri, but which also included certain measures that would have significantly weakened the leftists' influence. Probably distrustful of Sadiq's motives, Numayri responded by arresting him and imprisoning him at Gebeit.[37] The regime's uncompromising stand left the Ansar with no choice but to proceed with its second course of action, a course that eventually led to the well-known armed confrontation on Aba Island in the last days of March 1970.

Numayri's anti-communist, and successively pro-Islamic, measures after July 1971 were heartily welcomed by Sadiq, but they were not regarded as sufficient to bring about the desired political changes. Like Numayri, Sadiq believed that the parliamentary model had failed to solve the nation's problems and that it had served instead to maintain a discredited Westernized elite in positions of power.[38] He had also condemned sectarian rivalry in politics and, embittered by the political games of 'partyism' (*hizbiyya*), he had advocated, even before May 1969, the adoption of a popularly based one-party system as the most efficacious way of promoting economic and social progress.[39] But, unlike Numayri, he did not regard the 'permanent constitution' of 1973 as a completely satisfactory framework for such progress. In his view, the People's Assembly was not vested with adequate legislative powers and, with ministers responsible only to the President, its role was politically ineffective.[40] Moreover, he disapproved of the close connections between the SSU and the state or security organizations, believing them to be factors that transformed the People's Assembly from a 'representative' into a 'delegative' body.[41]

What he wanted to see was the dissolution of these bonds and the evolution of an independent, broadly based political organization which would enjoy genuine freedom of thought and expression. At the same time, he considered it essential to introduce certain amendments to the 'permanent constitution', with a view to establishing a *shura* assembly that would have both a truly representative character and the authority not only to re-enact provisions of the *shari'a* in the light of modern conditions, but also to validate existing modern legislation for which no provisions can be found in Islamic law. It is only in this way that the *umma* can effectively vindicate itself as the source of all authority (*sulta*) and the possessor of sovereignty (*siyada*).[42] For Sadiq, this was the fundamental pre-condition for the modernization of the *shari'a* and, concomitantly, of Sudanese society.[43]

The reconciliation agreement afforded Sadiq the opportunity to influence the course of the country's political development. His objective was to encourage Numayri to modify the political framework so as to allow broader political participation and freer political expression while at the same time reassuring Numayri that he did not want to see multi-party politics restored. As a basis for such a modification, Sadiq was prepared to accept the SSU as the country's only political organization. But to ensure effective popular participation in its policy-making processes, he called for a root-and-branch democratization both of the SSU and of the People's Assembly.[44] This was for him an essential pre-condition in return for his own participation in Numayri's government.

This institutional reform has become even more important following the Muslim Brotherhood's pre-emptive infiltration of the SSU. Like the Muslim Brothers, Sadiq believes that Islam plays a major role in the socio-political life of Muslims and that Islamic principles should be the main source of legislation.[45] But, unlike them, he does not subscribe to the belief that Islamization means the revival of certain *traditional* patterns and institutions. 'To try to resurrect them', he argues, 'is to try to shape contemporary society in the mould of a bygone intellectual and social past.'[46] The modern state and its institutions are for him new political phenomena. The original Islamic state does not resemble the modern one, and the function of *ahl al-hall wa'l-'aqd* ('those who loose and bind' – i.e., the *'ulama*) cannot be compared to that of present-day legislative assemblies.[47] This view is connected to his conception of the *shari'a*. For him, the Islamic code revealed by the Prophet Muhammad is sufficiently flexible to adapt to differences of time and place, with man himself entrusted to bring about such adaptation.[48] In order to be able to do so, however, 'the schools of Moslem law must be transcended in favour of a new position bound only by the Quran and Sunnah and capable of dealing with contemporary circumstances.'[49] He is convinced that Mahdist thought, by transcending sects and *madhhabs* (schools of law), and by drawing legislation from the original sources, could contribute effectively to Islam's accommodation with modernization and development. But, whereas the Muslim Brothers give prominence to the adoption of an Islamic constitution, Sadiq places greater emphasis on the prior fundamental adaptation of religious thought and institutions.

Besides Mahdist apprehensions about the Muslim Brotherhood's influence, there has been a growing opposition from the Khatmiyya and other Sufi orders. In their view, the Muslim Brothers underestimate the contribution of *faqihs* (legal experts) to Islamic jurisprudence, and emphasize instead the use of the Qur'an and Sunna as the only valid sources. Such Islamic legislation, without proper reference to procedures of *qiyas* (analogy) and *ijtihad* (independent judgement), is regarded as totally unacceptable. The Khatmiyya, in particular, view the Muslim Brothers as essentially Westernized Muslims, influenced by Orientalists in believing that Islam needs to be, and can in fact be, reformed.[50]

Like both the Muslim Brothers and the Ansar, the Sufi orders believe that the social and political institutions of the state should be Islamized. But they would not like to see Islamization take a form which could ultimately prove detrimental to their work. And yet the Muslim Brotherhood's potential to influence the formation of policy, and the growing political stature of Sadiq al-Mahdi, have merely served to intensify Sufi fears in this regard. Although reluctant to participate directly in a contest for political power, the *tariqa* leaders have none the less taken indirect measures to safeguard their interests. In 1978, on the personal initiative of Sayyid Muhammad 'Uthman al-Mirghani, they formed the Islamic Revival Committee to serve as a pressure group both within and outside the established political institutions.[51] In particular, Sayyid Muhammad 'Uthman has revived the traditional practice of touring his strongholds, ostensibly on ceremonial visits to open new mosques or schools, but probably also to demonstrate that Khatmiyya influence is still capable of responding vigorously to new challenges.

The stage is thus set for the Islamization of Sudanese politics in the 1980s. The struggle will probably centre on the various groups' determination to define the form that the Islamization of the state and its institutions should take. In this struggle, the divergence of Islamic ideologies will not be the only factor. The apprehensions and reservations of the southern Sudanese, the majority of whom are either Christian or pagan, will also have an impact. The regional autonomy of the southern region, which is guaranteed in the 'permanent constitution', should act as a device limiting the indiscriminate implementation of Islamic legislation within these areas. The politics of Islamization, therefore, will most probably be confined, at least for the foreseeable future, to the Muslim population in the northern and central Sudan. What that outcome will be, given the gradual spread of economic development and social change from urban to rural areas, only time can tell.

Notes

1. Ja'far Muhammad Numayri, *al-Nahj al-islami li-madha* (Cairo, al-Maktab al-Misri al-Hadith, 1980).
2. J. S. Trimingham, *Islam in the Sudan* (London, Oxford University Press, 1949), pp. 81ff. For a more detailed account of Arab penetration, see Yusuf Fadl Hasan,

The Arabs and the Sudan from the Seventh to the Early Sixteenth Century (Edinburgh, Edinburgh University Press, 1967).

3. For a general discussion, see Gabriel Warburg, 'Popular Islam and Tribal Leadership in the Socio-Political Structure of Northern Sudan', in Menahem Milson (ed.), *Society and Political Structure in the Arab World* (New York, Humanities Press, 1973), pp. 231–80.

4. John Voll, 'The Sudanese Mahdi: Frontier Fundamentalist', *International Journal of Middle Eastern Studies*, 10 (1979), 145–66; also P. M. Holt, *The Mahdist State in the Sudan 1881–1898* (Oxford, Clarendon Press, 1958), ch. 1.

5. John Voll, 'Mahdis, Walis, and New Men in the Sudan', in Nikki R. Keddie (ed.), *Scholars, Saints, and Sufis: Muslim Institutions in the Middle East Since 1500* (Berkeley, University of California Press, 1972), pp. 367–84. For a detailed analysis of the evolution of these alliances, see A. S. Cudsi, 'The Rise of Political Parties in the Sudan: 1936–1946' (unpublished Ph.D. thesis, University of London, 1978).

6. Yusuf Fadl Hasan, 'The Sudanese Revolution of October 1964', *The Journal of Modern African Studies*, 5 (1967), 491–509; also Ruth First, *The Barrel of a Gun: Political Power in Africa and the Coup d'Etat* (London, Allen Lane, The Penguin Press, 1970), pp. 222–77.

7. Peter K. Bechtold, *Politics in the Sudan: Parliamentary and Military Rule in an Emerging African Nation* (New York, Praeger, 1976), p. 215.

8. *Ibid.*, p. 225.

9. 'Chronology', *The Middle East Journal* (hereafter *MEJ*), 23 (1969), 377.

10. Gabriel Warburg, *Islam, Nationalism and Communism in a Traditional Society: The Case of Sudan* (London, Frank Cass, 1978), p. 164.

11. Numayri argues that he did not welcome such an alliance but that he felt compelled to accept it for fear that these leftists would have otherwise betrayed the preparations for the coup. See Numayri, *al-Nahj al-islami*, pp. 74ff.

12. *MEJ*, 23 (1969), 522.

13. Bechtold, *Politics in the Sudan*, p. 259.

14. Jaafar M.A. Bakhiet, 'The Politics of Native Administration, 1964–69', in John Howell (ed.), *Local Government and Politics in the Sudan* (Khartoum, Khartoum University Press, 1974), pp. 48ff.

15. *Ibid.*, 'Introduction', p. 8.

16. Numayri, *al-Nahj al-islami*, pp. 141–3.

17. *Ibid.*, pp. 127ff.

18. Bechtold, *Politics in the Sudan*, p. 275.

19. Idris Salim al-Hassan, 'On Ideology: The Case of Religion in Northern Sudan' (unpublished Ph.D. dissertation, University of Connecticut, 1980), pp. 175–6.

20. Numayri's Report to the First National Congress of the SSU, January 1974.

21. Bechtold, *Politics in the Sudan*, p. 261. Numayri admits that CPS manipulations had in effect diverted the May revolution from its original course. See Numayri, *al-Nahj al-islami*, p. 137.

22. *MEJ*, 25 (1971), 518.

23. Numayri, *al-Nahj al-islami*, pp. 144–5.

24. *Ibid.*, p. 132.

25. *Ibid.*, p. 156.

26. *Ibid.*, p. 343.

27. *Ibid.*, pp. 393ff.

28. *Ibid.*, p. 337.

29. *Ibid.*, p. 411.

30. *Ibid.*, p. 443.

31. To implement such a revision, two committees were established: A general committee, headed by the Chief Justice; and a technical committee, composed of nine

members and headed by the Attorney-General. The latter is responsible for undertaking research into original sources over the rights and duties of the individual and his relationship to society as a whole. In addition, it is authorized to re-evaluate existing laws, with a view to identifying contradictions with *shari'a* principles. The general committee, to which the technical committee reports, is charged with the task of recommending the necessary legislative and legal changes within the principles of its general terms of reference. The work of these committees has, however, progressed very slowly.

32. For a general discussion of some of the origins of the Muslim Brotherhood movement in the Sudan, see Salah el-Din el-Zein el-Tayeb, *KUSU: The Students' Movement in the Sudan, 1940–1970* (Khartoum, Khartoum University Press, 1971), pp. 43–5. For an analysis of its role in electoral politics, see Bechtold, *Politics in the Sudan*, ch. 7.

33. Interview, Muslim Brotherhood leaders, March and April 1981; see also Numayri, *al-Nahj al-islami*, pp. 61, 340, and 424.

34. *Ibid.*; also Numayri, pp. 26 and 362ff.

35. *Ibid.*; also Numayri, pp. 150 and 335.

36. The most prominent of these were Ja'far Shaykh Idris, who, as more fundamentalist in thought, considered Turabi extremely liberal on some ideological issues; Malik Badri, who believed that the movement should concentrate primarily on its educational mission; and Sadiq 'Abdullah 'Abd al-Majid, a pioneer of the movement since his student days in Egypt in 1946, who had some political reservations.

37. Sadiq al-Mahdi, *al-Musalaha al-wataniyya al-sudaniyya min al-alif ila al-ya* (n.d.), pp. 3–4; also *MEJ*, 23 (1969), 523.

38. Sadiq al-Mahdi, 'al-Fikr al-islami wa'l-dawla al-haditha', in his *Ahadith al-ghurba 'an al-thawra wa'l-islam wa'l-'uruba wa ruh al-'asr wa afriqiya* (Beirut, Dar al-Qadaya, 1976), p. 13.

39. Sadiq al-Mahdi, *al-Musalaha*, p. 33; also Numayri, *al-Nahj al-islami*, p. 222ff.

40. Interview, Sadiq al-Mahdi, November 1980.

41. Sadiq al-Mahdi, *al-Musalaha*, p. 65.

42. Sadiq al-Mahdi, 'al-Fikr al-islami', pp. 38 and 43–5.

43. Sadiq's argument rests mainly on his interpretation that a combination of factors had led to the stagnation of the *shari'a*. He identifies four such factors: (*a*) The practice of *taqlid*, which served as an 'intellectual strait-jacket'; (*b*) the imposition of despotic rule, which meant the monopolization of the policy-making processes; (*c*) the emergence of social and economic privilege, which subordinated public welfare to economic interest; and (*d*) the evolution of a quietist ethic by Sufi orders, which unintentionally allowed the survival of unjust conditions. See his *Social Change in Islam* (April 1980), p. 7.

44. Interview, Sadiq al-Mahdi, November 1980.

45. Sadiq al-Mahdi, 'al-Fikr al-islami', p. 43.

46. Sadiq al-Mahdi, *Social Change in Islam*, p. 10.

47. Sadiq al-Mahdi, 'al-Fikr al-islami', pp. 42–3.

48. *SUDANOW*, November 1979, p. 20.

49. Sadiq al-Mahdi, *Mahdism in Islam* (April 1980), p. 8.

50. Interview, Khatmiyya *shaykhs*, April 1981. For a more detailed account of the Khatmiyya order up to the late 1950s, see John Voll, 'A History of the Khatmiyya Tariqah in the Sudan' (unpublished Ph.D dissertation, Harvard University, 1969).

51. *SUDANOW*, November 1980, p. 41. Apart from the Khatmiyya, the other major orders represented on the Islamic Revival Committee are the Tijaniyya, Shadhiliyya, Qadiriyya, and Idrisiyya.

4   Ideological Politics in Sa'udi Arabia

JAMES P. PISCATORI*

Sa'udi Arabia evokes for most Westerners, though not for a great many Muslims, an image of Islam itself. The two holy cities of Mecca and Medina are there, of course, but what fascinates the West is the curiosity of an Islamic society rushing to modernize while a conservative dynasty constantly talks of Islamic commitment and occasionally applies the *lex talionis*. Although there was little Western public attention to Sa'udi Arabia before 1978 – it received, for example, only nine minutes' coverage per year on American television from 1972 to 1977[1] – today there is almost a fixation with the country and the stability of its regime. But there is a sharp division of opinion on the compatibility of development and Islam and of monarchy and Islam. With the bright light that the Iranian revolution has now created, some observers see great differences between Sunni Sa'udi Arabia and Shi'i Iran and conclude that the overthrow of the Shah presents no general lessons; other observers see the discontents of Sa'udis in a rapidly changing society with egregiously wealthy overlords and conclude that the royal family's end is imminent. I want to explain how it is that Islam has been central to the Sa'udi political process before attempting to suggest how it might be important in the future.

Islam and the establishment of the kingdom

Although many people regard the kingdom as far from, even as a perversion of, the ideal of the Islamic state, there is reason to think of Islam when talking about the Sa'uds. Indeed, since the eighteenth century they have prided themselves on the assiduous application of Islamic norms and practices. In 1744 an extraordinary alliance was

*I wish to thank J. Patrick Bannerman and Malise Ruthven for prodding, though they do not necessarily agree with, my thoughts.

56

struck between a local ruler and a local religious reformer, between Muhammad ibn Sa'ud and Muhammad ibn 'Abd al-Wahhab. The latter, disturbed by the obvious lapses in faith in the Prophet's peninsula, preached that God is indivisible, that veneration of saints verges on polytheism, that prayer is obligatory, and that the penalties of the *shari'a* must be upheld.

Muhammad ibn Sa'ud was impressed by this message of reform because of the beneficial effect it might have on regional politics. Ibn 'Abd al-Wahhab also saw the political ramifications clearly. According to Philby, the reformer told the prince: 'Be you too assured of honour and power, for whoso believeth in the One God and worketh His will, he shall have the kingdom of the country and its people.'[2] Without a doubt, Ibn 'Abd al-Wahhab also realized that his religious message would have greater impact with the support of strong and ambitious men like the Sa'uds. This convergence of political and religious interests led to an alliance of great importance: shortly after the two men exchanged their pledges of mutual support, what we can call the first Sa'udi state came into being. Between 1773 and 1819, the combined force united, for the first time since the days of the early Islamic community, most of the lands that make up the current kingdom.

This achievement came to an abrupt end in 1819, when the Ottoman government of Egypt became alarmed by Sa'udi power and by its threat to Damascus and Baghdad and to Ottoman control of the Pilgrimage. The Ottoman pasha, Muhammad 'Ali, invaded the state and razed the capital. It was not, however, the end of the Sa'ud–Wahhab alliance, which found a second political expression, this time centring on Riyadh and dating from the 1820s. It was less successful than the first. Opposition from the Ottomans, local rivals, and fighting within the family's ranks proved too much: the Sa'uds were forced to seek exile in Kuwait in 1891. But while it lasted, this state, like the first, had been beneficial to the Sa'uds since it allowed them to gain control of territory while putting them on the side of a great cause – removing unworthy innovations from the holy peninsula; and it had been beneficial to the zealots since it helped them to spread the word.

Perhaps the clearest expression of this combining of forces occurred in the early part of this century when 'Abd al-'Aziz (often known as Ibn Sa'ud) moved to recover and control what he now thought of as ancestral lands. To do so he initiated a unique experiment of settling certain nomads for the purpose of creating fixed territorial communities and of supplying him with recruits for a standing army. The first settlement consisted mostly of members of the Mutayr tribe, but eventually there were over two hundred communities involving most of the major tribes. The motivation was clearly Islamic: an adherent was called *akh*, or brother; the movement as a whole, the Ikhwan, or brotherhood; and each settlement a *hijra* – a migration from the corrupted to the purifying existence, just as Muhammad's 'flight' from Mecca to Medina had been. Of course, the implication that one was duty-bound to flee from the nomadic to the sedentary life fitted 'Abd al-'Aziz's designs, for once the bedouin became settled, they also became dependent on him for their livelihood.

Although some outsiders thought this dependence reduced them to virtual poverty,[3] they were organized into an effective military machine. Each *hijra* consisted of those who were on active duty, of reservists who normally engaged in pastoral pursuits but who could be mobilized quickly, and of those who could be 'conscripted' if the religious authorities (*'ulama*) declared that there was an emergency. 'Abd al-'Aziz was able to draw from these many thousands of troops, most of whom showed a fierce devotion to Islam. As one observer noted, they were eager to commit themselves to the death,[4] and, indeed, frightful excesses of violence occurred – for example, at Khurma in 1919 and Ta'if in 1924. Probably because of this zeal, they quickly succeeded in overwhelming the Rashids in the Najd, the central area of the peninsula, and the Hashimites in the Hijaz, the area along the Red Sea coast that includes Mecca and Medina.

A contemporary writer's evaluation was correct: 'Ibn Sa'ud has reverted to the time-honoured practice of using the religious beliefs of his subjects to help him forge a weapon with which to push forward his political dynastic ambitions.'[5] We would be unfair to conclude from this that 'Abd al-'Aziz insincerely endorsed the Ikhwan's values. There is no doubt that he believed in its *muwahhid* ('unitarian' or, popularly, Wahhabi) goals and that he himself was relatively devout, but just as clearly he could not have been unaware of its usefulness for establishing his right to rule. Whereas in the eighteenth century the Sa'udi and Wahhabi forces had used each other to roughly equal advantage, in the beginning of this century the Wahhabis' use of the Sa'uds became far less important than the Sa'uds' use of the Wahhabis. It is a pattern seen many times before in Islamic history: the fusion of temporal and spiritual authorities ends with the subjection of the spiritual.

Islam and the maintenance of the regime

Having created a nation-state by relying on a combination of force and ideological mobilization, 'Abd al-'Aziz found the combination useful for maintaining his rule. It is obvious that he and his successors have used Islam to legitimate their positions and policies – and, indeed, their very right to govern as a royal family. They have accomplished this by emphasizing their special role as guardian of the holy places, patron of the Pilgrimage, and promoter of Islamic causes throughout the world. Moreover, they have relied on the proposition that the Qur'an is the Sa'udi constitution to justify the monarchy. Kings are acceptable, according to this thesis, because everybody, including the king, must be subject to God's word. It is not surprising that this constitutional notion has favoured the Sa'uds: they have been able to rule without checks on their power while claiming to be deferential to the basic laws of Islam.

Specific policies also often help to validate the Sa'uds' right to rule. King Faysal, for instance, undoubtedly believed that pan-Islamic cooperation was desirable, but his timing in launching his scheme – when he was under attack from the immensely popular 'Abd al-Nasir – suggests that he saw pan-Islam as a way to counter the adverse effects that Nasirism or pan-Arabism was having on his regime's legitimacy. Sometimes, however, the Sa'uds have had to call on Islam for support, not of their royal birthright, but of ways they wished to exercise their prerogatives. For example, when 'Abd al-'Aziz made use of the radio and motor car and Faysal introduced the television and women's education, they had to answer the conservatives' vocal opposition by clever appeals to Islamic general principles. Islamic history also came in handy when 'Abd al-'Aziz imported infidel oil technicians: 'Showing a thorough knowledge of the Prophet's life and traditions, the King cited several well-attested cases when the Prophet employed non-Muslims individually and in groups. "Am I right or wrong?" The [*ulama*] replied unanimously that he was right.'[6]

In fact, until recently the Sa'uds have been able relatively easily to use Islam for legitimation. They have been able to do so for three reasons. First, there has been an absence of competing sources of legitimacy. With the possible exception of the Shi'a, to whom I shall refer later, ethnic and religious differences have not been very important and have not complicated national unity. By and large, the kingdom is homogeneously Arab and Suni; the kind of pluralism that makes Islam merely one of several keys to the individual's loyalty and identity, as in Iran or Syria, does not exist in Sa'udi Arabia.

Even the legendarily independent bedouin have not been resistant to national integration. In the early days of the kingdom, rivalry between the tribes had worked to 'Abd al-'Aziz's advantage because it prevented them from forming a united movement against him; and because they were poor, they were dependent on his largess. In the intervening fifty years, the Sa'udi government has gradually solidified its control over them: it has discouraged attachment to the *diras*, or traditional grazing grounds; it abolished the related *hima* system, whereby tribes held exclusive territorial rights to wells and even to villages; it nationalized the *qalamat*, or new water supplies, which, particularly in times of drought, led tribes to share resources regardless of their old habits and claims; and it has encouraged them to settle. The result is that tribal identifications have become weak and that, therefore, they are unlikely in the extreme to serve as the basis of an effective ideology. As the bedouin often say these days, 'All the land is the *dira* of the Sa'uds' (*al-ard kulluha dirat Al Sa'ud*).[7]

Outside ideologies, such as Nasirism, Ba'thism, or Marxism, have had only limited appeal and thus have not competed with Islam. This is due not only to the natural Islamic devotion of the Sa'udi people but also to the socialization that the young now undergo. Whether in the schools or armed forces, young Sa'udis are exposed to a way of looking at things which, to say the least, is hostile to the radical ideologies popular elsewhere in the Arab world. There is always the chance that they will rebel against the official line of thinking, but until now they seem to be conforming readily. As one researcher noted of a group of college students in 1968, 'There seems to be a willingness among most of our [subjects] to accept authority and to esteem it.'[8] It is unfortunate that more recent data are not available, but there is little reason to suppose that the observation is no longer relevant. Perhaps one sign that the Sa'uds continue to be successful in warding off alien ideologies is that a group of dissident students has attacked them for enslaving the people through 'indoctrination' (*al-ta'limat al-sa'udiyya*).[9]

Second, it has been easy for the Sa'uds to use Islam for legitimation because they have institutionalized the religious authorities *and* because they have given them wide functions. Since 'Abd al-'Aziz, who was committed to the Hanbali school of law, gradually replaced the antagonistic jurists of the Hanafi school in the Hijaz, the *'ulama* have had to depend on the government for their salaries and positions; they have become agents of the state. And because their methods of selection and education have been regularized, they have become bureaucratized. This pattern is not unique among Islamic countries, but what makes Sa'udi Arabia different is the extent of influence the *'ulama* have.

Until recently, for example, they have controlled education. Even now, when the two ministries of university and of pre-university education are modernizing the system, the *'ulama* run several institutes of higher learning, such as the Imam Ibn Sa'ud Islamic University in Riyadh. They are also in charge of the Pilgrimage, which brings over a million Muslims to Mecca and Medina each year, and they control the pious endowments (*waqfs*). They are the arbiters of social morality as well, controlling the Committees for the Exhortation of Good and the Suppression of Evil, which enforce the closing of shops at the prayer times and modesty of dress in the larger cities. In 1962 Faysal promised to reduce their power, and it is clear that they have become less active as they become more embarrassing to the Sa'udi government, which is worried about its reputation abroad. Nevertheless, because there has been a recent upsurge of conservative feeling throughout the country, which King Khalid shared, the religious police are not likely to be abolished altogether.

Furthermore, the *'ulama* have direct political influence because of their long-standing connection with the elite itself. The leading *'ulama* are from important families, like the Al al-Shaykh who are descended from Ibn 'Abd al-Wahhab, and their ties to the Al Sa'ud are particularly close. It is natural, therefore, for the Sa'uds to call on them to approve decisions that go to the heart of the regime's stability. For example, the religious establishment was called on to support the decision in 1964 to depose 'Abd al-'Aziz's incompetent son, Sa'ud, and to replace him with another son, Faysal. More recently, King Khalid and Crown Prince Fahd (yet other sons of 'Abd al-'Aziz) were careful to secure a *fatwa* (religious opinion) to legitimate their actions to end the Great Mosque takeover.[10] They certainly could have acted without a *fatwa*, but asking for one cost them nothing and probably gained them something important in the long run – a reaffirmation of the Sa'uds' special role as protectors of the holy places and, thus, of their primary claim to govern.

Third and last, the Sa'uds have been able to use Islam for legitimation because they have followed a flexible approach towards Islam itself. Rather than being rigid in the interpretation and application of Islamic law, they have been largely skilful in making it compatible with a modern society; in doing so, they have tended to fulfil the people's demands for measured change and to make themselves popular. This is a point which is generally overlooked, probably because historians emphasize the puritanism of the Wahhabis, and journalists make much of the intolerance of the religious police. Both, of course, are accurate, but they present an incomplete picture of the current complexity of Sa'udi life. Indeed, contrary to what we might expect, the Sa'udis have made innovations remarkably easily.

One reason why they have been capable of changing is the flexibility of the Hanbali school of law. The conventional Western wisdom on this subject is exactly the opposite – that the Hanbalis are the most unbending of jurisprudents and that, accordingly, they have impeded legal development in the one country where they are dominant. However, this view misinterprets Hanbali conservatism: there must be faithful adherence to the Qur'an and the *hadiths* (the traditions of the Prophet), but when these have nothing to say on a subject, there are no rigid guidelines. In practice this attitude has translated into the assumption that an innovation is permissible unless there is a clear textual prohibition of it. The manoeuvrability this provides is compatible with with the consistent Hanbali emphasis on *ijtihad*, or independent reasoning. Hanbalis, particularly the great fourteenth-century jurist, Ibn Taymiyya, have always held that the *'ulama* should rely on their own judgement when the Qur'an, the traditions, and the authoritative consensus of the Prophetic community are vague. Over time, the exercise of this independent judgement has had salutary results. For example, whereas the Hanafi school makes only the closest relatives responsible for the care of the impoverished or ill, the Hanbali school broadens the responsibility to include all relatives who stand to inherit from them; Iraq and Jordan accepted this interpretation as more just.

In addition to relying on the built-in flexibility of the Hanbali school, the Sa'udis have resorted to other ways of making acceptable changes. One is the selective choice of legal opinions (*takhayyur*) to justify one's position. In the early days of the kingdom, 'Abd al-'Aziz encountered difficulties in persuading the *'ulama* to call upon non-Hanbali sources, and he eventually ruled that judges were to rely principally on six Hanbali texts.[11] At the same time he stressed that they could consult other schools when their own was unclear on, or did not address itself to, the question at hand. This might seem unnecessary since, as we have seen, the Hanbali school is permissive, but the king and his successors knew that in the justifying of a legal policy any text is better than none. In the Mining Code, for instance, the Sa'udis rely on the clearer position of the Maliki school that minerals should not fall into private hands under any circumstances.[12]

Another way of facilitating change is administrative discretion (*siyasa shar'iyya*). Since the eleventh century it has been a way for rulers to exercise some freedom within the bounds of the divine legislation (*shari'a*). The Sa'udis show their sensitivity to this by hesitating to use the word *qanun*, which implies a legislated enactment, and by preferring the more neutral word *nizam* when they speak of a 'law' that they have brought into effect. But, whatever the terminology, they have not been passive. For example, they introduced the Commercial Code as early as 1931, and revised it, according to the Western-influenced Ottoman Commercial code, in 1954; they also introduced the Labour and Workmen Law in 1970. The Social Insurance law, promulgated in 1970 as well, indicates how the government can change traditional law by administrative discretion. Rather than following the customary laws of inheritance when an insured worker dies, the regulation limits the circle of relatives who may inherit and qualifies the rights of inheritance of some of them (the deceased's father, for example, must be over sixty years of age and unable to work).[13]

Related to administrative discretion is sovereign prerogative (*takhsis al-qada*), by which the Islamic ruler may make institutional changes. The Sa'udi government changed the court system in 1927, 1931, 1936, and 1952. Most important, it created appellate institutions, so that the citizen now has recourse beyond the *qadi* (judge) who first hears the case: he can go to the Court of Cassation and the Supreme Judicial Court. He also can appeal to the Board of Grievances, which was set up in 1955, if he is the victim of an administrative injustice. The government has also set up a tribunal under the Labour and Workmen Law to hear and resolve labour disputes and to impose appropriate penalties,[14] and, more generally, in 1971 it substituted for the office of Grand Mufti a Ministry of Justice.

By all these ways, then, the Sa'udis have shown that they are willing and able to adapt to modern conditions and to complement the *shari'a* with new pieces of legislation and new institutions. This flexibility has helped the elite to keep pace with many social developments and so to present itself as a prudent government: its attitude to Islam has affected its capacity to use it for legitimation.

Opposition to the regime

From this discussion, it would appear that Islam is the main pillar of the Sa'udi regime, but it would be wrong to conclude that it will always be so or even that it will always be a stabilizing element. Because the kingdom is now undergoing the unprecedented strains of rapid development, it is possible that Islam will have a role to play in attacks on the government. But before we can assess the likelihood of that, it is necessary to review the rapid changes which, in under forty years, have moved Sa'udi Arabia from being a recipient of Western subsidies and loans to being a governor of the International Monetary Fund. In this period, it has begun to industrialize, to import large numbers of foreign workers, and to construct an extensive social welfare system. Several consequences are apparent.

One is the rapid growth of bureaucracy. If an American diplomatic observer could write in 1941 that 'there is no government organization in Sa'udi Arabia in the generally accepted sense of the term',[15] it is clearly a different case now. Only two ministries, Foreign Affairs and Finance, existed in 1932, but today there are twenty-two. Government has become the largest employer, generating reams of regulations and official forms for every sphere of life. Though it is a cumbersome development, perhaps inhibiting creative responses to the dilemmas of modernization, it constitutes a kind of institutional check on royal absolutism.

A second consequence is the development of a technocratic or modernizing middle class. New wealth has created new educational and job opportunities, and many beneficiaries are now important bureaucratic officials, including cabinet ministers. They are particularly important in the Ministries of Petroleum, Finance, Commerce, Agriculture, Communications, and Information, although they are present in every government bureau. They are characterized by having received secular and advanced foreign training and by being irritated with some of the more conservative of the *'ulama*. The religious police embarrass them, and they are uncomfortable with some of the restrictions still imposed on women. If they are cool or, at best, indifferent towards the religious leadership, most of them are not anti-royalist. Writing in 1973, William Rugh noted that 'the New Middle Class does not really compete with the princes. In business, the two groups sometimes form naturally beneficial partnerships.'[16] While the young men of this middle class meet socially with their peers from time to time, there is no evidence yet that these groups, or *shilal*, are the nucleus of a political movement.

A closely related consequence of the kingdom's modernization is that there are now a number of well-educated, foreign-trained members of the royal family itself. Most notably, the sons of King Faysal are making an impact. Prince Sa'ud, the Foreign Minister, is often mentioned as a worthy candidate for the throne, and Prince Khalid is proving to be an effective governor of 'Asir. Other princes are assuming responsible positions, and it is perhaps likely that they will be spokesmen for liberalizing, albeit moderate, reforms.

A final consequence is that modernization is victimizing significant numbers of Sa'udis, as it does the poor, the illiterate, and the rural in virtually all developing countries. In Sa'udi Arabia the rush for a more efficient and self-sufficient economy has led to the consolidation of farmlands, resulting in small landholders seeking brighter futures in the cities. There they complicate an already difficult situation with inadequate social services, scarce and exorbitantly priced housing, and few jobs. Illiterate, as 80 per cent of Sa'udis still are, and lacking marketable skills, these rural dispossessed stand a good chance of becoming the urban dispossessed.

But even the educated young may prove to be victims. As their numbers swell, their chances of finding satisfying employment diminish because of the limits of the economy's absorptiveness and the presence of large numbers of foreign workers. Indeed, the government intended that 1.3 million students would be in the primary schools and 21,000 students in the high schools by 1980.[17] The number of girl students was to rise to almost half a million at school at all levels. Because these students have benefited from the first fruits of modernization, they have come to expect unlimited progress;[18] they are bound to meet disappointment.

These changes suggest that although there is relative tranquillity now, the Sa'udi regime might come under attack if it continues to deny a political role to the bureaucrats and intellectuals, or if it fails to redress injustices that the development process creates. There certainly have been oppositional movements in the past, but they have been unsuccessful in posing a serious threat and in gathering popular support. The most celebrated example is the defection of Princes Talal, Badr, 'Abd al-Muhsin, and Fawwaz, all sons of 'Abd al-'Aziz, to the Cairo of 'Abd al-Nasir. Critical of the spendthrift ways of King Sa'ud and the political conservatism of the regime generally, in 1962 they proclaimed themselves the Arab Nationalist Front and pledged themselves to the creation of a 'free Sa'udi Arabia'. They seemed to have a reasonable chance of succeeding, since Sa'ud had brought the country to bankruptcy, and the Egyptians, having intervened in the Yemeni civil war, were on the borders of the kingdom. Yet Faysal, as prime minister, soon did much to set the Sa'udi economic house in order, and

Egyptian troops became caught in the tribal and political entanglements of the Yemen. Pragmatic to a fault, the princes came to see no future in Cairo and so, suitably penitent, they returned to Riyadh in 1964. King Faysal and, later, King Khalid displayed the judicious magnanimity for which their father was noted, and made their brothers welcome; as one example, Talal, who admitted that he had been taken in by 'lustrous slogans and promises',[19] is now Sa'udi representative to Unesco.

Another prince, the conservative Khalid ibn Mussa'id, led an abortive attempt in 1965 to close the new television station in Riyadh. At the time Faysal was at an Arab summit meeting, and thus some people believe that Prince Khalid was seeking to take advantage of the king's absence to stage a coup with the Muslim Brotherhood's help.[20] At the end of 1966 the Sa'uds had to worry about yet another threat, this time from the leftist Union of the People of the Arabian Peninsula, which claimed to have sabotaged the major oil pipeline and to have set bombs in several Sa'udi cities.[21] The government placed blame squarely on 'Abd al-Nasir, whom it accused of dispatching teams of saboteurs to disrupt public order and 'to tamper with holy sentiments'.[22] Moreover, in 1969 there was an attempt by air force officers to overthrow the monarchy and to establish a 'Republic of the Arabian Peninsula.'[23] Many of the two to three hundred arrested were high-ranking and thought to be in sympathy with the technocratic middle class. Since this unrest came on the heels of the successful Libyan coup, the nervousness of the Sa'uds was understandably pronounced.

Even greater anxiety, however, was to occur in late 1979 with the startling events in Mecca. They were startling because the Sa'uds, and some of the rest of us, had assumed that the systematic rooting out of dissidents in the early 1970s and the policy of coopting potential trouble-makers would forestall a major attack on the regime. Yet here was an odd group of well-armed zealots who threw the country into almost two weeks of turmoil. A significant number of Sa'udis and other nationals (about two hundred) felt so strongly about the regime's impiety that they ignored the Qur'an's promise of death for the 'unbelievers' who violate Islam's holiest place (2:191).

Indeed, the group's leaders, Juhayman ibn Muhammad al-'Utaybi and Muhammad ibn 'Abdullah al-Qahtani, were upset by what they saw as the Sa'uds' sinfulness and were intent upon creating a new, truly Islamic, state. Although reliable information is hard to come by, it is widely believed that al-'Utaybi, the more important of the two, had been a student at Medina University but that he became dissatisfied with an Islamic education which failed to reach its logical conclusion – to teach that the Sa'uds were un-Islamic. Taking to the countryside, he began to preach a message that the Ikhwan had delivered in the late 1920s: the Sa'uds had become too powerful, rich, and corrupt; they were not protecting Islam from the unbelievers; and they actively courted foreigners. But he also referred to the idea of the Mahdi, which had had no precedent in Ikhwan thinking, and came to see al-Qahtani in this role. The uncompromising message and the messianic fervour apparently account for the devoted and well-funded following he attracted, and for the danger they posed to the regime: 'Juhaiman's band drew its strength from the same source as the Saudi state, from a militant piety almost as old as Islam itself.'[24]

At the same time as the siege of the Great Mosque was going on, there were riots among the 200,000 to 300,000 Shi'a of the Eastern Province. It was the beginning of 'Ashura, the time Shi'is remember the repression they have endured throughout Islamic history, including Sa'udi history. Although the Shi'a constitute 35 per cent of the Arabian American Oil Company's work-force, they have never felt that they were benefiting as much as the Sunni majority from the oil wealth they helped to create. They have also felt discriminated against by the Jiluwis, the often harsh governors of the province. These riots in several Gulf towns, during which approximately fifteen people were killed, were a more violent repetition of events earlier in the year when news of Khumayni's revolution generated considerable excitement among the Sa'udi Shi'a. A sign that Shi'i unrest has continued is that the government has acted to break up political activities of recent pilgrims to Mecca, though it is not clear whether these activities have consisted of more than the distribution of Iranian-inspired literature.[25] Another more ominous development for the regime is that several Sa'udis participated in December 1981 in the predominately Shi'i effort to overthrow the government of neighbouring Bahrain.

We can see that the picture of opposition is complex. On one hand, there is evidence that most Sa'udis have undergone the changes of the past decade or so without becoming revolutionary. This seems particularly true of the bureaucrats and the technocrats, who have been conscious of who their paymasters are and relatively content with the *status quo*. On the other hand, there are signs that not everyone is satisfied and that many people, particularly among the young, the religious, and even parts of the new middle class, wish to see major changes. The periods when these have been most active have been the early 1960s and the early 1980s, when first 'Abd al-Nasir and then Khumayni loomed menacingly on the Sa'udi horizon.

Prospects for the Sa'udi order

Despite these problems, we must not underestimate the Sa'uds' resourcefulness. By using force and manipulating an Islamic ideology, the Sa'uds have been able to create a nation-state and to foster a general loyalty towards themselves as a kind of super-tribe. And now that modernization is producing stresses and strains, they are showing again how resourceful they are, identifying and responding to the two likely groups of dissenters to their rule: the secular radicals and the religious conservatives. As is so often the case in connection with Sa'udi Arabia, we do not have enough information about the former to know how many there are or, in fact, who they are. But the attempted air force coup, the continuing propaganda blasts from the Union of the People of the Arabian Peninsula (now based in Beirut), and the constant grumblings from Sa'udi students abroad[26] suggest that there is solid sentiment for a radical and probably secular revision of the way Sa'udis are governed. By way of response, the regime devotes large sums of money to improving the lot of those who would be most likely to feel this way: the civil servants and the military. Salaries, for instance, were to rise 40 to 80 per cent for most public employees in the budgetary year 1981–2.[27] More important, the government has indicated that it is moving towards the establishment of new, purportedly more democratic institutions. By now this is a well-rehearsed response to political turmoil. In the face of the royal defections and the general unrest of 1962, Faysal promised that he would establish regional consultative assemblies and curb the power of the religious authorities. In the uncertainty following his death in 1975, Fahd pledged that the assemblies would be forthcoming. They never were.

More recently, however, the occupation of the Great Mosque seems to have prompted the government to take its commitment more seriously. Fahd announced that a 'basic law of governance' was to be prepared, and in March 1980 King Khalid appointed a constitutional committee to consider some two hundred proposed articles. These concern principally the establishment of a consultative assembly (*majlis al-shura*) and new 'modes of governing'.[28] Since those who dominate the committee are traditionally educated, it is unlikely that they will go further and suggest the formation of political parties or trade unions, which are generally rejected as divisive and hence contrary to the Islamic notion of unity among the believers. Although many observers have been sceptical about whether real constitutional changes would come about, it is noteworthy that Prince Nayif, the chairman of the constitutional committee and Minister of the Interior, stated in April 1981 that the king would soon start consideration of the committee's suggestions,[29] and that Prince Fahd said in March 1982 that the assembly would come into being shortly.[30]

The government is also paying attention to the religious conservatives. It knows, for example, that although the *'ulama* are part of the elite and depend on it for most of their income, they also have enormous prestige throughout the country, primarily because of their erudition. Individuals, like Shaykh ibn Baz, the leading religious authority, stand above reproach and their opinions carry great weight (even though they are not always accepted without criticism). There is also a widespread feeling that the *qadis* are fair and that justice is served in the *shari'a* courts. Although the Sa'udi religious authorities are not as organized as the Iranian *mullas*, they have much the same effect as informal social agents. For example, they often act as marriage counsellors, mediators in disputes, and intermediaries between the individual and the increasingly impersonal bureaucracy. The *'ulama* also have a small degree of financial independence because of their control of income deriving from the *waqfs*, particularly that which arises from the *ribats* (hostels endowed for the poor making the Pilgrimage to Mecca).[31] Moreover, Medina University has been a centre of Muslim Brotherhood thinking, which often has been at variance with the official ideology. For all these reasons, then, the government cannot take the religious establishment for granted. And, as the disturbances in the Eastern Province showed, it cannot assume the loyalty of the Shi'i officials, whom it has barely recognized and whom it has actively discouraged from performing their customary roles.

To mollify the religious conservatives, the Sa'uds have toned down their earlier emphasis on rapid development (although their is no sign that they are slowing down development in practice). It is now thought not to be a good idea to speak so forcefully, as the former newspaper editor Turki 'Abdullah al-Sudayri did,[32] of rapid technological and economic progress as the best way to protect Islam. There is also stricter control on the large numbers of expatriate workers in the country: workers with expired visas or invalid work permits are being expelled, and the religious police are intensifying their supervision of how foreign women dress. There has even been a report that the government now claims the right to detain foreigners who are found more than thirty miles from their home and who are without authorization from their employers.[33] The government is also tending to the neglected and volatile Eastern Province by pouring in large sums of money and by favouring it with more frequent royal visits.

But the question that everybody seems to be asking these days remains: is this enough? Many people seem to be answering 'no'. In fact, some observers of the kingdom assume that the actions I have outlined are stopgap measures at best. There are two arguments along these lines. One is that their traditional Islamic ideology has led the Sa'uds into a trap: they have had to abandon the ideology because it has prevented them from modernizing; in doing so, however, they have lost the rationale for their rule. Helen Lackner, for example, thinks that only 'the shell of Wahhabism' remains, for 'enforcement of this ideology naturally means that neither political nor religious developments consistent with the technological advances of society can be countenanced.'[34] But, as I argued earlier and wish to re-emphasize here, the Sa'udis have been more successful than is commonly thought in adapting their ideology to desired changes.

The other, and, to my mind, more convincing, argument that the association of the Sa'uds and Islam may prove to be counter-productive points to the disappointing standard of behaviour of the royal family. This argument holds that although individual princes have offended the devout before, the instances of offensive behaviour seem greater now that the treasury is overflowing. Corruption among the elite, among the princes and the favoured businessmen, is being increasingly condemned. Everyone is aware that vast sums of money change hands to secure contracts or to bypass red tape; and many find this incompatible with Islam's teachings on fairness in economic transactions. There has also been a surprisingly widespread feeling that the attackers of the Great Mosque erred in their choice of target but that they expressed valid objection to the decline of public morality. From this argument's perspective, then, the regime's vaunting of its attachment to Islam may be having the ironic effect of making it illegitimate.

One could argue that the Sa'uds faced illegitimacy before, at the time of 'Abd al-Nasir's attacks, and that they succeeded in avoiding it then. But there are perhaps two differences now: the threat does not come from secular Arab nationalists, but from those who espouse the same Islamic ideology that the Sa'uds say they are espousing; and the Iranian revolution, in spite of its being a particular, national, revolution, has posed a general Islamic challenge to the validity of monarchies.[35] The Sa'uds' history indicates that they were least able to use their Islamic ideology when, in the period 1902–12, they were fighting their ideological colleagues – the Rashids, who were also followers of Shaykh Ibn 'Abd al-Wahhab.

The Sa'udi story has always been the story of overlapping interests, but it has also been the story of shared values. It would seem to be in the interests of most citizens to support the royal family, and for the 'Wahhabis' to continue to accept their subordination to the Sa'uds: the regime is rich and has much to offer; there is no clear alternative to the Sa'uds; the course of the Iranian revolution is giving rise to second thoughts, especially in the middle class, on the desirability of radical change; and the Islamic ideology has been adaptable. Yet, precisely because the Sa'uds claim to be so Islamic, the decisive field of action may yet be that of ideology – not in the sense of whether it is compatible with the modern age, but in the sense of whether the Sa'uds are seen to be faithful to it.

Notes

1. In the same time period, Israel received an average of 91.3 minutes' coverage per year; Egypt, 41.5 minutes; and Lebanon, 29.8 minutes. See William Adams and Phillip Heyl, 'From Cairo to Kabul with the Networks, 1972–1980', in William C. Adams (ed.), *Television Coverage of the Middle East* (Norwood, New Jersey, Ablex, 1981), p. 9.
2. H. St John Philby, *Sa'udi Arabia* (Beirut, Librairie du Liban, 1968), p. 39.
3. Political Resident, Bahrain to Secretary of State for the Colonies, Telegram (P) No. 59–T (20 Mar. 1928), India Office Records, R/15/5/30.
4. Captain J. F. Rabino (Assistant Political Officer, Basra), 'Note on the Akhwan' (n.d.), India Office Records, R/15/2/34.
5. Phoenix, 'A Brief Outline of the Wahabi Movement', *Journal of the Central Asian Society*, 17 (1930), 414.
6. Minister, Jidda to Secretary of State, Letter No. 35 (4 Dec. 1944), American National Archives, Record Group 59, State Decimal Files 1940–4.
7. F. S. Vidal, 'The Evolution of the "Dirah" Concept and Bedouin Settlement in Arabia', unpublished paper delivered at the Middle East Studies Association Meeting, Los Angeles, 1976.
8. Levon H. Melikian, 'The Modal Personality of Saudi College Students: A Study of National Character', in L. Carl Brown and Norman Itzkowitz (eds.), *Psychological Dimensions of Near Eastern Studies* (Princeton, Darwin Press, 1977), p. 180.
9. ''Anasir al-du'f lada al-hukm al-sa'udi', *Sawt al-tali'a* (n.p., n.d.), p. 30.
10. *Al-Riyad*, 6 Muharram 1400 (25 Nov. 1979).
11. But the Sa'udis now rely on two main compilations of the Hanbali texts: *Kitab sharh al-muntaha* and *Kitab sharh al-iqna*.
12. *Nizam al-ta'din*, issued under Royal Decree No. 40, 11 Ramadan 1384 (5 Feb. 1963) (Mecca, Matba'at al-Hukuma, 1384/1964), esp. p. 5.
13. *Nizam al-ta'minat al-ijtima'iyya*, issued under Royal Decree No. M/22 of 6 Ramadan 1349 (Mecca, Matba'at al-Hukuma, 1389/1970), p. 10.
14. *Nizam al-'amal wa'l-'ummal*, issued under Royal Decree No. M/21 of 6 Ramadan 1389 (Mecca, Matba'at al-Hukuma, 1389/1970).
15. Legation at Cairo to Secretary of State, Strictly Confidential Memorandum, Enclosure No. 1 to Despatch No. 110 (12 Sept. 1941), State Decimal Files 890F.00/70.

16. William Rugh, 'Emergence of a New Middle Class in Saudi Arabia', *The Middle East Journal*, 27 (Winter 1973), 15.
17. Ghassane Salameh, 'Political Power and the Saudi State', *Merip Reports*, no. 91 (1980), p. 16.
18. See Muhammad Abu Ashi's lament of youthful attitudes in '*Ukkaz*, 8 Rajab 1401 (12 May 1981).
19. *The Times*, 21 Feb. 1964.
20. *Al-Anwar*, 26 Sept. 1965.
21. *Al-Ahram*, 21 Dec. 1966; 22 Jan. 1967.
22. *The Times*, 7 Mar. 1967.
23. *The New York Times*, 9 Sept. 1969.
24. James Buchan, 'The Return of the Ikhwan', in David Holden and Richard Johns, *The House of Saud* (London, Sidgwick & Jackson, 1981), p. 514.
25. *The Financial Times*, 13 Oct. 1980. See *The Observer*, 11 Nov. 1979, for a report that the government prevented pro-Khumayni demonstrations during the 1979 Pilgrimage.
26. Sa'udi students abroad have produced monographs on such topics as 'Saudi Justice', dealing mainly with *The Death of a Princess* incident, and 'Political Opposition in Saudi Arabia'. Many students have come to change their views on women after living abroad. See, for example, Abdullah Saleh al-Banyan's findings with regard to Sa'udi students in the United States in 1971–2: *Saudi Students in the United States: A Study of Cross Cultural Education and Attitude Change* (London, Ithaca Press, 1980), p. 68.
27. *Arab News*, 15 Mar. 1981 (9 Jamad al-Awwal 1401); 6 May 1981 (2 Rajab 1401).
28. *Al-Jazira*, 22 Safar 1400 (10 Jan. 1981).
29. *International Saudi Report*, 1 (27 Apr. 1981), 2.
30. *Al-Siyasa*, 4 Jamad al-Thani 1402 (29 Mar. 1982).
31. Aharon Layish, ''Ulama and Politics in Saudi Arabia', unpublished paper delivered at the Binational Conference on Islam and Politics in the Modern Near East, Bogaziçi University, Istanbul, 11–13 Aug. 1981.
32. *Al-Riyad*, 9 Muharram 1400 (20 Nov. 1979).
33. *The Times*, 11 Feb. 1982.
34. Helen Lackner, *A House Built on Sand: A Political Economy of Saudi Arabia* (London, Ithaca Press, 1978), pp. 215–17.
35. I may have insufficiently weighed these factors in the conclusion to my article, 'The Formation of the Sa'udi Identity: A Case Study of the Utility of Trans-nationalism', in John F. Stack, Jr (ed.), *Ethnic Identities in a Transnational World* (Westport, Greenwood Press, 1981), p. 134.

5 The Islamic Factor in Syrian and Iraqi Politics

MICHAEL C. HUDSON*

Reports from Syria and Iraq leave little doubt that religion is playing an important role in the current political conflict. What some describe as the most massive repression in modern Syrian history has been directed against the acts of protest and terrorism carried out by the Muslim Brotherhood. In Iraq, the leading Shi'i Muslim leader, Muhammad Baqir al-Sadr, was executed in April 1980; this was merely the most dramatic in a series of crackdowns against Shi'i religious opponents since the early 1970s. In view of other manifestations of religious struggle in the region – the Iranian revolution, the Lebanese civil war, the challenges from fundamentalist Islamic groups in Sa'udi Arabia and Egypt – one can only conclude that Syria and Iraq too are in the throes of an 'Islamic resurgence'.

Nobody can ignore the possibility that an assassin's bullet or a skilfully executed coup might propel 'Islamic' elements into power in Damascus or Baghdad at any time; yet to argue that the current situation indicates a fundamental trend towards Islamic dominance may be to misread what is really happening in these two countries. In order to understand the situation, one must discard any essentialist idea of 'Islam' as some kind of disembodied spirit or mentality, and concentrate instead on its observable features. It is useful simply to consider Islam (*a*) as actors and social structures – that is, individuals, groups, and organizations with religious identities and functions; and (*b*) as ideology – politically relevant Islamic symbols, values, and beliefs. By sticking to specifics in this way, one is in a better position to judge the power and influence of individual Islamic actors and the importance of programmes legitimated on Islamic grounds.

It is also helpful in mapping out the features of Islam in Syrian and

* I would like to express my appreciation to John Alexander, Michael Eisenstadt, Tracy Hall, and Amel Hashim for their help and comments.

Iraqi politics to draw a distinction between the *political culture* broadly conceived – that landscape of important political values and norms – and the *political process* in a narrower sense – the arena of competition for power and what David Easton has termed the 'authoritative allocation of values'. Islam obviously is an important ingredient in Syrian and Iraqi political culture, and its manifestations vary according to different social and ethno-sectarian groupings. However, it is not clear whether its net effect is integrative or disintegrative. Within the political process itself, one can draw a further distinction between the function of Islamic actors and ideology in legitimating and strengthening incumbent regimes, on the one hand, and opposition movements, on the other. It is essential, finally, to recognize that political culture and political process in Syria and Iraq are not static phenomena. Each is affected by fundamental changes in the demography, social class structure, and economy ('modernization') in each country and also by the regional and international political environment. Thus, to discover trends in the growth or decline of 'the Islamic factor', one must try to extrapolate from these internal and external socio-political processes. Two questions need to be discussed. First, with respect to political culture in Syria and Iraq, how is modernization affecting the importance of religion? In particular, is the secularization that many theorists see as an inevitable by-product of modernization causing sectarian divisions within the Islamic community to grow at the expense of the universalistic 'Islamicness' that colours the whole society, including even the non-Islamic minorities? Second, with respect to the political process, how are current socio-political and regional trends affecting the Islamic actors and structures that support the incumbent regimes or the opposition movements?

Political culture

Any survey of that constellation of political values that has shaped thought and action in the eastern Arab world in this century would emphasize first the overwhelmingly Islamic affiliation of the population and the fact that Islamic influence is broad and pervasive, affecting the customs, norms, and practices of Muslims (of whatever sect) and non-Muslims too. Thus, Jacques Weulersse, the anthropologist of the 'Alawis, emphasizes the thoroughgoing Islamicness of society in general, above and beyond sectarian identification. Similarly, Michel 'Aflaq, intellectual founder of the Ba'th Party and a proponent of secularism, insists that Islam is a vital component of Arabism and should be recognized and honoured as such.[1] Although Islam may be pervasive within a given population, its political significance and expression still differ across its socio-economic groupings. Thus the popular Islam of the poorer classes, especially in urban areas, is symbolically rich, intensely held, and socially conservative – and therefore effective for political mobilization – whereas the Islam of the wealthier, educated classes is more intellectualized, compartmentalized, and liberal.

Notwithstanding the pre-eminence of Islam, however, the region is honeycombed with parochial ethnic-sectarian communities, Muslim and non-Muslim, lending a heterogeneity to its political identities and values. Albert Hourani and other historians have noted the distinctive localism and parochial nature of Syrian society, attributing it in part to geographic factors which facilitate isolationist attitudes.[2] It is essential to comprehend the nature of the relationships between identity groups. These 'boundary relationships' are neither uniform nor static. For example, in Syria and Lebanon the social distance between Maronites and Sunnis is probably greater than that between Greek Orthodox and Sunnis. The interaction between 'Alawis and Sunnis in Syria is probably quite limited, whereas that between Druze or Christians and Sunnis may be quite extensive. In Iraq, with just over half the population Shi'i Arab, Sunni–Shi'a relations on the whole seem smooth but vary by region and social class; whereas Kurdish–Arab separation may be greater, depending on the political circumstances, inasmuch as ethnic-national rivalries tend to outweigh religious similarities. Comparisons are risky, but it is arguable that sectarian particularism, or even hostility, though present in varying degrees throughout the Arab East, was probably more severe in Lebanon (where it in fact became institutionalized in the confessional political system) than it was in Syria (where confessionalism was at least formally avoided) or in Iraq (where there was an evident, albeit poorly assimilative, relationship between Sunnis and Shi'is).[3]

A third observation is that economic cleavages underlie and to some extent explain sectarian separateness and hostility in Syria and Iraq. The historical social and economic inferiority of the 'Alawis is well documented, and if today the 'Alawis are in control of a vastly more powerful state apparatus, the resentment on both sides caused by this turning of the tables must be explained by more than doctrinal theological differences. The same point is made repeatedly by Hanna Batatu in his monumental study of Iraq with respect to Sunni–Shi'a differences: 'In brief, the Sunni–Shi'i dichotomy coincided to no little degree with a deep-seated social economic cleavage.' And, commenting on the resistance in the Shi'i quarters of Baghdad to the Ba'thist coup of 1963, he cautions us not to overemphasize the sectarian element, because of the economic division: 'Shi'ism . . . has here for long been by and large the ideology of the underdogs, just as Sunnism is that of the socially rich dominant classes.'[4]

The fourth main point that emerges from a survey of political culture and subcultures in the Fertile Crescent is that Islam is but one of several important ideological and philosophical strands. One of these strands – secularism – has been spreading at the expense of Islam ever since the establishment of the modern Middle Eastern state after World War I. Partly because of its mixed ethnic-sectarian character (as Ibrahim Ibrahim has noted), Syria became a centre of secular nationalist ideologies, such as Syrian nationalism and Ba'thist Arab nationalism.[5] The emergence of the Palestine issue in the inter-war period also had a strong effect in Syria and Iraq, and exacerbated frustrated nationalist aspirations. In addition, social reform ideologies had an impact, and the penetration by Europe left its mark on an ideologically diverse area. Unlike Iran and (to a lesser extent) Egypt, where ideological currents could not deeply penetrate the mass of the religiously homogeneous, self-contained, and impoverished populace, Syria and Iraq were more exposed, more diversified, and hence less open to domination by Islamic ideology and Islamic actors. This is not to say that Islam was or is unimportant, but rather that it is not all-important. Even though certain nationalist parties have faded, the increasingly educated populations of Syria and Iraq today still appear deeply committed to goals that include the recovery of Palestine and other 'lost' Arab territories, some form of democracy or political participation, some form of socialism or social justice, some degree of freedom of expression, continuing struggle against superpower 'neo-imperialism', and – not least – economic development.

Can we say that a desire to Islamize further is sufficiently widespread and intense to belong in this political lexicon? Does the apparent consensus on these other concerns apply also to Islamic reform? To an outside student the question is not easy to answer, even though in the last decade Islam has become increasingly evident politically. In certain neighbouring countries the answer would seem to be more clearly yes; Kuwait, for example, has returned a number of fundamentalist Muslims in its recent parliamentary elections (at the expense of secularist Arab nationalists), and in other Gulf states, especially Sa'udi Arabia, there are signs of fundamentalism gaining influence. In Jordan the Muslim Brotherhood appears to have quite a following, and in Egypt the assassination of President Sadat in October 1981 by Muslim fundamentalists dramatically reveals the force of Islamic political revival. But whether the violence and repression involving Islamic opposition groups in Syria and Iraq indicate a general Islamic mood, or are tied to specific political conditions, is hard to say. It is also difficult to ascertain whether the Islamic factor derives its influence from a deep-rooted desire further to Islamize Syrian and Iraqi society, or whether it is used as a means of achieving nationalist and other non-religious goals. In short, the evidence of a new and pervasive Islamic religiosity in Syrian and Iraqi political culture is ambiguous at best; but one does not observe the kind of intense Islamic ground-swell that typified Ayatullah Ruhullah Khumayni's revolution against the Shah of Iran.

Political process

If the significance of the increase of Islamic symbolism in Syrian and Iraqi political culture is hard to ascertain, so too is the emergence of the Islamic factor in the political process of these two countries. In the Ottoman Empire and its successor states, Islam as ideology was a pillar of system legitimacy, although today it is no longer the only important one. To be sure, most of the modern Arab states publicly stipulate that Islam is the religion of the state and/or the source of legal authority. Even the most radical-secular regime, that of the People's Democratic Republic of Yemen, has struck an accommodation with Islam; none has gone nearly as far as Turkey under Atatürk to extirpate religious influence. Nevertheless, nearly all Arab states have come to assert administrative power over the formal Islamic actors and structures. The successor states to the Ottoman Empire now regulate, subsidize, and direct the religious functionaries – *shaykhs, mukhtars, qadis,* and *'ulama* – and the Muslim legal and educational institutions. Jamal 'Abd al-Nasir brought al-Azhar under his control, and even Sa'udi Arabia under Faysal established governmental dominance over the successors of Ibn 'Abd al-Wahhab.

Islam and the regime

Syria and Iraq have both been under Ba'thist rule for well over a decade. Although the Ba'th Party is a secular party, it too has made its accommodation with religion by honouring Islam as an essential component of the Arab national culture. But it cannot be said that either Ba'thist regime has assigned Islam to a central or unique place in its legitimacy formula. Each is, of course, a minority regime: the 'Alawis are only about 12 per cent of the Syrians, and the Sunnis are less than half of the Iraqis (and the Arab Sunnis only about 20 per cent). The two regimes, however, have sought simultaneously to placate and to dominate their religious establishments. Saddam Husayn's regime has enjoyed partial success in maintaining loyalty from some prominent Shiʻi personalities, but not all – as the Muhammad Baqir al-Sadr affair showed all too grimly. The Sunni religious establishment presumably is more cooperative. Saddam has also spent a great deal of additional money on both Shiʻi and Sunni religious shrines, mosques, and activities. In Syria the story is much the same. President Hafiz al-Asad's response to the anti-regime violence of the Muslim Brotherhood reveals a constant theme that the regime is acting in the interests of true Islam against 'gangsters' in the pay of Israel, the Lebanese Phalangists, the Iraqis, or the Americans. On occasion a group of *'ulama* will issue a public statement defending the government and attacking the Muslim Brotherhood.[6]

Thus the two regimes seek to monopolize the religious establishments – Shiʻi in Iraq, Sunni in Syria – with only partial success in each case. But since both regimes are identified with a minority religious sect, it must also be asked to what extent their legitimacy derives from their religious sectarian base as opposed to a more 'ecumenical', all-Islamic position. In the case of Iraq there is little evidence that the Saddam Husayn regime seeks or derives power by identifying itself as distinctively Sunni and appealing to that community on doctrinal grounds. It happens that the key power-holders are predominantly but not exclusively Sunni, and that the inner circle of Takritis are Sunni. But the ties that bind and identify the inner circle seem to be the ties of kinship and the ideological characteristics of the Baʻth. Perhaps because Sunnis have traditionally dominated Iraqi politics and because their Sunnism is so entrenched in Iraq (and throughout the Muslim world), they are not so sharply identifiable on a sectarian basis. Sunnism, as such, therefore, is not particularly important politically.

The same cannot be said for Syria and the 'Alawi-dominated Asad regime. As a small, compact, and socially inferior sectarian group, the 'Alawis have been historically visible and vulnerable. Their recent ascendancy at the expense of the largely Sunni commercial ruling bourgeoisie has made them a communal target; and their esoteric beliefs are seen as sufficiently deviant to inspire accusations from the urban Sunnis that they are not Muslim at all. There is little dispute among observers that 'Alawis have come to occupy key positions in the regime, notably in the army, such as the command of the Saraya al-Difaʻ and the Saraya al-Siraʻ. ʻAlawi domination of the officer corps is attested to by the fact that 286 of the 300 candidates attending the school for artillery officers in Aleppo at the time of the massacre of July 1979 were ʻAlawi.[7] Dawisha notes, however, that 'an examination of the Syrian high policy elite in the period 1970–5 in no way suggests a striking preponderance of ʻAlawis.'[8] Yet van Dam and Batatu, among others, point to the crucial security-related positions as dominated not only by ʻAlawis but by ʻAlawis of President Asad's tribe.[9]

Is it correct, then, to conclude that the Asad regime derives its cohesion from common religious-sectarian identification and doctrine? To be sure, the Asad regime is perceived and presented in this manner by its various opposition movements, especially the Muslim Brotherhood; and the targeting of prominent officials and personalities (even many far removed from power and politics) for assassination on the basis of sect alone has surely been designed to foment religious tension. But there is little evidence that this regime is governed primarily by sectarian considerations. Asad himself goes to great pains to stress the ʻAlawi sect's full membership in the Islamic community and to argue that religion should be excluded from politics – except as a general moral guide. This secularism, of course, has exposed him to attack by conservative Sunnis, who complain that he is indeed excluding religion from its proper socio-political function. His reliance on non-ʻAlawis in high policy-making posts outside the most sensitive security positions has already been noted. Furthermore, a close examination of the ties that bind his inner circle suggests not so much a religious-sectarian linkage as a kinship and tribally based structure. Batatu puts the matter persuasively: 'the ruling element consists at its core of a close kinship group which draws strength simultaneously but in decreasing intensity from a tribe, a sect-class, and an ecologic-cultural division of the people.'[10] Religion, in short, does not provide the only, or even the main, basis of the Syrian regime.

Islam and the opposition

Turning now from the incumbents to the opposition, one finds religious sectarianism playing a far larger role in both countries. Although Islam is something of a mask for various opposition forces whose purpose is more power-seeking than religious, it is in fact more significant in the analysis of the opposition than it is of the incumbent regime. So it is important to look closely at Islam as ideology, and as actors and structures, in order to ascertain the prospects for opposition in these two surprisingly long-lived Ba'thist regimes.[11]

The first thing to note is the obstacle that the opposition in virtually all Arab regimes faces today: the growth of the power of the state. Technology has tended thus far to favour the incumbents, who now dispose of formidable political resources. They exert influence through the more extensive media and educational instruments of the state. They are more capable of surveillance and repression. The growth of the military, the establishment of the single-party state, and the ability of the regime to coopt potential opposition leaders all make effective opposition much more difficult than before. But evidently the accumulation of these formidable weapons has not brought about a corresponding increase in the legitimacy of the ruling elites, and they have been exceedingly cautious about permitting participation and 'loyal opposition' by elements outside the ruling group. Perhaps this is because the incumbents are simply selfish and power-hungry; but even the most saintly rulers might find the riddle of power-sharing hard to solve in polities such as Syria and Iraq, where the issues are so intense, the institutions so untested, and the problem of subversion from outside so pervasive. Furthermore, modernization has increased the mobilizational capabilities of the opposition as well as of the incumbents. Not only is there the expansion of a politically relevant population for the opposition to exploit; there is also the powerful backlash effect of the regime's new repressive capabilities. The Shah's Iran stands as example of the power of a modernized Third World regime that sowed the seeds of its own destruction. To what extent is it an object lesson for the ruling elites of Syria and Iraq, especially in the way that a religiously inspired opposition could triumph over the most advanced technology of repression?

Consider the position of an opposition leader in Syria or Iraq today. What strategy can he employ to attain power? If he is already a member of the ruling circle, he can hope to make a coup from within through a conspiracy. If he is outside the regime, he must mobilize mass and key sectoral support. While presumably there are a great many elements potentially available to join an opposition front, given the narrow and exclusivist character of the regime, it is difficult to mobilize them because of the regime's surveillance capabilities mentioned above. Furthermore, the task is complicated by the regime's ability to pre-empt or monopolize important symbols, such as struggling for Palestine and against imperialism, working for social justice and economic growth, and so on. Ba'thism as an ideology has made much of these legitimacy resources. What about religion? On this score both regimes would seem to be vulnerable, owing to their minority character. Moreover, charges of corruption and despotism carry greater weight if presented as violations of Islamic norms. In Iran, religion proved to be the indispensable fuel for igniting a broad-based opposition movement and the glue for holding it together. Of all the social structures that might have served as a base for opposition, only the religious organizations of the *mullas* in the urban slums and rural villages had not been effectively penetrated by the secret police, Savak. Buffered, as it were, by these Shi'i networks, a variety of organized groups of varying political hue were able to erode the Shah's position. Behind the banner of religion, a nationalist movement was able to crystallize in opposition to a regime that was suddenly vulnerable to charges of not just errors, but sins. Use of the religious weapon intensified and magnified the conflict.

Can a religious strategy do the same thing for the opposition to Asad and Saddam Husayn that it did for the anti-Shah forces? Let us briefly analyse the opposition in both countries, focusing on the ideological and structural dimensions, in order to assess the significance of the Islamic factor in each. We may begin by advancing eight general propositions:

(1) Islam as an opposition movement is limited by the sectarian and ethnic pluralism of society.

(2) It is limited by the relative 'thinness' of Islamic personnel and organizations that are independent of the state.

(3) It is limited, in parts of the wealthier and more educated strata, by the influence of secularism as a political principle and by the secular nature of competing political ideologies.

(4) Modernization (especially education and urbanization) in the poorer income groups has probably strengthened their Islamic identity and knowledge, just as it has exposed them to a variety of other ideas and experiences.

(5) By virtue of the moral certainty and the intensity of commitment associated with any religious political ideology, Islam may be especially effective in mobilizing those disadvantaged by socio-political change and those convinced that the existing system of rule is fundamentally evil.

(6) Islamic opposition holds several basic ideological values and goals that are widely held in the rest of society; this means (a) that it competes with the ruling incumbents for 'authentic possession' of these values, and (b) that there is at least a philosophic basis for cooperation with some of the non-Islamic opposition forces.

(7) Structural development and cooperation with other opposition groups, however, may be impeded by the doctrinaire and inflexible attitudes that characterize religious militants, and by the fear and suspicion that their potential allies may hold towards them.

(8) Finally, the prospects for effective Islamic opposition may increase with increasing repression by the regime (as the 'martyrdom' effect develops), but will then decrease if the state can bring overwhelming repression to bear.[12]

It is evident that some or parts of these conditions favour the development of an Islamic opposition while others hinder it. Let us now analyse the Islamic opposition in Syria and Iraq in light of these eight propositions.

Syria

Syrian society, we have seen, cannot be said to display the kind of Islamic homogeneity that characterizes, say, Iran, Egypt, or Sa'udi Arabia. As already noted, approximately two-thirds of Syria's population is Sunni, while perhaps 12 per cent is 'Alawi; Orthodox Christians and Druze constitute the remaining major communities. All four groupings are important; an opposition movement like the Muslim Brotherhood that is militantly committed to the Sunni persuasion may face fundamental difficulties in raising support from the others. Beyond this basic condition, however, is the probability that a history of openness to a variety of influences has softened the strictness of Islamic political commitments in Syria.

In terms of organizational density and autonomy, there appears to be little evidence in modern Syrian politics that the religious establishment itself was a centre of power, or that mass-based Muslim opposition groups exerted significant influence. The Muslim Brotherhood in Syria never took root as its parent body in Egypt did, nor did it develop the local-level 'thickness' of the Iranian religious establishment. The Brotherhood, according to Seale and others, played a relatively marginal and ineffectual role in the 1950s.[13]

What of Islam in the middle and upper classes? In the 1960s, the Sunni urban middle- and upper-class establishment underwent such internal fragmentation – notably a series of purges within the Sunni members of the officer corps – that there was little in the way of a community from which effective opposition to the 'Alawi-Ba'thist-military faction could be mobilized.[14] In fact, in the upper reaches of Syrian society, where political power lay, the main ideological struggles involved Ba'thist and Nasirist Arab nationalism, Greater Syrian nationalism, communism, and liberal parliamentary capitalism. All of these tendencies were predominantly secular, and, as noted, the Muslim Brothers were at best secondary or tertiary actors on the stage. The wealthy, educated middle and upper classes and the political intellectuals were on the whole not very interested in Islam. It is only belatedly, after a decade and a half of Ba'thism, that Islam is becoming interesting to the displaced and largely Sunni upper bourgeoisie.

But rapid modernization, with its heavy urban migration and social dislocations (aggravated by the 1967 and 1973 wars and the Lebanon intervention since 1976, and indirectly by the regional oil boom) seems to have facilitated the growth of Islamic opposition in Syria. Urban migration by the 'Alawi and other rural beneficiaries of Ba'thism may have strengthened support for the regime in the capital of Damascus, but in the other main cities – Homs, Hama, and Aleppo – this influx threatened the long-established, largely Sunni urban lower classes. It is plain enough that an Islamic-spearheaded opposition has generated mass urban support which the regime has found hard to suppress. In 1973 Muslim opposition took to the streets in the bazaars of Hama, Homs, and Damascus to protest the failure of the regime to strengthen the place of religion in the new constitution by stipulating that Islam would be the religion of the state, and it was not really satisfied by the regime's response: an undertaking to include a clause requiring that 'Islam shall be the religion of the head of state'.[15] The widespread violence against the regime reached a climax in 1979 and 1980, but by the end of 1981 had diminished considerably. Nevertheless, sporadic and spectacular acts of terrorism continued, such as the bomb blast in Damascus in November 1981 that killed over 200 people. And in February 1982 a major rebellion broke out in Hama. Although confined to that city, before it was finally contained several weeks later, over 2,000 people were reported to be dead or wounded and large sections of the old city were reduced to rubble as a result of the regime's draconian response.

The Muslim opposition ideology in Syria displays both righteous certainty and a bitter hatred towards the Asad regime that seems calculated to arouse the most intense mass support. The following excerpts are typical examples of the language of religious opposition politics. In August 1979, for example, the first issue of the clandestine Muslim Brotherhood publication *Al-Nadhir* proclaims 'the beginning of a long journey in the way of establishing the desired Islamic Society, and in the way of demolishing the despicable rule of ignorance . . . We cannot see better proof that Allah has ordained everything than the attempts on the lives of the criminals Hafiz and Rifaat al-Asad, and we believe that Allah has His destiny in store.'[16] Similarly, the 'Declaration and Program of the Islamic Revolution in Syria' describes the Ba'th

Party in power as 'a total disaster . . . [It] squashed freedom, abolished political parties, nationalized the press, threw people into prison, and hanged those who dared to voice their disapproval.' Elsewhere it states: 'We hope that the followers of the 'Alawi sect – to which the people's affliction, Hafiz Asad and his butcher playboy brother, belong – will positively participate in preventing the tragedy reaching its sad end.' To remedy these intolerable conditions, 'The Islamic Revolution will rely on Allah alone, adhere to His laws and course, and work without discrimination towards the betterment of the nation.'[17] The legitimacy of the movement's programme is attested to with numerous citations from the Qur'an and classical Muslim scholars.

If one were to envisage certain key values as political resources for which incumbents and various opposition groups compete in their struggle for legitimacy and power, among the most important in Syrian political culture would be (in no particular order) internal stability, social justice, government consistent with Islam, Arab unity, Palestine, economic development, political participation, and freedom. Syria's Ba'thist government, of course, has attempted to deliver on all these issues and has placed special emphasis on its fidelity to the Arab and Palestinian causes, the achievement of economic development and social justice through socialism, and the promotion of political freedom and stability. The Islamic opposition severely condemns the regime on all these counts. The literature of 'the Islamic revolution' identifies the regime's stability and order as terror and repression, its social justice as corruption and favouritism for the party elite, its rule as the very antithesis of Islamic government, its performance on Arab and Palestinian matters as false and hypocritical, its economic policies (in agriculture, especially) as ruinous, and its commitments to participation and freedom as ludicrous.[18]

The question that intrigues political observers is the extent to which the Islamic opposition has succeeded or failed in convincing public opinion that it, rather than the regime, can best maximize these values. The regime, with all the informational means at its disposal, can make a case for its anti-Israel and anti-Zionist credentials, and points to the 1973 war as a comparative victory; and it also can claim greater fidelity on these issues than many other Arab regimes. But the stories of scandal surrounding the 1967 defeat and the bloody conflict with the Palestinians and the National Movement in Lebanon are seized upon by the opposition to show the contrary. The regime can back its claims to progress on the domestic front with positive aggregate growth statistics and visible development in public works and construction, and even to an unaccustomed period of political stability; furthermore, it incessantly portrays the Muslim Brotherhood as a tool of Zionism and imperialism and as responsible for fomenting violence and terrorism against innocent citizens. In view of the polarization between the regime and the militant opposition, it is plausible to imagine the ordinary Syrian privately condemning both, hoping to avoid involvement, and thus in effect casting a passive vote for the incumbents.

If the competition between the Islamic opposition and the Asad regime to dominate basic values is a close one (with the regime in a stronger position, one suspects), an equally interesting question is whether there are ideological grounds for cooperation between the Islamic opposition and other forms of opposition in Syria. Taken at face value, many of the positions of the Muslim organizations are shared by other parties or interest groups: among them, greater militancy towards Israel and the United States, more support for the Palestinians, a more open and democratic political system, and greater social justice (with less corruption) at home. Most important may be a shared revulsion at the excesses of the Asad regime. The comment of a left-wing Syrian intellectual, speaking of the Muslim Brotherhood, illustrates the situation: 'Very few people actually support the Ikhwan's ideas. But everybody supports the Ikhwan in its acts against the regime. If the Ikhwan had a political programme, [it] could seize power tomorrow.'[19] Indeed, there is evidence that the opposition is not just one organization but a number of Islamic and non-Islamic groups. The Islamic element consisted in 1979 and 1980 of three or four banned parties, identified collectively by the authorities as the Ikhwan al-Muslimun (The Muslim Brothers), based in Aleppo, Homs, and Hama; they include the Islamic Liberation Party, the Islamic Liberation Movement, and the Youth of Muhammad. These groups were said to include 'well-trained urban commando units, armed with rockets and all sorts of light arms, which have assassinated scores of regime supporters'.[20] As for the non-Islamic element, some observers believe that the Ikhwan enjoys widespread but largely passive support among the non-Islamic opposition because it is the only structure capable of leading the struggle against what has become (to many) a closed tribal-sectarian dictatorship. In Syria some of the non-Islamic opposition elements have given active support: according to reports, dissident Ba'thist factions, communists, a radical leftist organization known as the Red Brigades, the lawyers' association, merchants, and professional people have participated in public and clandestine protests.[21] The assassination in Paris in July 1980 of a founder of the Ba'th, Salah al-Din al-Bitar, allegedly by a Syrian government hit team, was dramatic evidence both of the extent of the opposition and of the lengths to which the regime could go to eliminate it. Some of this opposition support may stem from less than altruistic motives. According to one observer, 'Behind the mask of religion stands the Khumasiya, the wealthy former owners of Syria's largest industries, who suffered from Ba'th nationalization measures in the 1960s and now would like to regain their former position.'[22]

As for structural coordination, without having access to the murky and violent world of anti-regime politics, one can only speculate about the extent to which Muslim groups can develop a broad front against a regime as well-established as Hafiz al-Asad's. Doubtless the heavy-handedness of the regime itself has generated opposition from many quarters and induced a degree of cooperation that has not existed in the past. Yet despite a number of common goals, one might suppose that virtually all the other currents of opposition, inasmuch as they are basically secular, would harbour profound uneasiness towards the Muslim organizations who, once in power, might display the kind of despotism, confusion, and arbitrary use of authority that has marked the Islamic revolution in Iran. A relaxation of extremely coercive measures by the Asad regime might, therefore, lead to a weakening of such collaboration as may have existed between the Islamic and non-Islamic opposition.

Finally, the history of the Asad regime seems to illustrate the proposition that the cycle of opposition violence and regime repression continues to escalate until such time that the regime can bring to bear such extreme coercion that opposition is virtually destroyed.[23] This trend was visible in Syria from the early 1970s until a paroxysm of violence was reached in 1979 and 1980, during which very destructive acts of terrorism attributed to the Muslim Brotherhood were answered with equally terrifying mass reprisals by the regime's Special Forces and Defence Forces. Overt acts of opposition declined markedly in 1981; but, as we have noted, a major outbreak of fighting occurred in early 1982, and it appears that the regime has not definitively triumphed over its opponents.

Iraq

As in Syria, there is reason to suspect that Islam is not as uniform or as deeply rooted in Iraqi political culture as it is in other Muslim societies, such as Iran, Arabia, or northern Africa. Historically, Islam in Iraq is an overlay on earlier civilizations whose traces (and differences with Islamic customs) are evident not just in the excellent Iraq Museum. While over 90 per cent of Iraq's population is Muslim, just over 50 per cent are Shi'i; of the remainder some 20 per cent are Sunni Arabs and 18 per cent are Sunni Kurds. Kurdish opposition, of course, has been a perennial feature of Iraqi politics. Since independence, however, religious sectarian opposition has been far less evident. It is important to recognize that the Islamic opposition to the Ba'thist regime led by Saddam Husayn eschews defining the conflict in sectarian terms; thus, the Da'wa Party and other groups do not see themselves as Shi'is fighting the oppression of a Sunni government, but as spokesmen for all the Muslims of Iraq – Shi'i and Sunni, Arab and Kurd – against an evil secular government.[24] For its part, the regime also insists that there is no Sunni–Shi'i conflict; rather, it claims that the problem is one of Persian-inspired subversion, which uses Islam as a cover against an Arab nationalist government that fully respects Islam in both of its major denominations. To the extent that there are Sunni–Shi'i divisions, therefore, this may present as many, if not more, problems for the Islamic opposition than for the regime.

On the structural level, too, Iraq's Islamic opposition displays a certain weakness, for, like Syria, it lacks the 'thickness' of Islamic organization that is typical of Iran and Egypt (whose government moved to crack down on 40,000 unregistered mosques shortly before Islamic fundamentalists assassinated President Sadat). Batatu draws a revealing comparison: there was perhaps one *mulla* for every 308 Iranians in 1979, whereas in Iraq (in 1947) there was a person 'employed in the religious services' for every 562 Iraqis.[25] The smaller size of the Iraqi religious establishment in absolute terms as well – 7,763 in 1947 and possibly around 22,500 at present (if it has grown proportionately with the population) – leaves it more vulnerable to state surveillance and control. He also reports a singular scarcity of religious institutions in the predominantly Shi'i rural districts – only one for every 37,000 persons – which suggests a lack of mobilization capability.

Iraq's modern political history, like Syria's, is dominated by secular actors and ideologies. The middle- and upper-class elites have expressed themselves, for the most part, in the language of nationalism and development. The British, the Hashimite monarchy, and the post-revolutionary regimes did not seek to encourage religious political expression. At least until the end of the 1970s the process through which power devolved onto a rural, middle-class, professional elite did not assume either a sectarian or a religious colouration, as it had done to some degree in Syria; and the principal nodes of serious opposition have been secular in their inspiration: liberals, Nasirists, communists, and Kurdish nationalists.

The pace and extent of social change in Iraq, however, have certainly had (from the regime's point of view) both positive and negative results as regards the Shi'is, who have been the most affected. The newer, sprawling, and predominantly Shi'i working-class quarters of Baghdad have spawned conspiracy, protest, and violence against several regimes, although until now this opposition has not been expressed in religious terms. At the same time the mainly Shi'i areas of southern Iraq have been deliberately favoured in the government's welfare and development programmes, giving many Iraqi Shi'is a positive interest in the present system. Nevertheless, the establishment in Najaf in the late 1960s (during Ayatullah Khumayni's exile there) of the Islamic Da'wa Party aroused the concern of the Iraqi authorities, presumably because they feared that the exploitation of Islamic symbols and values for political purposes could have an explosive effect in mobilizing the uprooted poorer elements against the regime. The same fears presumably motivated the regime to execute the Imam Muhammad Baqir al-Sadr on 9 April 1980 and to outlaw the Da'wa Party. Whether these dramatic steps weakened the Islamic movement or, on the contrary, stimulated latent religious loyalties by the creation of an authentic martyr remains to be seen. One thing is clear: the invective and moral condemnation directed by the Iraqi Muslim opposition towards the Saddam Husayn government are no less intense than those with which the Syrian Muslim Brothers condemn Hafiz al-Asad.[26]

How successful are the Iraqi Muslim opposition elements in competing, either with the regime or with non-Islamic opposition elements, for 'ownership' of important, widely shared values? As in Syria, the Islamic opposition in Iraq attempts to outbid the regime in terms of its achievements or fidelity towards the struggle against imperialism and Zionism abroad and the development of a prosperous and socially just society at home. The Ba'thists in Baghdad are accused of serving the interests of the superpowers, especially the United States, by making war against the sacred Islamic revolution in Iran, and by acquiescing in Israel's conquests and collaborating with un-Islamic, imperialist, client regimes in Jordan, Sa'udi Arabia, and the Gulf. The regime, however, is not necessarily perceived as vulnerable in the field of Arabism; its stands on Arab issues are strong compared with many Arab regimes; moreover, they are incessantly emphasized in the state-controlled media. The regime, for its part, accuses the Islamic groups of being tools of American imperialism. On domestic issues, against impressive evidence of socio-economic development in Iraq, the opposition makes charges of massive corruption, mismanagement, and poverty;[27] but again the regime can reply effectively with its highly visible development projects. Surely the central issue is the legitimacy of the regime itself: to the claims of the Ba'th one-party government that it is the authentic voice of the people and that it is instituting democratic procedures (such as restoring elections and the parliament), the Da'wa charges that the reality is tyranny. Authentic government must be subservient to and consistent with the will of God; and the institutions of the Islamic state must be subject to the guidance of a wise and prestigious Islamic legist or *faqih* (or committee of *faqihs*) who, by interpreting the sacred texts, can best elucidate the will of the living (but hidden) infallible Imam, Muhammad al-Mahdi. The raw tyranny of individuals or factions (such as the present rulers in Iraq) is inadmissible, as are the political theories associated with Western liberalism and Soviet Marxism.[28]

The Islamic opposition to Ba'thist rule in Baghdad is not the only form of opposition; there are dissident Ba'thists, communists, and Kurds among others. Given the capabilities of the central government, there is a compelling need for cooperation among all elements of the opposition, Islamic or otherwise, but how easy is this to achieve in light of their different goals and priorities? For example, the Da'wa Party, which claims to be the leading Islamic opposition group in Iraq, makes clear its deep hostility to communism and nationalism. Criticizing the view that the Communist Party is one of the vehicles for Shi'a opposition, a spokesman states that, to the contrary, 'Another rival for Islamic opposition is the Iraqi Communist Party.' And in the same article he bitterly and sarcastically attacks the Ba'th Party and its founders, stating that the Da'wa 'very strongly denounces nationalism in all its forms and equates it, according to Islam, with racism.'[29] The article also disputes allegations that the Da'wa has agreed to participate in the Iraqi Front of Revolutionary, Islamic, and National Forces (discussed below) because some of its constituent groups are nationalists (dissident Ba'thists and other Arab nationalists, or Kurds) or communists and secular socialists. Thus it would appear that coordination is a serious problem on ideological grounds.

Even within the Iraqi Muslim community, the doctrinal differences between Shi'ism and Sunnism may be deeper than the Da'wa is willing to admit. In its treatise on Islamic government, the party distinguishes two views on the holder of the executive office. There is the Sunni view, which emphasizes the importance of *shura* (consultation) in the selection of this person: his legitimacy rests upon having been elected by a majority of the community, whether or not he is a *faqih*, as long as he does not oppose the opinions of the *faqihs*. The Shi'i view, on the other hand, makes it a precondition for 'the person in charge to be a *faqih* in addition to being equitable and efficient, and it does not accept a non-*faqih* to take charge merely because the majority of the nation votes for him.'[30] The declaration observes (perhaps disingenuously) that a 'compromise' can be reached by accepting the second view, because although the first view does not insist that the executive be a *faqih*, it does not insist that he *not* be one either. Since the second view is categorical in its insistence on the necessity of a *faqih*, then it should prevail. Whether such a solution is actually acceptable to Sunni legists, let alone to Iraqis who believe in democracy, is far from clear.

On structural grounds, too, there is evidence of fragmentation, although there is a dearth of precise information on the identity, strength, and interrelationships of the various organizations. The Da'wa, the most religiously oriented movement, is thought to enjoy more widespread support – notably in the holy cities of Najaf and Karbala and in the lower-class Shi'i quarters of Baghdad – than other similar organizations. According to Batatu, however, the Da'wa itself is factionalized between those who favour a reformist and those who favour a revolutionary approach to the present Iraqi regime. Furthermore, according to various observers, the execution of Imam Muhammad Baqir al-Sadr in 1980 dealt a severe blow to Da'wa; this claim, however, is sharply disputed by Da'wa spokesmen, who claim that in fact the martyrdom generated 'hundreds, nay, thousands' of volunteers, making it unnecessary for the movement to recruit members any longer.[31] Another sign that reports of the decline of Da'wa may be premature was a claim that the group was responsible for a serious coup attempt in Bahrain and the demolition of the Iraqi embassy in Beirut in December 1981.[32] Shortly after the execution of Imam al-Sadr a group calling itself the Islamic Action Organization split off from Da'wa, in order to pursue a more militant programme of violence and armed attacks, but to what extent the two groups coordinate activities is not clear. Although basically an Iraqi organization, the Da'wa is faithful to Imam Khumayni and is presumably supported to some extent from Iran, a relationship that has become something of a burden since the outbreak of the Iraq–Iran war.

A distinctly different grouping known as the Mujahidin was, according to Batatu, formed in Baghdad in 1979. It was influenced by the unfolding Islamic revolution in Iran, although it was linked neither to Imam Khumayni (as the Da'wa has been) nor to the Iranian Mujahidin-e Khalq, with its Islamic Marxist colouration.[33] Smaller than the Da'wa, it is composed of 'modern' educated professionals who are reputed to be energetic and effective. As a rival to the Da'wa for Iraq's Muslim 'constituency', its existence would appear to illustrate the problems of developing a coherent religious opposition.

The outbreak of the Iraq–Iran war in September 1980 witnessed a growth and dynamism among other opposition groups even as Da'wa was allegedly suffering its fragmentation and decline. According to press accounts, three new fronts were formed: the Iraqi Front of Revolutionary, Islamic, and National Forces (IFRINF), the National Democratic Front (NDF), and the Jama'at al-'Ulama (Community of 'Ulama). In the IFRINF, the most important of these groupings, can be found the Iraqi Kurdish Democratic Party (led by two sons of the late Mustafa Barzani), a group of dissident military officers led by General Hasan Mustafa Naqib, and a group of pro-Syrian Iraqi Ba'thist politicians led by Baqir Yassin. Syria reportedly has lent support to this front. [34] Also allied with it is a Shi'i grouping known as the Mujahidin. From the available accounts it appears that this grouping is the same as the Mujahidin organization discussed above; in any case, it is clear that it is not the Da'wa. In fact, the Da'wa firmly denies any association with it because of its alleged communist and nationalist tendencies and, indeed, denies the existence of any separate Mujahidin organization, explaining that all Da'wa (and Muslim) strugglers are generically known as *mujahidin*.[35] In the NDF, which is supported by Syria, are found exiled Iraqi communists, the Kurdish Democratic Union of Jalal Talabani, and seven smaller parties. Of the various groupings, the NDF appears to be farthest to the left, the most secular, and the least susceptible to cooperation with Islamic opposition movements. The third front, the Jama'at al-'Ulama, has been formed by Ayatullah Muhammad Baqir al-Hakim, a brother of a leader of Da'wa, to try and unite the divided religious opposition. To date, none of the fronts has shown any signs of being able or willing to cooperate with one another, or with the Da'wa or the Islamic Action Organization.

The future for the Iraqi opposition in general, and the religious opposition in particular, may be shaped by the regime's coercive capabilities and policies. As in Syria, the government has responded to the rising level of religious protest in the late 1970s and 1980 with massive crackdowns, and some observers believe that these repressive measures weakened the opposition decisively. Thus Gurr's hypothesis about the curvilinear relationship between violence and regime repression appears to be borne out. At the same time the Iraqi government was able to channel substantial funds into Shi'i religious structures; in this it was more fortunate than the Syrian regime. A new factor, however, has been introduced by the seemingly interminable Iraq–Iran war which, if it continues, could weaken the regime's ability to contain the various strains of opposition at home with either the carrot or the stick.

Conclusions

The legitimacy formulas of regimes and oppositions cannot be specified in an historical vacuum. To explain the emergence of a serious religious opposition in Syria and Iraq at this time and to assess its future, one must study this opposition in a context of internal social change and external (regional and international) political pressures.

A well-known theory of modernization sees 'Islamic resurgence' as the product of the accumulated psychological frustrations of people buffeted by social change. The return to Islam is a defence mechanism against the demands of a society that challenges traditional values and identities. There may be some truth in this in so far as it applies, let us say, to the practice of young women in Arab universities adopting the veil and conservative clothing. But it is not persuasive as a general explanation for the reappearance of fundamental Islamic movements in the political arena. If the Muslim masses who marched against the Shah were outraged at the alleged moral corruption of that regime, they (and the important non-religious elements that joined them) were acting in rational pursuit of clear political objectives: the oppressiveness of a particular ruling establishment and its subservience to an outside superpower. The same may be said for the assassins of Anwar al-Sadat. To be sure, modernization and the government's grandiose policies of development played a part, but not by creating psychological disorientation and triggering alleged Islamic fanaticism or xenophobia; rather, in objective terms, they disrupted the livelihood and life-style of hundreds of thousands of people – displaced peasants, the urban poor, and parts of the labour force and business community that were being denied a share in the disposition of the country's oil wealth. In Egypt we have seen a similar increase in socio-economic tensions as the country's recent aggregate growth created dislocations within the lower-middle-class and poor sectors. Modernization along these lines creates conditions under which people can be mobilized for opposition. In Iran and in Egypt, Islamic ideological symbols are pervasive and effective mobilizers of these unhappy people, and a substantial infrastructure of religious personnel and movements exists; and so 'Islam' emerges as an important legitimacy resource for the opposition. The case in Syria and Iraq is somewhat different, even though both countries have also witnessed modernization and fundamental shifts in the power of social groupings.

Syria in the 1970s experienced substantial economic growth, partly as a result of the new oil wealth accruing to the oil-exporting countries. Despite corruption and inefficiency, there was considerable infrastructural development in public works such as roads and construction, and a consequent influx of rural people into the cities, Damascus especially. There was also a much-noted increase in the living standards and economic opportunities of 'Alawis, whose officers dominate the regime, often at the expense of the Sunni landowners and businessmen of Hama, Homs, and Aleppo. There were three important political consequences of these factors which bear upon the role of Islam in Syrian politics today. First, the general country-wide growth of infrastructure strengthened the regime by increasing its presence and its patronage throughout Syria. Second, the socio-political victory of the 'Alawis, reversing their historical degradation, enhanced the sense of 'Alawi identity to 'Alawis themselves while also generating a high degree of visibility to non-'Alawi Syrians – a visibility often accompanied by resentment. Third, the fact that Syria's traditional ruling establishment, which happened for the most part to be Sunni, had been decimated by a series of political upheavals beginning even before the 'neo-Ba'th' coup of Salah Jadid in 1966, left the field of opposition open to Muslim Brothers because the previously dominant elements – Nasirists, 'national' Ba'thists, and assorted other groupings (inside and outside the army) – were seriously divided among themselves. Given the new visibility of the 'Alawis, the possibility of crystallizing an opposition on religious grounds was enhanced. Furthermore, the Ikhwan may to some extent be the façade behind which a number of displaced secular but nominally Sunni elitist groups have mobilized, using the power of Islamic ideology to legitimate their own specific interest in overthrowing this regime.

Changes in the regional picture also stimulated religious opposition to the regime. The Asad government's negative attitude towards the Palestinian resistance movement in 'Black September' 1970 and in the Lebanese civil war in 1976 – however 'necessary' it may have been in strategic terms – certainly created hostility on religious as well as national grounds. The triumph of Khumayni as a Muslim (overshadowing his Shi'i affiliation) over the Shah constituted a positive demonstration of the power of religion, notwithstanding the fact that the Asad regime developed a close relationship with the Ayatullah's government. The surge of Muslim militancy in Egypt, dramatized in the assassination of Sadat, the official toleration of anti-Asad Islamic movements in Jordan, and the assistance from Iraq to any groups opposed to Asad were also favourable for Islamic opposition in Syria.

In Iraq the example of Islamic political action elsewhere in the Middle East has also acted as a stimulus for the Da'wa and other Islamic groups. In this case, of course, the impact of the Iranian revolution is stronger, more direct, and far less ambiguous than in Syria. The Saddam Husayn regime may have a slight advantage over Syria in handling regional Islamic pressures, partly because of its increasingly cool relations with the Soviet Union. Iraq also has placed itself squarely among the Sunni Islamic states and the various Islamic organizations and has joined them in condemning the Soviet intervention in Afghanistan. But the war with Iran, as already mentioned, poses a serious challenge to the regime. Internally, Iraq's oil wealth provides the regime with considerably greater capability than is available to Asad's government to coopt the potential opposition, religious or otherwise. The largely Shi'i south of Iraq has benefited substantially from the oil wealth, and some observers believe that the regime is not exaggerating much when it claims that Iraq's Shi'a put their Iraqi and Arab identity ahead of their sectarian beliefs. With a relatively effective governmental bureaucracy, the Iraqi regime has a better chance of easing the strains associated with growth and internal urban migration than, let us say, is the case in Iran or Egypt.

But in Iraq (as in other Arab countries) there is a limit to the regime's ability to depoliticize its environment. Issues of who shall govern, the bases of political authority, and the extent of political participation cannot be permanently smothered by cooptation, coercion, and administrative capability. Despite its awareness of its problem and its serious efforts to broaden its base through the recent elections and Saddam Husayn's travels through the country, the Iraqi regime still rests disproportionately upon a small coterie of kinsmen from Takrit. Even though it is much more adroit than was the Shah's regime in identifying itself with Islamic values and symbols, it is still a closed system with many enemies among the Kurds, the Shi'a, and those strata that have supported the communists and various Arab nationalist factions in the past. Clearly there are many differences between the Iranian and Iraqi situations, most of which suggest that the Islamic factor is less strong in Iraq. Perhaps to an even greater extent than Iran under the Shah, Iraq under Saddam Husayn is a regime whose party, parallel associations, and security services have penetrated the society thoroughly. And yet there may be one similarity. Just as the religious infrastructures emerged in Iran as the only major part of society that escaped penetration by the regime, something of the same situation may be true for Iraq. Despite the comparative weakness of the religious infrastructures there, Shi'i Islam – because it is a key identity symbol for what is still a relatively deprived social stratum – may yet present the most favourable vehicle for the various opposition currents to exploit in the future.

As perhaps the most pervasive set of values in Syrian and Iraqi society, Islamic principles are a political resource which an opposition can use to outbid an incumbent regime, particularly at the point at which the regime is provoked into highly oppressive counter-measures. Other ideologies and interest groups can for the time take shelter behind the religious vanguard. The problem for the opposition, however, is that the religious vanguard may lack sufficient ideological appeal and structural coherence to combat the highly organized state, army, and party.[36] These incumbency institutions can stake out their own important claims to ideological legitimacy in national, social, and even religious terms; and so many Syrians and Iraqis in all walks of life derive benefits from them (regardless of how despotic they may be) that the religious opposition cannot mount the sort of massive and pervasive demonstrations of public support that eroded the authority of the Shah. Instead, they (or other elements acting in their name) must resort to assassinations, armed attacks, and acts of terrorism. It is doubtful whether Islamic fundamentalism alone is sufficient to rally the many different facets of opposition in these mixed and fragmented societies; and it may even be too doctrinaire and parochial to mobilize all the potential opposition that exists. The national issue would seem to have a wider, more pluralistic appeal if it can be wrested from the state – no easy matter, as we have seen.

Notes

1. Jacques Weulersse, *Paysans de Syrie et du Proche-Orient* (Paris, Gallimard, 1946), p. 68; and Michel 'Alflaq, *Fi sabil al-ba'th* (Beirut, Dar al-Tali'a, 1959, 1963), pp. 43–6.
2. Albert Hourani, *Syria and Lebanon: A Political Essay* (London, Oxford University Press, 1946), ch. 1.
3. Hanna Batatu, *The Old Social Classes and the Revolutionary Movements of Iraq* (Princeton, Princeton University Press, 1978), p. 36.
4. *Ibid.*, pp. 45, 983.
5. Ibrahim Ibrahim, 'Islamic Revival in Egypt and Greater Syria', in C. K. Pullapilly (ed.), *Islam in the Contemporary World* (Notre Dame, Indiana, Crossroads Books, 1980), pp. 158–70.

6. For example, the Damascus domestic broadcasting service of 6 June 1980 (as reported in the *Foreign Broadcast Information Service Bulletin,* Washington) reports President Asad's meeting with a delegation of *'ulama.* Asad is reported as saying: 'The state takes care of religion and calls for adhering to it. Being religious is totally different from killing innocent people and following Zionist and imperialist plans'. At the end of the meeting 'the *'ulama* stressed their full support . . . against all conspiracies'.

7. According to information reported in the Egyptian Muslim Brotherhood magazine, *al-Da'wa* (Cairo), August 1979, p. 10, as reported and translated by the Joint Publications Research Service of the US Government.

8. Adeed Dawisha, *Syria and the Lebanese Crisis* (London, Macmillan, 1980), p. 60.

9. Nikolaos van Dam, *The Struggle for Power in Syria* (New York, St Martin's Press, 1979), pp. 61–3; Hanna Batatu, 'Some Observations on the Social Roots of Syria's Ruling Military Group and the Causes for its Dominance', *The Middle East Journal,* 35 (1981), 331–44.

10. Batatu, 'Some Observations', p. 331. In a study of the attitudes of Syrian Ba'th Party members, Hinnebusch finds a significant Islamic commitment, particularly among lower-class party members. It is wrong, therefore, to conclude that the essentially secularist Ba'th regime is isolated from Syrian society in general, a majority of which exhibits certain non-secular attitudes; 'instead the contradiction has penetrated into the regime'. He also finds mitigating trends in that secularism appears to be increasing with increasing education, and because a substantial proportion of his respondents indicate only 'some' role for Islam in the state. Raymond A. Hinnebusch, 'Political Recruitment and Socialization in Syria', *International Journal of Middle East Studies,* 11 (1980), 143–74, esp. 155–6.

11. See also Michael C. Hudson, 'Islam and Political Development', in John L. Esposito (ed.), *Islam and Development: Religion and Sociopolitical Change* (Syracuse, Syracuse University Press, 1980), pp. 1–24.

12. On this point generally, see Ted Robert Gurr, *Why Men Rebel* (Princeton, Princeton University Press, 1970), ch. 8.

13. Patrick Seale, *The Struggle for Syria* (London, Oxford University Press, 1965), *passim* and pp. 180–1. The Muslim Brotherhood '. . . did not succeed in using this Islamic approach as a political instrument for rallying the youth of the country in a highly-disciplined, paramilitary mass movement. Its influence was widespread, but diffuse and politically ineffective' (p. 180).

14. On this process, see van Dam, *The Struggle for Power in Syria,* esp. ch. 3; also Itamar Rabinovich, *Syria Under the Ba'th, 1963–66* (Jerusalem, Israel Universities Press, 1972).

15. On the history of the issue of religion and state in Syrian constitutions, see George Jabbour, 'Safhat min al-tatawwur al-dusturi l'il-qatr al-'arabi al-suri hatta thawrat adhar' ('Pages from the Constitutional Development in the Syrian Arab Region until the March Revolution'), pp. 13–33 in *al-Dustur al-jadid* (Damascus, Syrian Writers' Federation, n.d. [1974?]), pp. 25–6, 31–2. See also Abbas Kelidar, 'Religion and State in Syria', *Asian Affairs,* 61 (1974), 16–22.

16. Abstracts from the English edition of *al-Nazeer (Al-Nadhir),* no. 22 (31 August 1980), pp. 1–2. The rest of the pamphlet contains news about *mujahidin* attacks and massive repression by the regime.

17. The Higher Command of the Islamic Revolution in Syria, 'Declaration and Program of the Islamic Revolution in Syria', Damascus, 9 Nov. 1980. Signed by Sa'aid Hawa, Ali Baianoni, and Adnan Saaduddeen. pp. 8, 11, and 12.

18. 'Declaration and Program', pp. 12–59.

19. Quoted by Helena Cobban in *The Christian Science Monitor,* 10 Dec. 1979. Interestingly, the Ikhwan in November 1980 presented a political programme in consider-

able detail in the Declaration cited in note 17 above, but it did not lead to a resurgence of opposition in general.

20. *The Christian Science Monitor*, 7 Nov. 1980.
21. See Stanley Reed, 'Little Brother and the Brotherhood', *The Nation* (16 May 1981), pp. 592–6.
22. Faris Glubb, 'Assad Manages to Hold On', *Middle East International* (13 Feb. 1981), pp. 12–13.
23. Gurr, *Why Men Rebel*, pp. 240–1.
24. 'A Message of Imam Al-Sadr the Martyr, to Iraqi People', statement, in Arabic and English, issued by the Islamic Revival Movement (POB 5789, Washington, DC 20014, n.d.).
25. Hanna Batatu, 'Iraq's Underground Shi'i Movements: Characteristics, Causes, and Prospects', *The Middle East Journal*, 35 (Autumn 1981), 578–94, esp. 583. The Iraqi data on persons employed in the 'religious services' also include persons such as servants in mosques who are not authoritative men of religion, so Iraq's population per clergyman figure is probably even higher.
26. It is ironic but not surprising that the intensity of the ideological conflict in these two neighbouring countries does not deter the secular regime in the one from supporting the religious opposition in the other; similarly, the religious opposition in the one is conspicuously mute about the sins of the secular regime in the other.
27. See, e.g., *Islamic Revival*, March–April 1981, p. 7.
28. See Muhammad Baqir As-Sadr, *Contemporary Man and the Social Problem* (translated by Yasin T. Al-Jibouri, Tehran, 1980), esp. pp. 165–74; and the Islamic Da'wa (Call) Party, 'The Form of Islamic Government and Wilayat al-Faqeeh' (Bethesda, Md., The Islamic Revival Movement, 1981).
29. Dr Abu Ali, 'Misconceptions about Iraqi Muslims: An Iraqi Corrects *The New York Times*', *Islamic Revival*, October 1981, pp. 11–13.
30. 'The Form of Islamic Government and Wilayat al-Faqeeh', p. 6.
31. Abu Ali, 'Misconceptions about Iraqi Muslims', p. 13.
32. As reported in *The New York Times*, 17 Dec. 1981.
33. Batatu, 'Iraq's Underground Shi'i Movements', p. 578.
34. Jonathan C. Randal, 'Iraqi Opposition Groups Organize, Argue and Hope in Damascus', *The Washington Post*, 18 Feb. 1981; and Edward Cody, 'Kurds Join Other Rebels in Effort to Overthrow Iraqi Rulers', *The Washington Post*, 7 Jan. 1982.
35. Abu Ali, 'Misconceptions about Iraqi Muslims', p. 12.
36. For an interesting study of the growth and penetration of Ba'th and state institutions in Syria, see Raymond A. Hinnebusch, 'Party and Peasant in Syria', *Cairo Papers in Social Science*, vol. 3, monograph 1 (Cairo, The American University in Cairo, November 1979).

6 Popular Puritanism versus State Reformism: Islam in Algeria

JEAN-CLAUDE VATIN

In Algeria, as in many Muslim countries today, Islam tends to support the ideology of both the government in office (which uses religion to reinforce the social consensus while enforcing its own cultural despotism) and those who openly oppose the government. These apparently contradictory functions may well have to do with the nature of Islam itself.

Muslims have succeeded in building what Marshall Hodgson termed a new society, a 'vision', a 'venture'.[1] Islam – the act of submitting to God – is much larger than a religion: it is a total system, a self-contained whole. But it is also a language. As such it has been the *political language* either of times without politics – that is, without an independent political structure – or of times offering no possibility for popular political expression. Thus in many countries it has been an arena for both open and underground debate; and in Algeria it has been, and still is, the language of both power and resistance to power.

This does not obscure the importance of either the Qur'an or the Sunna, or of the spiritual values attached to them. Nor does it reduce Islam to pure ideology, manipulated both by the government for self-justification and by political opponents for the purpose of dissent; the links between religious fervour and belief on the one hand, and political attitudes on the other, have always been close. Still, there is no question that, since its origin, spiritual Islam has been manipulated on many levels for materialistic purposes. First, it has been used by the believers themselves, for whom it was only natural to relate the precepts of God to the process of selecting leaders, as well as to the entire hierarchical structure of privilege and influence. Second, it has been used by political leaders seeking legitimacy. Third, it has been employed by reigning sovereigns aiming to reinforce their control over society: caliphs, sultans, *mahdis*, *marabouts*, *'ulama*, and *shaykhs*, in various contexts and at different times were the agents of such manipulation. Governments today tend towards the same behaviour.

But we are now also facing the conjunction of the 'repoliticization' of Islam at the popular level and 'political spirituality':[2] that is, religion as used by the state, and by the political elite, who tend to rely on the sacred sources (texts and traditions) in order to obtain the consensus necessary for secular undertakings. The people resent the state's monopolistic control over the language of Islam, and they have tried to find in orthodoxy itself elements that could be used to break this monopoly. The chapter that follows is an attempt to illustrate in the Algerian case how popular puritanism, which has become the language of the state's critics, tends to check 'state reformism', which has been the means of power for almost two decades. Political strategy and religious tactics, governmental phraseology and Muslim vocabulary – until now consistently intertwined in the Algerian consensual society – are becoming differentiated. Between official (or national) Islam and popular Islam, there are intermediaries that may try to manipulate the latter to put pressure on the former.

At the popular level: a disconcerted society

There have been many signs of an Islamic revival in Algeria during the past ten years.[3] This is largely attributable to two different factors. The first is the comprehensive character of Islamic fundamentalism – i.e., the unification of a civilization and a religion. This implies that there exists some sort of Islamic system, so that what happens in one part of the *umma* is not without effect in the rest of the community of Muslim believers. Thus, traces of various Islamic resurgence movements, such as the Iranian revolution, can be spotted in Algeria. The second factor is more localized: it is that Algeria is a socio-religious cat's-cradle of communities and groups having particularities of their own. In short, Algerians are undergoing an Islamic revitalization partly because of external influences, and partly because of problems peculiar to Algeria itself. Strikingly, this revival has been characterized more by an increase in religious fervour, of religiosity (some might even say bigotry), than by the development of religious belief or spirituality.

There has been much evidence of a return to an excessive scrupulousness in religious matters. For example, ten years ago, in the streets of the main Algerian cities, one would have seen only very few girls wearing the *hijab* or *thawb* – what is often referred to as the '*shari'a* dress' or the 'Muslim sisters' costume'. This trend started in 1967, and remained confined for some years to the Faculty of Letters in Algiers among groups inspired by such 'post-*'ulama*' leaders as Malek Bennabi.[4] The movement was known for its proselytism, although this was unsuccessful, and its dogmatism. Religious conservatism was, at that time, recruiting its followers from among a limited number of students of Arabic and Muslim studies, who gave the impression of having been bypassed by the educational system, and behaved as if the university were still controlled by French-speaking educators. Their determination for greater Islamization seems to have been identified with a desire for a more rapid Arabization, so that the latter appeared as a mere device for gaining access to those jobs more or less monopolized by their French-speaking co-religionists.

Today more cities are bearing witness to the development of such practices. The number of women wearing the symbolic dress has increased, not only because the number of universities has been increasing (one in 1962, three in 1965, eighteen projected),[5] with more girls attending courses and passing examinations, but also because social pressure is stronger. Some women themselves regard this as a way of showing their 'Islamicness'. As for men, they encourage such dress for their wives and daughters, particularly since the proportion of the former seeking jobs and of the latter attending school is greater than ever. Families claim that the *hijab* is good protection in cities where sexual harassment, coarse language, and youngsters' aggressiveness are on the increase. This argument, however, is far from convincing. After all, there has always been a national costume: the veil or *ha'ik*, which is white in most of the country (though there are some exceptions; it is black in Constantine, for instance). This was the traditional feminine apparel (outside the Berber regions at least), not the *hijab* or semi-chador imported from the Middle East. Times have changed since Frantz Fanon demonstrated that wearing the veil – especially at the end of the colonial period, when the French had tried to 'liberate' native women by asking them to abandon it – had a political, then nationalist, meaning. Today the system of political symbols has been modified under social influence: the *hijab* is no longer a sign of a sense of national community but of a cultural and religious affiliation.[6]

Another significant development is the number of people going to the mosque, especially on Friday, among whom there is an increasing proportion of young men and adolescents. Although the exact figures are not available, the increase over the past fifteen years is apparent even to the casual observer. Connected with this are the people's recent demands for permission to pray near their places of work: offices, factories, public buildings, and the like. Still another manifestation has been the establishment of what could be called a new religious conformism. Even families of the upper social strata, who had not felt compelled to respect the revived Islamic values and who might have believed (until recently at least) that puritanical Islam was good for the masses, are discovering that social obligations are being penetrated by the injunctions of religion. The bourgeois ethos is being permeated by Qur'anic moral obligations, which formerly were thought to be for others. Strangely enough, the rules now tend to be enforced by the young generation, rather than by the old.

The ostentatious references to revived traditions and moral values, as well as the use of the *hijab*, could be read as the latest fashion in a society whose social code has been so heavily damaged – both by colonization and by the political and economic transformations which followed independence in 1962 – that it is now willing to adopt certain changes, whatever they are. In fact, however, these trends show how much public opinion has been attracted by the Muslim normative system which has been manipulated by both the conservative and the radical proponents of fundamentalism. A common orthodoxy is spreading over the different social strata.

People are turning, or returning, to Islam because they are looking for answers to the problems of today: a rapid industrialization that has not fulfilled its promise, an incomplete and not wholly successful agrarian revolution, growing urbanization, unemployment, inflation, and cultural and social tensions. There is certainly cause for popular dissatisfaction. There was an emphasis on industrialization, for example, in the Boumédienne period, especially between 1970 and 1979. It was, however, an illusion to believe that heavy industry could be built up in a society the majority of whose population was rural, without alienating the agricultural capital from which Algeria could benefit once French troops returned home. Moreover, the opting for heavy industry did not simply mean steelworks, foundries, chemical factories, oil refineries, and gas liquefication. It also implied recruitment of highly qualified personnel, importation of foreign technology and experts, close links with the world capitalist market, economic organization and structure closely linked with the political apparatus, and, last but not least, transformation of the Algerian society as a whole. But technocrats within the state bureaucracy of the national firms, because they were administering a key sector of production, believed that their political autonomy was almost unlimited. Furthermore, they came to think that what was good for the national oil company, Sonatrach, was good for the nation.

Algerian economic planning, which had tended to be much more systematic than that of other Middle Eastern countries, could keep the whole population at bay with the myth of industrialization as the only socially integrative and economically constructive force leading to independence internationally. However, threatening clouds were appearing; some of the plans were not bearing the expected fruits. Economic development did not bring wealth except to a minority, and industrialization became synonymous with Westernization. Prices rose, while unemployment remained the rule. One million workers, about a third of the total active male population, were forced to look for jobs in Europe because of the lack of opportunity in Algeria itself. And productivity declined in the self-administered sector of production (*autogestion*), especially in agriculture, in spite of its use of the best part of the land. For example, two-thirds of the production of cereal comes from the private sector, although it is less developed than the public sector.

The agricultural 'revolution', which was supposed to make Algeria self-sufficient in food production, proved to be totally inadequate: one-third of oil revenue was said still to be devoted to importing food; nor was it possible to span the increasing income gap between urban and rural areas. Despite the new cooperatives, the 100 'socialist villages' built (among the 1,000 promised), and the distribution of 600,000 hectares to landless peasants by the government, dissatisfaction prevailed. A new system of economic exchange, with tightened governmental control over the market and a shift away from promoting self-sufficient agricultural production to promoting intensive product specialization, has also not been successful. The total amount of cereals, for instance, has been decreasing, and the production figures for other agricultural products have remained unchanged. Moreover, *autogestion* workers and cooperative farmers have been leaving the farms and looking for better employment in the cities – until recently at least, when Colonel Chadli Benjedid's government decided that the monthly minimum wage in the rural areas would be put on a par with that in industry. This, in turn, has resulted in the cost of agricultural production in Algeria now being one of the highest in the Third World.[7]

Two general situations are noteworthy. First, the level of poverty is on the rise for a large part of the population; its direct impact can be seen in the widening gap between the 'new bureaucracy' or 'new bourgeoisie' (that is, the urban middle class) and the rest of society.

Second, there has been an atmosphere of political confusion, which peaked during Boumédienne's last months of office; the serious illness of a still young president was not revealed by the national press and there were widespread rumours of fierce competition between potential successors. After Boumédienne's death in December 1978, the army's attempt to impose its own candidate was another shock. Most people were expecting a regenerated party, the National Liberation Front (FLN), to oversee the constitutional transition – which it did according to the letter of the law, but not with regard to political realities. The new government had neither the legitimacy of its predecessor nor a leader with Boumédienne's charisma.

Although there was no significant political instability, people were anxious about the future. Their concern was about economic and political problems, and they had no channels for protesting against these. Moreover, they could not resist linking this concern to something which they could feel but not define: some called it moral decay; others, Westernization. A certain number thought that a solution might be found in a return to the 'Islamic personality'. A general dissatisfaction thus opened the way for intermediary groups to serve as critics not only of the Western-oriented economic policy (with the conspicuous consumption indulged in by a social minority), but also of a central government unable to perform its job. A puritanical, revivified Islam could be effectively used for criticizing official actions, while also providing a political lever for popular and not just traditionalist movements.

At the intermediary level: Islamic mobilization

There are two possible agents between the people and the ruling class that could play a part in the future by using Islam as the political language: the Islamic movements and certain key social groups. The fact of popular dissatisfaction makes particularly important those outside the state apparatus who have the power to interpret the various rules and codes. The result is that there are now disputes over the interpretation of Islamic dogma – i.e., disputes mainly between, on the one hand, those who seek to interpret Islam in order to restore the original religious law and to impose themselves as the religious and moral leaders of the community, and, on the other, those who want to assure that Islam will lead to real equality, socialism, and modernization.

The orthodox or conservative fundamentalists, or 'Islamists', have existed in Algeria for some time.[8] They had their cultural association (Al-Qiyam), their leaders (Malek Bennabi, Dr Khaldi, among others), their review (*Humanisme musulman*), their meetings, and their followers. During the Ben Bella period, they made every effort to be recognized as the true and only heirs of the reformist *'ulama* of the 1930s to 1950s. When in 1965, Ben Bella was overthrown by a military coup, they profited from the occasion by entering the political arena and presenting themselves as the guardians of pure Islam; their goal was to have their say in all matters, including governmental decisions. However, they entirely misinterpreted the situation: the exclusion of the neo-Marxist group from the higher echelons of power was not meant to make room for Muslim dogmatism. After the period 1968–70, the government and particularly the provisional secretary of the F L N, Ahmed Kaid, seemed to rely for a time upon the Islamists in order to eliminate the leftist influence within national organizations and especially in the National Union of Students. When this attempt was checked, the Islamists' power waned, and less was heard from a movement that seemed to be limited to groups of intellectuals clustered in certain cities. Moreover, their association, Al-Qiyam, was outlawed. The regime itself, having chosen to focus on socialization, economic development, and agrarian revolution, looked for support from the left and was prepared to get it through the Parti de l'Avant-garde Socialiste. It thus appropriated the Islamic vocabulary again and left that language no other medium in which to express itself.

Until 1975, the Islamist movement remained quiet, although its members participated in the debate on Arabization, which became their favourite theme. They were also known for their resistance to the nationalization of land, as well as for their support of Shaykh Noureddine, one of the former leaders of the defunct Association of Reformist 'Ulama, who had signed a declaration in March 1976 condemning Boumédienne's policy. In actuality, it was the National Charter that offered the Islamists a new opportunity to be heard. Since then they have been able to press openly for Arabization, and generally to argue that systematic Islamization should be carried out and that the state should act in accordance with Islamic values as defined in the Qur'an and *shari'a*. In so arguing, they have invoked the constitution and the National Charter of 1976 in order to affirm that Islam is the religion of the state.

Their strategy has been to force the central authority to provide proof of its conformity with Islamic tradition, claiming that in so doing they speak for the whole nation. Whenever they deem it possible, they have gone a step further and tested governmental capacities, while always trying to make a spiritual and moral force into an influential pressure group. For example, until recently, they have known that the economic choices made by the regime were not to be criticized, that some matters belonged to the domain of the president. But they also have known that religious and moral questions, such as family law and the law governing personal status, can be subject to their influence. Through Shaykh 'Abd al-Rahman al-Jilali's open condemnation of birth control they have resisted family planning. They have encouraged a strong respect for Islamic law every time the subject of the family code is raised, and the most recent draft of the code appears to have been greatly influenced by traditional views, particularly regarding women.[9]

In fact, the movement has no coherent doctrine of its own, or indeed programme. It is more an assembly of tendencies – the accidental conjunction of groups acting separately in different parts of Algeria – than a defined network, with any visible structure. It bears no resemblance to the kind of religious party noted by Ali Merad in the 1940s.[10] It has no militants, no hierarchy either, as far as we know, and few religious activists. Its influence derives from the desire of a bewildered people to find some form of Islam that will protect them from the uncertainties of development.

There is evidence of such feelings in both the city and the countryside, as well as of the way Islamists are canalizing them. One finds, for example, that not all modern mosques have been built by the government. Some of them have been constructed from the donations of local inhabitants. These private mosques now have their *imams* (prayer leader) and *talaba* (lecturers), whose services are paid for by the neighbourhood. Unless some part of the funds comes from other Muslim countries, such as Sa'udi Arabia, it seems that believers are raising enough money to build their own places of worship, to have their own *imams*, and to have their children educated by their own Qur'anic teachers. In this way they are freed from state reformism and national culture, as interpreted by state-appointed religious personnel. Around Ben Aknoun, a suburb of Algiers, in a place that people still refer to as 'Climat de France', the private mosque attracts more people for the Friday prayer than does the nearby official mosque.

Another indication of the informal network among Islamists is the amount of money collected in the name of people or groups supporting religious values, although the collectors are not known as Muslim activists. Similarly, parents are often told that a certain shopkeeper will provide their daughter (who is attending the *lycée*) with a *hijab* – without charge. Another indicator is the increasing number of petitions addressed to those who run factories and public buildings. These demand that workers and civil servants be allowed to observe the requirements of their religion: that they be allowed to pray freely; that alcohol be prohibited in the canteens; that preachers or Islamists be given free access to economic and administrative facilities.

In the universities, the Islamist current is no longer controlled by a small group of established traditionalists. Other students have joined, and paradoxically they come less from the humanities than from the social sciences, mathematics, physics, and engineering. Even the Institute of Law in Algiers, which in the past had remained relatively calm, has been affected. In December 1979, Muslim students who had gone on strike occupied one of the five large lecture rooms and converted it into a mosque. One year later (probably on the recommendation of the Minister of Higher Education and Scientific Research) neither the dean of the institute nor the rector of the university dared to have them evicted.

In spite of private donations, of private mosques and schools, of militants collecting funds and shopkeepers giving assistance, of students being more deeply involved, there is no such thing as a religious party. None the less, the Islamists have a sound case as well as a potential social base. Their argument is that state reformism leads to the glorification of the state rather than to the glorification of Islam. The nation-state has nationalized religion, to the detriment of the community of all Muslim believers. In so doing, the state has worked counter to the plan of the Prophet: to have all Muslims under one banner within one entity, the *umma*. The social base of this conservative movement of fundamentalism is not obvious. From whom does it recruit? The answer is not clear, but the deprived lower middle class and the sub-proletariat of the cities and the rural areas might find in these arguments and in the new puritanism a means for rebelling against the way of life and privileges of the ruling class.

Thus far, there is nothing new in all of this: conservatism has always existed in the religious field. But what does represent a rupture with the past is the impact of the Iranian revolution among Islamists themselves as well as among the people. The overthrowing of the Shah, of a powerful state structure, by a Muslim ideology used by *mullas* and *ayatullahs* who could be described as traditionalists, came as a shock. Suddenly, Tehran's religious leaders demonstrated that Islamic traditionalism could indeed produce a revolution. Their Algerian counterparts (there is no such clergy in Sunni countries) felt that they could rid themselves of the infamous label of reactionary. They could thus argue that their policies were aligned with those of a modern country having a programme of social and industrial reform. Of course, this position would hinder the other current of fundamentalism, which has also tried to use Islam as an instrument of modernization.

Radical (or revolutionary) puritanism is somewhat closer to the Libyan model, while the conservative tendency seems more akin to that of the Sa'udis. Like the conservatives, the radicals call upon Islam in general, and the Prophet in particular, to provide the country with spiritual guidance. But they want more. They believe that Muslim puritanism should be put into practice, in order, first, to prepare for a truly egalitarian society and, second, to find within Oriental tradition, Muslim culture, and the Algerian personality the means for a form of development as little derived from the West as possible. They use the Islamic vocabulary to proclaim revolution, and demand the purification of economic and political life, starting with politicians and technocrats and including merchants and other tradesmen. They truly believe that Islam and socialism can mesh and that they can have, as Bashir Hajj 'Ali (poet and secretary-general of the former Algerian Communist Party) said, 'the Qur'an in one hand and *Das Kapital* in the other'. They also refer approvingly to Iran as an example, although they would probably be on the side of the Marxist groups that Khumaynists are now fighting.

Like the conservatives, they derive their arguments from the constitution and National Charter, but unlike them they emphasize the substance of both documents regarding a progressive Islam. Thus, they can explain to the people what their demands should be and can clarify for the leaders their duties as well. They also ask that Boumédienne's policy be enforced. It is for this reason that they quote the late president's statements in support of social and economic reform; they present him as the founding father of modern Algeria, whose heritage should be respected and whose example followed. Their goals are to advance national revolution with the help of Islamic ideology and to sustain the tradition of the war of liberation. Moreover, they require that the impetus to realize these goals be maintained; they feel the Chadli government's recently demonstrated inclination to adopt some of their Islamic rivals' views is a threat to Boumédienne's heritage. They resent what they call religious extremists, particularly since these, for the moment at least, seem to be more in favour with the masses.

Both currents, conservative and radical, have common elements. They both seek popular support, particularly from members of the resource-less, destabilized, or disinherited strata who have no class-consciousness, and for whom Islam – as a culture and as a religion – is identified with the model of an egalitarian society, of men equal before God. They

take advantage of the cultural emptiness and economic instability that
have characterized periods of transition. Likewise, they profit from the
fact that the senior staff of both administration and state-run firms,
personnel in the national and local assemblies, and educators are either
ambivalent or reluctant to express their views and orientations. The
Islamic intermediaries feel that, within a 'detribalized', shattered society,
people need what Anthony Wallace called 'revitalization movements'.[11]
They sense people's longing for a return to community, although the
radicals think that the answer lies in the nation, whereas the Islamists
think that it lies in the *umma*. At any rate, both Islamic groups seek
to play the role of irreplaceable agents in the process of social and
ideological reunification.

Neither current, however, has a proper programme, and neither is
in a position to conceive one that goes to the heart of Algerian politics.
Neither group wishes to overthrow the government or change institutions, in which, incidentally, each is represented. The aim of both groups
is to have influence, not responsibility. Their idea is to condition society
in such a way that it could be mobilized to put pressure on the political
apparatus. However, because of their loose structures and mixed social
bases, they may not be the best agents for politicizing the traditional
Muslim symbols and transforming the national political culture.

It may be that the tension that results from social groups competing
with each other will do more to politicize Islam and make its vocabulary
attractive. Today the middle peasantry (landowners of ten to fifty
hectares), a community of 140,000 people owning about half of the
private land in Algeria, is a particularly apt example of these social
groups. It is fearful of losing access to jobs, administrative and political
positions, and wealth. It is among the sons of the middle peasantry
who have emigrated to the cities that we find the supporters of a return
to Islam, the leaders of fundamentalism (both Islamist and radical),
the men working towards a systemic and general Arabization.[12] The
urban middle class of shopkeepers and functionaries (200,000 members
approximately) is also eager for its share of profit and power or, at
the least, to maintain its privilege. The conflict between reformist Islam
and popular Islam might yet dull the social opposition between these
two parts of the middle class. For now each of them – the rural, and
the merchant and bureaucratic – is trying to win some support within
the population; the former has not yet proved successful even with the
lever provided by the latter's unconvincing programme of modernization.

A second possible increase of social tensions could come from the gap between the modern and the traditional sectors, and, more precisely, between the working class on the one hand and the bazaar on the other. For quite a while, the two sectors' moral attitude towards working conditions had been very similar: economic austerity, low consumption, a certain number of working hours. Thus the real gap was between peasants and people in the cities. Today, both attitude and practices have diverged. The working class (not so much the private one in smaller companies or family firms with lower wages, but the public one which is still growing and is dominant now) has greater consumption and more leisure hours – mostly because of shorter work time – than the bazaar sector.[13] In the working class, for instance, the traditional male–female division of labour has been questioned, as more women are working and more girls going to school than before. For the bazaar merchants, these industrial ethics look revolutionary and dangerous; they cannot accept them. Furthermore, they see that technocrats, politicians, and workers all tend to hold the same views about culture, leisure, consumerism, and money; these are the views of Westernization. As for them, they want to keep to austerity, male–female segregation, family work, and a clear separation between work and leisure, as God and the Prophet ordained. Puritanism is thus a way to condemn new trends within Algerian society. Popular *imams* and political censors have recently noticed that the bazaar population can be mobilized through the use of a limited number of 'moral concepts'. The government itself is very well aware of this, as its socio-political base has moved from the rural middle class (after independence) to a 'new technocracy' allied with part of the urban middle class. These contradictions between major social groups are a potential source of crisis. In this sense these groups could become 'Islamic actors'.

At the state level: political monopoly

In Algeria, there had been various forms of Islamic-based resistance to the central powers during the pre-colonial and colonial periods.[14] There was also a long tradition of official religion – i.e., of Islam being closely associated with the state. Between 1830 and 1962 the French government remained a patron of the mosques as well as the employer of the religious personnel attached to them, despite the formal separation of the state from the Catholic Church at the beginning of the twentieth century in France itself. The colonial government's Director of Algerian

Affairs (Directeur des Affaires Indigènes) had been keeping a close eye on the official religion as well as on its informal mystic variant, that of the 'saints' (*marabouts*) and Sufis.

From the 1930s onwards, a revived Islam began to operate as a counterbalance to French influence, because it was the only local means for collective expression of opposition to the Europeans. By presenting to the Algerian community a set of renewed values, the Association of Reformist 'Ulama and its leader Ben Badis developed an Arab-Muslim national identity capable of countering colonial domination.[15] In this way, Islam and nationalism became closely tied until 1962, even if parts of the liberation movement, the 'Messalists' and the Association of Algerian Workers in France (Fédération de France) of the FLN, had a more secular outlook. Although the '*ulama*'s association did not succeed in making Islam the dominant force during the war of liberation (1954–62), reformist principles were recognized as constituting the base of the established religion after independence was declared. In fact, politicians of opposing views sought legitimacy through the main commonly accepted source: the Islamic vocabulary. In so doing, they were able to make sacred the political formulas as well as to imbue the national code with Muslim overtones.

After Ben Bella's replacement by Colonel Boumédienne in June 1965, the most pressing issue was the restructuring of the state apparatus. This led to a type of state control over religious activities and discouraged any form of local autonomy, whether religious, cultural, or social. The message of modernization and the decision to impose socialism, as a means of promoting economic development, were conveyed through state channels: political discourses were transmitted by means of a religiously influenced vocabulary. For instance, Islam was said to be compatible with socialism, once it had been adjusted to a modernization process which was still derived from the Western experience. It was demonstrated that, according to reformist doctrine, a return to religious orthodoxy would not preclude social reform and industrialization; in fact, Islam was nationalized. It was used to reinforce national cohesion. The Algerian state tolerated no political party outside the FLN, ignored social classes, and dismissed all types of religious organizations and propaganda that did not come from its own initiative.[16]

In the early 1980s, the government is still striving to control the Islamic sphere, or at least to monopolize the Muslim language for its own benefit. It attempts to counter opposing leaders, clans or groups by the use of religious dogma. It discredits other interpretations of Islam in order to enhance its own. For quite some time it has had two basic weapons at its disposal: the institutionalization of religious activities (which implies a ban on any Islamic groups that challenge it) and the recruitment of new supporters by means of concessions to specific popular demands and a greater use of Islamic symbolism.

The state monopoly over religious activities has relied in the first place on its own official network: the Ministry of Religious Affairs (Wizarat al-Shu'un al-Diniyya) and the mosques and personnel attached to them. The formal organization of religion – in a country where Islam is proclaimed *the* religion of the state and where only 100,000 out of twenty million inhabitants are not Muslims[17] – is now in the hands of the Minister of Religious Affairs. The head of the ministry has always been a man known for his close affiliation with the Islamic and political establishments. After independence, the first person to be appointed was Tawfiq al-Madani, a former leader of the Reformist Association of 'Ulama and later a member of the Algerian government in exile. A subsequent minister, Mouloud Kassim, demonstrated in the early 1970s that governmental policies were not contrary to popular traditional demands: he, better than anyone else, was able to explain modernization in terms of Muslim values. After Boumédienne's death, Shaykh 'Abd al-Rahman Chibane became minister. A former professor of Arabic language and literature at the Ben Badis Institute in Constantine, he may be linked both with the Reformist Association of 'Ulama and its publications (especially *al-Bassa'ir*) and with the national movement of liberation, since he had been a high-ranking member of the FLN during the war of liberation.[18] Almost twenty years after the declaration of independence, he is still the perfect symbol of the official dualistic formulation of legitimacy: the cultural *and* the historical, the reformist *and* the revolutionary, the religious *and* the political.

The ministry itself has been recently reorganized, according to two decrees of 9 February 1980, and its functions have been more explicitly delineated. The minister is 'in charge of preparing the coming generations for a better understanding of Islam, both as a religion and as a civilization, as a fundamental component of the Algerian personality' (Article 2); the ministry's tasks are the administration of the religious institutions, the extension of Qur'anic education (Article 4), the development of Islamic studies (Article 5), and the explanation and dissemination of 'socialist principles embedded in social justice – one of the essential elements of Islam' (Article 6).[19]

For the moment, the minister's main concern is probably religious administration. One of his problems is related to the control of the mosques. There are an estimated 5,000 public mosques of different types (*jami'*, *masjid*, *musalla*), most of them devoted to the Maliki rite, with a few Hanafi and Ibadi buildings. There is a further number of private mosques, for which no information is available. The 1980 text does not explicitly state that all mosques should be registered, but it certainly emphasizes that the ministry should watch over their 'religious orientation'. The ministry is also required to check their property and real estate, and, finally, to supervise the educational training of their personnel.

Related to this last is the problem of how to provide the same standard of education for the personnel of both private and public mosques. Although we do not have figures for the personnel of private mosques, such as the 'flying *imams*' (unofficial leaders of prayer), we do know that there are about 5,000 people in charge of the public mosques. Semi-official data mention 2,881 *imams*, 1,397 *mu'adhdhins* (summoners to prayer), and 905 *qayyims* (caretakers),[20] who receive a permanent salary from the ministry. In addition, there are other agents of Islamization, such as the appointed preachers, religious teachers, and instructors, who, though attached not to mosques, but to different institutions and offices, come under the aegis of the ministry. The government's aim is to make sure that all these people are provided with similar and adequate education. But it has had difficulties, since the traditional *madrasa*, or school, disappeared and the Islamic Institutes that had been programmed when Boumédienne was still in office have never come into being. According to the Minister of Religious Affairs himself, in an address to ministry personnel in January 1981, three-fifths of the *imams* in official mosques are not sufficiently qualified to comment on the Qur'an and the Sunna accurately.[21]

This situation – the lack of competence of the state *imams* and the existence of private *imams* – clearly could not be allowed to continue, and the government has made various attempts to deal with it. The first plan, to create several Superior Islamic Institutes, with university-level faculties where classical Arabic, theology, and Islamic culture would be taught, was abandoned towards the end of the Boumédienne period. President Chadli's new policy appears to have been influenced by the promulgators of this original plan, among whom 'Abd al-Hamid Mehri, the present Minister of Information and Culture, probably played a more important role than, say, Dr Taleb Ibrahimi, Minister-Counsellor to the President, who, writing under the pen-name of Ibn el-Hakim, frequently represents neo-reformist views.[22]

Both the Fourth Congress of the FLN (27–31 January 1979) and the succeeding congress for the preparation of the five-year plan of June

1980 had recommended that religious education be extended. It was suggested that a complete system of Islamic education, with a Faculty of Shari'a at the top, should be devised. This plan, which has been discussed since, did not make clear what the stages or what the final curriculum would be. But there now exists in Algeria a new type of Islamic institute: a 'centre for the training of *imams*'. At least one of them is operating today, in Meftah (south of Algiers, near Blida), with eleven more being opened in the near future.[23] This would mean a total of 500 students preparing for the imamate. The ultimate goal is to create one such centre in each *wilaya* (department). A post-graduate institution would probably free students from the necessity of going abroad for a degree in Islamic studies in such well-known centres as Cairo or Tunis. The new Superior Institute of Islamic Studies (Al-Ma'had al-A'la li'l-'Ulum al-Islamiyya) will be opened soon in a building attached to the 'Abd al-Qadir mosque in Constantine – itself still under construction after more than ten years of work. Two others may be erected soon in Algiers and in Oran.[24]

What is noteworthy about this general project is that it can help the government to regain full control of that part of the religious arena which is attached to the mosques. If the government is successful, the private sector's capacity to affect the state monopoly will be sharply reduced. Were the system extended to the whole country, no one without an institute degree would be allowed to lead the prayer in a mosque. There would, in fact, no longer be the distinction between official preachers, who follow the guidelines of the Islamic commentaries issued by the Ministry of Religious Affairs, and private preachers, who freely select and comment upon their own topics.

Clearly, this educational scheme for *imams* represents a direct threat to the growing influence of private Islam. It will most likely lead to one of the masked battles in which Algeria specializes. Indeed, the government's hesitation in implementing the project suggests that this is already under way. In the long run, however, a well-organized state structure for the creation of *imams* could lead to the formation of an institutionalized clergy. Today, a hierarchy of 5,000 people does not constitute a pressure group. Tomorrow, however, three or four times that number, with a far better education, would represent a unified body with a community spirit of its own. Although they would not enjoy the financial support that the Iranian clergy has had, they would make the Algerian Islamic system unique among Sunni countries.

It has been noted that one of the tasks of the ministry was the development of Islamic studies. Implicit in this is the responsibility for making known Muslim tradition and Islamic ideology and principles. The available instruments are Seminars on Islamic Thought, which the ministry 'organizes', and other religious institutions and cultural circles that it 'guides' (Article 5, Decree 80–30). Despite the impressive number (715) of Islamic associations (*jam'iyya islamiyya*) under the aegis of the ministry, which might be used as instruments for taking readings of local activity, and despite the existence of certain Islamic cultural centres (*markaz thaqafi islami*), the most effective forums for action are the Seminars on Islamic Thought and certain periodicals.

The first Seminar on Islamic Thought was convened in 1969. Three sessions were held in that first year; thereafter it became an annual event. Batna in the Aurès in 1978, Tamanrasset in the Hoggar in 1979, and Algiers in 1980 were the locations of recent conventions when intellectuals, theologians, academics, and politicians met together. Algerian representatives have the opportunity of meeting linguists, Islamologists, philosophers, and theorists from all over the world, as well as a number of important Algerian students. Here one can observe the official interpretation as well as other trends in Islamic political thought. One may also analyse the evolution of clan relationships as they are presented in the lectures and talks of radical or conservative fundamentalists. The seminar also provides a useful opportunity for observing who, among the Algerian establishment, is asked to speak and with what effect they do so.[25] The debates are generally open and passionate, and often have to be toned down in the official annual publication (published in both Arabic and French by the ministry).[26] Whatever the personal interest of either the participant or the observer, the seminars provide the government with an excellent instrument for popularization, for propaganda, and for its own interpretation of national reformism, as well as a means of contact with Islamic scholars from other Muslim countries.

With regard to periodicals, two reviews deal directly with questions related to Islam. They are both controlled by the ministry. The most important one, *al-Asala*, is a monthly publication whose first issue came out in 1971. *Al-Risala*, another monthly, started only in March 1980 and seems to have been planned mainly for adolescents. The purpose of the editor is to spread the official view regarding theology and law and to give answers to more popular problems. Some of the contributors are well-known authors, others are obscure civil servants and intellectuals. Most of the articles have been written by Algerians, but there are also some by foreigners, even non-Muslims. Important *fatwas*, or legal opinions, are sometimes included. Despite the formal style and official interpretations of both journals, an attentive reader will notice differences between the issues throughout the years as well as between contributors. It is even possible to guess the major tendencies of the moment, the conflicting interpretations, the rivalries between clans and persons. By focusing on the two publications controlled by the ministry (and there are no others in this field, since no private Islamist review is permitted), one can get a good picture of the way the bureaucratic apparatus manages religious affairs.

There are other means available, such as the control of the yearly Pilgrimage to Mecca, to which the regime can resort. Some of these involve other ministries, such as the Ministry of Information and Culture, which controls the mass media as well as films, theatres, exhibitions, and festivals. The part played by a semi-official press and television has been more and more marked. One can observe a more systematic reference to Islamic questions in French as well as in Arabic periodicals.[27] Television, although it still shows films produced in the West, has adhered to Muslim morals; it has also addressed itself at length to the Islamic character of the Algerian community. The national publishing and distributing company (Sned) reinforces the monopoly of the state over various publications. In this domain as in others, although there is not overt censorship, the surveillance of a whole sphere of expression (cultural, religious, and political) has been well organized.

The Ministry of Interior Education, Higher Education, and Scientific Research and the Ministry of Justice have also had their part in the socialization of state reformism. But there is a specific institution which should not be overlooked, since it is the official structure in charge of interpreting Islam on some ambiguous or disputable points. The function of *ifta* (issuing *fatwas*) is fulfilled by the Islamic Superior Council (Al-Majlis al-Islami al-A'la), a body appointed by the government and presided over by one of its members, selected from among the most distinguished scholars (today, Shaykh Hammani). Normally, most of the *fatwas* given by the council would not have much overtly political significance. Nevertheless, in Algeria, because the government has almost always interpreted Islam in order to justify its policies, *fatwas* are as political as they are religious. The regime needs a body of learned men who can demonstrate that whatever choices are made are well founded. There have thus been some judicial interpretations supporting the nationalist way of implementing the Islamic ideal in Algeria.[28]

The regime may use other channels, if needed, to facilitate the nationalization of Islam, a process that has coincided with the urbanization of Islam. Its main purpose, to be the sole organizer of the Islamic resurgence in the country and to use it as an instrument of unification, leads it to seek the elimination of Islamist movements and the systematic reduction of the influence of other religions and sects.[29] With regard to the Islamist groups, the government has said that any criticism of its policy on religious grounds will be construed either as a return to traditional practices, to superstition and neo-paganism, or as a ruse of political opponents whose aim is to undermine the national consensus. For instance, in the summer of 1968, there were violent incidents near Mostaganem in which a branch of a local Sufi brotherhood was involved. Ignoring social difficulties in the area, the state-run newspaper, *El-Moudjahid*, immediately blamed the trouble on mystical and obsolete forces.[30]

Having crushed any form of rural Islam, which the reformist *'ulama* had so sharply criticized, the government turned against urban Islamists. As already mentioned, the Al-Qiyam Society was dissolved (and its periodical banned) in 1966, and then outlawed in 1970. In 1971, 'devout activists', who were reported to have created a subversive organization, were arrested. Since then, there have been repeated rumours of the existence of a new movement, Ahl al-Da'wa, which was reported to have taken shape in the cities, especially in Algiers, Constantine, Médéa, and Ghardaïa.[31] By spring 1981, it was clear that there was widespread unrest. In May of that year, in Sidi Bel Abbès, Algiers, Annaba, and Bedjaïma, Muslim activists, whose core of Islamic students had apparently provoked the incidents, attacked public buildings, notably university and prefecture buildings, and destroyed card-indexes and administrative documents. In Annaba, according to *Le Monde*, more than thirty persons were severely hurt, among whom, allegedly, four were killed during the clashes and the subsequent police repression.

In other words, the consistent strengthening of the government and the nationalization of Islamic ideology had not succeeded in silencing criticism. The disturbances of May 1981 probably had social and economic causes – unemployment and inflation – and the use of Islamic language did not mean that segments of the population had suddenly turned Islamist. Nevertheless, only a year after the sharp clash that had occurred in Kabylia over Berber culture, such clear signs of unrest could not be ignored. In a speech made on 20 May in Saïda, President Chadli took a moderate line. He claimed that there was no inconsistency between the government's determination to stamp out religious violence and the concessions it was now making – not for the sake of the Islamists, but on behalf of those who could be influenced by their slogans.[32]

In actuality, President Chadli's policy is one of procrastination. So far as I am aware, none of the popular *imams* in the suburbs of the big cities who were known for criticizing the regime and its policies has been arrested or even forbidden to preach. Obviously, the government does not want to make heroes or martyrs of them. Although it has relied on the police for reports on the activities of urban Islam, the regime has refrained from attacking this popular base openly. At the same time, it has given proof of its own respect for Muslim observances. There have been several such assurances recently. Friday is now the official day of rest, rather than Sunday. The proposed family legislation, as already noted, is under review again. Formerly, the Boumédienne government wanted a family code that was neither in compliance with the Islamists' desiderata, since this would conflict with its modernist image, nor shaped by the 'social-nationalists', because that would make the conservatives hostile. Today the presidential position encourages the Islamists to believe that they can influence the final drafting of the text. In order to avoid being suspected of Islamic deviationism, the government has tried to refrain from provocative decisions and to adopt some of the puritanical themes.

The recent campaign, initiated by President Chadli himself, to purify the morals of the political and technological class might contribute to the same end. By replacing some of its ministers and dismissing high civil servants and businessmen in national firms, the government is demonstrating that it is ready to apply Qur'anic principles to its own personnel. Furthermore, it is slowing down the policy of industrialization. This might very well satisfy those groups who advocate not so much a rigid adherence to religious norms at the national level as a form of modernization compatible with the Arab-Islamic tradition. They hold that any form of progress should be based on Muslim resources and thus should be less dependent on foreign investment and Western technology.

Education is another field in which the state can demonstrate its orthodoxy. We noted that in 1976 the whole education system had come under the direct control of the government. Christian schools disappeared, and Qur'anic schools came under the aegis of the Ministry of Education. Since 1980, there have been many critics who believe the nationalization of Qur'anic instruction is a form of secularization. Both in the elementary and in the secondary schools children were said to have no religious education any more, which could be obtained only in private Qur'anic schools, some of which were still functioning.[33]

Faced with a general demand to reintroduce the Qur'anic tradition in children's schooling, the Algerian government has drafted a new project. Its aim is not to reintroduce the old system but to make room for religious education within the existing programme. Learning the Qur'an by heart, in the government's view, is less important than absorbing the basic principles of a culture and a way of life. The main function of Islamic education, to quote the recommendations of the FLN's Fourth Congress of 1979, is 'to explain the real causes of the decline of the Muslim world, which must now go beyond the reformist experience and lead directly to social revolution'. There are plans to open 160 Qur'anic schools between 1981 and 1986. It has even been suggested that special 'Islamic sections' should be created as an alternative for children in the *lycées*. There are in fact two options for the government: to allow a parallel system of Qur'anic education to develop, or to reintroduce official Islamic courses in all schools. Most probably, the government will do its best to demonstrate that the second solution is the better, since this will help to maintain its own monopoly while seeming to conform to popular wishes.

So far, the state has not exhausted the possibilities for countering the Islamic resurgence, although some of the usual tricks are no longer effective. For instance, the hyper-Islamic proclamations of former Ministers of Religious Affairs (like Mouloud Kassim) – which sounded more extremist than the Islamists' propaganda itself and were aimed at undermining it – are no longer convincing. Nor is the practice of using historical Islam to legitimate present Islam as interpreted by the state bureaucracy. Solemn announcement and official speeches quoting Muslim concepts are less effective in winning people over than they used to be.

But there are more subtle policies at the state's disposal. One is readily accomplished – finding support among the intelligentsia. Among Arabic-speaking intellectuals, who have long felt deprived of cultural leadership, there are several who would regard it as an honour to act as cultural spokesmen for their country. Others might look for a professorship, some office, a seat of authority or, more simply, prestige.[34] French-speaking intellectuals and academics are clearly losing their influence while the government is looking for support among well-known Islamic theorists and scholars. Furthermore, by letting such people publish books that do not absolutely conform to the Islamic doctrine of the established institutions,[35] the regime demonstrates its open-mindedness. Its efforts to help former *marabouts* and *'ulama* to adapt to modern times, and especially to prosper politically in local and departmental elections, are part of the same policy.[36]

The state has other means at its disposal for countering the problems of Islamic criticism and the new waves of dissatisfaction. It can provide a new Islamic vulgate, which could borrow from that of the Islamists without reinforcing their position. It can accept the *doxa*, or opinions, of the moment to comply with popular demands. It might explain that 'violent Islam' is contrary both to Qur'anic doctrine and to national interest, as indeed President Chadli said in his speech after a clash between police and Islamists in Laghouat in October 1981.[37] Certainly the state apparatus, with its judiciary, police, and army, could itself use force to suppress local movements inspired by a revived puritanical Islam. However, fundamentalism is an ideology more than anything else.[38] And it is unclear whether the type of 'managerial state' which now exists in Algeria is equipped to deal with ideological questions adequately.

Notes

1. See Marshall Hodgson, *The Venture of Islam: Conscience and History in a World Civilization* (Chicago, University of Chicago Press, 1974), pp. 71–99, as well as his use of such concepts as 'Islamicate' and 'Islamdon', pp. 57–60.
2. See Ali Merad, 'L'idéologisation de l'Islam dans le monde musulman contemporain', in Centre de Recherches et d'Etudes sur les Sociétés Méditerranéennes (hereafter CRESM), *Islam et Politique au Maghreb* (Paris, Centre National de la Recherche Scientifique, 1981).
3. For example, see the articles in CRESM, *Annuaire de l'Afrique du Nord*, vol. 18 (1979) (Paris, Centre National de la Recherche Scientifique, 1980) by Mustafa-Kamel Bougerra (pp. 111–21); Yamina Fekkar (pp. 135–46), and Souad Khodja (pp. 123–34). Also see Susan E. Marshall, 'Islamic Revival in the Maghreb: The Utility of Tradition for Modernizing Elites', *Studies in Comparative International Development*, 14 (1979), 95–108.
4. Bennabi is author of *Vocation de l'Islam* (Paris, Editions du Seuil, 1954); *al-Zahira al-Qur'aniyya* (Beirut, Dar al-Fikr, 1968), translated from *Le Phénomène coranique; essai d'une théorie sur le Coran* (Algiers, En-Nadha, 1946).
5. According to the Minister of Higher Education and Scientific Research, A. Brehri (9 Feb. 1980). In fact, thirteen *new* universities would be created during the period of the five-year plan (1980–4). The programme defined by the National Charter of 1976 referred to a total of about thirty universities, approximately one for each *wilaya* or department.
6. On this question, see two articles, one by S. Khodja, the other by N. Chellig Aïnad-Tabet, in Christiane Souriau (ed.), *Le Maghreb musulman en 1979* (Paris, Centre National de la Recherche Scientifique, 1981).
7. Statistics cited during the third congress of the National Union of Peasants (*UNPA*), convened in January 1982 in Algiers, illustrate the sorry condition of agriculture. The official *Recensement général de l'agriculture* will provide updated data. Among recent studies on rural Algeria, see Rachid Benattig, 'Facteurs de transformation et de stagnation de l'Algérie rurale', *Peuples Méditerranéens*, October-December 1981, pp. 23–35.
8. 'Islamists' could also be called 'organic fundamentalists' (for lack of a term equivalent to the French *intégristes*, with reference to the Catholic traditionalists). Conservative

fundamentalism also refers to the puritanical trend of those who believe in the revelation of the truth sanctified by tradition.

9. However, this new draft, the third since independence, has encountered strong resistance, especially among women, to such an extent that the government might decide to postpone its promulgation.

10. Ali Merad, *Le Réformisme musulman en Algérie de 1925 à 1940* (Paris, Mouton, 1967).

11. Anthony F. C. Wallace, 'Revitalization Movements', *American Anthropologist*, 58 (1958), 264–81. According to Wallace, 'A revitalization movement is defined as a deliberate, organized, conscious effort by members of a society to construct a more satisfying culture', p. 265.

12. Peter von Sivers, 'Rural Demands and Governmental Responses in Algeria', unpublished paper, conference on 'Social Movements in the Middle East', Mount Kisko, New York, 14–17 May 1981.

13. Peter von Sivers, 'Work, Leisure and Religion: the Social Roots of the Revival of Fundamentalist Islam in North Africa', in CRESM, *Islam et Politique au Maghreb*, pp. 355–70.

14. Jean-Claude Vatin, 'Religious Resistance and State Power in Algeria', in Ali H. Dessouki and Alexander Cudsi (eds.), *Islam and Power* (London, Croom Helm, 1981).

15. See Ernest Gellner, 'The Unknown Apollo of Biskra', *Government and Opposition*, 9 (1974), 277–310; Merad, *Le Réformisme musulman*; Fanny Colonna, 'Cultural Resistance and Religious Legitimacy in Colonial Algeria', *Economy and Society*, 3 (1974), 233–52.

16. On these questions – i.e., the relations between Islam and socialism and the nationalization of the Islamic system of references – see Jean Leca and Jean-Claude Vatin, *L'Algérie politique, institutions et régime* (Paris, Fondation Nationale des Sciences Politiques, 1975), pp. 259–62, 304–31; Hubert Gourdon, 'Citoyen, travailleur, frère: la deuxième constitutionalisation du système politique algérien', *Développements politiques au Maghreb* (Paris, Centre National de la Recherche Scientifique, 1979), pp. 99–121.

17. Although the reference 'Islamic' is not mentioned in the country's official name. Algeria is still a 'Democratic Popular Republic', which means it is a direct derivation from Marxist-style language and not from the Arabic and Muslim one. On this question, see Roger Gruner, 'Place de l'Islam dans les Constitutions du Maghreb', *L'Afrique et l'Asie modernes*, no. 130 (1980), pp. 39–54; Henri Sanson, 'Statut de l'Islam en Algérie', CRESM, *Annuaire de l'Afrique du Nord*, 18 (1979), 381–90.

18. According to *al-Sha'b* (9 July 1980), A. Chibane is still a member of the Superior Islamic Council. Quoted from Christiane Souriau, 'Quelques données comparatives sur les institutions islamiques actuelles au Maghreb', CRESM, *Annuaire de l'Afrique du Nord*, 18 (1979), 346, note 19.

19. Texts in *ibid.*, pp. 348–52.

20. *Ibid.*, p. 354.

21. According to *El-Moudjahid*, 6 Jan. 1981.

22. Ibn el-Hakim, 'Reflexion sur la personnalité algérienne', *El-Moudjahid*, 25 Mar. 1981.

23. In Tamanrasset, Sidi Okba, Sidi Abderrahman Jellouli, Cheloum al-Id, *et al.*

24. Souriau, 'Quelques données comparatives', pp. 372–3. The *imam* of the five prayers and the *imam* of the Friday prayer, who now spend one year at the Institute (the *baccalauréat* now not being needed), would spend two years instead. As for the 'superior *imam*' (*imam mumtaz*), he would stay three years altogether, at the

Insitutute of Islamic Science (where a *baccalauréat* would be requested). See p. 371.

25. For example, Shaykh Bouamrane's remarks regarding Charles de Foucauld, the Catholic monk – remarks uttered in the very place where he lived in the Hoggar – were interesting. See also Dr Bouamrane's contribution in *Hommes et Migrations*, Doc. 986 (1 Mar. 1980).

26. The national press has consistently provided reports of the seminars. Summaries and accounts are also provided by participants in foreign periodicals. See the thirteenth seminar's report in *Revue de l'Occident Musulman et de la Méditerranée*, 29 (1980), 162–5, for instance.

27. Two recent examples of semi-official interpretations can be found in the daily *El-Moudjahid* (French edition). See, among others, Mahfoud Smati's 'Islam et société', in the 21–22 Aug. 1979 issue, and Ahmed Aroua's 'Les Conditions de la renaissance de l'Islam' in the 27 July 1979 issue.

28. There are *fatwas* which deal with the obligation of the fast, as adapted for an industrialized society. Another prohibits the drinking of beer. Cf. Souriau, 'Quelques données comparatives', p. 365.

29. At the end of 1969, Methodists and Jehovah's Witnesses were expelled from Algeria. In 1976, all religious schools, including Catholic schools with 70,000 pupils were nationalized. On the status of the Catholic school, see H. Sanson, 'Statut de l'église catholique au Maghreb', in CRESM, *Annuaire de l'Afrique du Nord*, 18 (1979), esp. 386–8.

30. *El-Moudjahid*, 20 July 1968.

31. Mentioned by several observers, although none of them was able to give valuable information regarding the group's activities and organization. See G. Grandguillaume, 'Relance de l'arabisation en Algérie', *Maghreb-Machrek*, No. 88 (1980), p. 59.

32. *Le Monde*, 24–25 May 1981.

33. See Fanny Colonna, 'La répétition: Les Tholba dans une commune de l'Aurès', CRESM, *Annuaire de l'Afrique du Nord*, 18 (1979), 187–203.

34. For a tentative typology of intellectuals' political attitudes, see Jean-Claude Vatin, 'Introduction à Islam, religion et politique: communauté islamique et états musulmans: renaissance religieuse ou adaptations politiques?', *Revue de l'Occident Musulman et de la Méditerranée*, 29 (1980), 3–14.

35. 'Abd al-Razaq Guessoum, *'Abd al-Rahman al-Tha'alibi wa'l-tasawwuf* (Algiers, Société Nationale d'Edition et de Diffusion, 1978); 'Ammar al-Talibi, *Ara al-khawarij al-kalamiyya; al-mujaz li-Abi 'Ammar 'Abd al-Kafi al-Ibadi* (Algiers, Société Nationale d'Edition et de Diffusion, 1978).

36. Hugh Roberts demonstrates that this has been its policy in Kabylia. See his 'The Conversion of the Mrabatin in Kabylia' in CRESM, *Islam et Politique au Maghreb*, pp. 101–25.

37. *Le Monde*, 6 Oct. 1981.

38. A symptom of the day: Ben Bella, after having been released from prison, criticized the government's policy in Algeria, using the Islamic rather than the neo-Marxist vocabulary of his years in office (1962–5), and advocated a return to Muslim tradition!

7 Sufi Politics in Senegal

DONAL B. CRUISE O'BRIEN*

Sufism is the Senegalese mode of Islamic devotion. More precisely, to be a Muslim in Senegal is almost automatically to be affiliated to a Sufi order (*tariqa*). Three of these orders, Qadiriyya, Tijaniyya, and Mouride, clearly control the eminently political world of Senegalese Islam: while some 85 per cent of citizens profess Islam (at least to state demographers), some 90 per cent of these Muslims are situated in one or other of the *tariqas*.[1] The leaders of these orders, *marabouts* or living 'saints', thus have extensive spiritual clienteles which may readily be turned to political account: each local Sufi lodge (*zawiya*) is a centre of power, political and economic as well as spiritual. This ultimately sacred power may be said to rise from the tombs of the order's local saints, tombs which attract crowds of pilgrims hoping for the blessing of saints both dead and living. Saintly *baraka*, or spiritual grace, can guarantee salvation to the Sufi disciple in the next world; saintly wealth and political influence can at least hold out a promise of some material assistance here below. Whether in the present or the hereafter, saintly assistance effectively is purchased – by the disciples' labour and pious tributes. This *baraka* is most potent in the local saintly tomb and lodge, and it is not surprising that at a popular level the gift of *baraka* is confused with the possession of material wealth and power.

The structure of Senegalese Sufism

Each Sufi *tariqa* ('way', order, brotherhood) has some minimal dis-

* I wish to record my thanks to the Social Science Research Council and to the School of Oriental and African Studies for making possible a research trip to Senegal (December 1980–January 1981) devoted to the study of recent developments in the politics of local Islam. This visit afforded the opportunity to update the findings of two previous spells of field research in Senegal (in 1966–7 and in 1975) and to assess the potential for fundamentalist Muslim reform in Senegal.

tinguishing features, the use of a particular prayer formula and (sometimes vestigial) devotion to the memory of the order's founding saint (variably distant in time and space). The Qadiriyya's foundation is the most remote in both time and space, taking us away to Baghdad and back by eight centuries. Qadiriyya is a global order, owing its presence in Senegal largely to the early nineteenth-century missionary activity of Moorish lodges to the north of the Senegal river. It cannot be termed an organization (scarcely, indeed, a brotherhood), since its disciples owe allegiance to a variety of local religious leaders, and lack any kind of common discipline, either spiritual or material. All Qadiri chains of spiritual initiation ultimately reach back to the order's remote and distant past, but awareness of this common spiritual history is limited to the saintly and learned few. For the ordinary illiterate disciple the initiation that counts is that of his local *shaykh*, and the notion of Qadiriyya as an entity is scarcely operative. Because it is thus fragmented, Qadiriyya is politically weak (only one *zawiya*, that of the Kunta at Ndiassane in Kayor, can be accounted anything like a political cell). The order also has a smaller popular following than either of its principal local rivals: at the last demographic estimate, in 1957–8, Qadiri disciples numbered 302,957, or 13.5 per cent of Senegal's total population.[2] Since national politicians value the support of Sufi notables in rough proportion to their popular support, Qadiriyya counts for little in Senegalese politics – above all, for want of what politicians see as discipline and cohesion.

The next Sufi order in historical precedence is the Tijaniyya, founded in Morocco by Ahmad al-Tijani (d. 1815) and propagated in the Senegal region by the warlike efforts of Hajj 'Umar and his successors in the mid- to late-nineteenth century.[3] Tijani disciples retain some attenuated links with Morocco, but Tijaniyya in Senegal is organized around a few great lineages and lodges: the Niasse family at Kaolack, the Tall family on the Senegal river, and above all the Sy family at Tivouane. Tijaniyya is to this extent subject to internal divisions which readily take on a political character, but there is sufficient cohesion to make each of the main lodges (especially that of Tivouane) well worth the assiduous attention that is paid to it by national politicians. Tijaniyya in 1957–8 was estimated to have much the largest following of the three main Sufi orders: 1,029,577, or 45 per cent of the total population.[4]

The Mouride order is the only *tariqa* to have a purely Senegalese character: created in the 1880s as an offshoot of Qadiriyya by Amadu Bamba, it is centred on the founder's tomb in Touba. It is properly thought of as a brotherhood because it has more cohesion than any other Sufi order. There are occasional personal and lineage squabbles, but ultimately no Mouride contests the authority of the founder's single acknowledged heir (Caliph-General). In numerical terms, Mourides rank second – in 1957–8 they were estimated at 423,273, or 18.5 per cent of the total population[5] – but, in political terms, their solidarity gives them a strong claim to primacy.

However one may rank the Sufi orders in Senegal, or by whatever criteria (political or other) one differentiates between them, one cannot escape the fact that Sufism *is* Islam in Senegal. Almost 80 per cent of the population in 1957–8 (1,778,658 of 2,260,136) were classified as affiliates of a Sufi order. One is, of course, dealing here with Sufism as a demographic category, which does not tell one much about the realities of popular belief. What the figures mean is not that there is a mass obsession with the teachings of Sufi mysticism, but rather that among Senegalese Muslims the great majority owe a spiritual, and in varying measure material, allegiance to a sacred dignitary who in turn recognizes himself to be part of a given Sufi *tariqa*.

Under the general rubric Sufi, there may be all kinds of local possibilities, ranging from a pious association of holy men to a popular brotherhood, almost Sicilian in style; but, whatever the variations, the political importance of Sufi notables remains inescapable. This form of Sufi dominance is in large part a legacy of French colonial rule: given scant administrative resources (in finance and personnel), the colonial government adopted a strategy of indirect rule that relied heavily on native intermediaries. For a variety of reasons, including simple recognition of majority local preference, the officially nominated 'customary chiefs' were given an arbitrary administrative handling, whereas the Muslim saints were used extensively and effectively as intermediaries between the colonial government and the population.[6]

The political strength of Senegalese Sufism owes much to French indirect rule, under which the brotherhoods flourished more than ever before, but it also owes a lot to the particular local example of the Mouride Brotherhood – founded, as it was, at the very moment of French conquest of the Senegalese interior. Mourides showed that *tariqa* organization could be turned to account under colonial rule, notably by groundnut cultivation in the service of a saintly establishment. The colonial government saw in the groundnut the salvation of the country – in clear harmony of interest with the holy men, who turned their disciples to work for their personal salvation on the *zawiya*'s estates. As the saints became wealthy on the strength of the disciples' unpaid labour, they also became politically powerful within the French framework of indirect rule. The Mouride example proved to be an inspiration to the leaders both of Tijaniyya and, to a lesser extent, of Qadiriyya.[7] Thus it was that under colonial rule Sufi dignitaries became the dominant political force in rural Senegal, particularly in the area to the north of the Gambia river.

Challenges to Sufi dominance

Senegal's politically dominant form of institutionalized Sufism, especially in its Mouride version, did not go altogether unchallenged from within the Muslim community, even under colonial rule. As early as the 1920s urban reformers began to speak for an Islam that was less willing to compromise with pagan tradition, more assiduous in popular religious instruction, and less enthusiastically preoccupied with the 'things of this world'. There has also been a small Sufi intellectual element which shared the reformers' reservations about the conduct of some *tariqa* leaders. Despite differences, however, on matters of religious purity, it is still true to say that a substantial part of the Senegalese Sufi world is involved in a continuing process of conversion to Islam. Occasional outbursts of Mahdism, as well as the development of new *zawiyas*, attest to the continuing vitality of the local Sufi tradition. Urban reformist *'ulama* could, at some future date, challenge the Sufi saintly hierarchies, but their hour seems distant yet.[8]

Since the nationalist agitation of the late colonial period (1950s) – when the *marabouts* were stigmatized from the left as colonial puppets, feudalists, charlatans, and more besides – the secular challenge to Senegal's Sufi establishment has come from various quarters. The holy men survived this urban tempest of secular and youthful rage, while the nationalist movement itself lost momentum with the granting of Senegalese independence in 1960. Socialism as a secular counterpart to nationalism has, of course, proved more durable, but there are many rival socialisms in Senegal, and none is incapable of some accommodation with the entrenched political positions of the Sufi hierarchy. When a socialist political programme has the effect of expanding the state's power and bureaucracy, the governing Parti Socialiste is as sensitive as any of its colonial predecessors were to the need for Sufi maraboutic support to ensure popular compliance with its programmes.

Of all the secularizing tendencies in Senegalese society, the most powerful is not an ideological or explicitly political one, but the continuing penetration of French culture, principally through the medium of French-language education. This language is familiar only to an urban elite (not more than 10 per cent of the population can speak French at all fluently, and less than 1 per cent use French as the language of the home),[9] but education in a French-language school (and university) is a prerequisite to clerical employment, whether in the state service or in private business. Members of the Senegalese elite necessarily write in French, and naturally take on many French tastes and values while acquiring this valuable linguistic skill. Dress, cookery, entertainment, as well as style of political discourse, all show a Gallic influence. But in religious matters (despite a certain lack of enthusiasm which has much to do with the French style of *laïcité*) a French outlook has never been decisive. Roman Catholics are a declining minority (some 5 per cent of the total population), and that minority is not distinctively part of the elite. The bulk of the national elite is at least nominally Muslim, even if willing enough to take advantage of the continuing French presence in independent Senegal.

French cultural penetration is not, in fact, much resented, even by the 'anti-neo-colonial' younger generation. (There is, of course, a sound material logic to the hypocrisy of educated youths who can rail at the evils of cultural colonialism while themselves profiting from French education – and no question, apparently, of what will happen when *their* children go to school.) Arabic-language education remains marginal, largely confined to devotional purposes and without impact in the modern sector of employment. Articulate (if often incoherent) opposition to the dominance of the French language comes less from representatives of Islam than from the publicists of Senegal's major national language, Wolof. In the capital city, there is a Muslim reformist minority which certainly desires greater official support for Arabic-language instruction, but even within this group the prevalent attitude to French education is one of resignation. In terms of urban culture at least, France rules.

The political history of independent Senegal has been dominated by the advocate of Francophile *négritude*, Léopold Sédar Senghor – President from independence in 1960 until his resignation at the end of 1980. Senghor's two decades as a Roman Catholic head of state in a largely Muslim country have often been remarked upon by foreign visitors, but no local opposition spokesman succeeded in making a popular political issue of his Catholicism. Senegal has operated since independence with a constitution proclaiming the secular (*laïc*) status of the country's government, and this option for official *laïcité* has no doubt reflected presidential preference. While the government avowedly stands above religious partisanship, citizens are free to follow their own religious preferences (within, of course, the limits of the law). There would seem to be no reason for Muslims as a body to feel themselves to be disfavoured by political authority, no reason for the notion of citizenship to conflict with adherence to local Islam. In fact one could argue that local Sufi Islam had already gained in so many respects under the infidel colonial government's Nazarene rule that the notion of an Islamic subject had prepared the way for that of the post-colonial Islamic citizen.

More directly pertinent to the regime's survival amid the intricacies of local political intrigue has been the formidable political skill of its first president. Léopold Senghor even managed to turn his anomalous religious status to political advantage, and to present himself to notables of all local Sufi orders as a neutral arbiter of factional disputes within the Muslim community. His careful dispensation of official patronage through these same notables did much to strengthen the government's position, particularly in the rural areas, as did his conspicuous attendance at all major Sufi gatherings. All political parties since Senegal's independence have attempted to gain the support of Sufi notables, but in the politics of patronage the government clearly has more than a head start. The governing party can also use the machinery of state to keep a fairly comprehensive police surveillance of the *zawiya*'s internal and external political affairs.

Whereas the political structure of independent Senegal seems to be relatively solid (at least in comparison with neighbouring states), the same cannot be said for the country's economy. France's colonial legacy was one of massive budgetary reliance on a single crop, the groundnut, which was apparently well suited to the sandy soils and light rainfall of Senegal north of the Gambia river. A series of drought years, from 1965 onwards, led to the desertification of the northern groundnut zone, and brought massive migration from the country to the towns. At the same time the towns, especially Dakar, have been privileged in public and private investment, with a substantial growth of light industry on the Cape Verde peninsula in the 1960s. (Thus whereas in 1960 local manufactures accounted for just under 17 per cent of Senegal's total exports, in 1970 this figure had risen to 40 per cent.[10]) Subsequent developments in the world economy, notably the huge rise in the price of oil since 1973, and more recently the imposition of very high interest rates for investors, have of course severely restricted industrial development. However, the economy's urban bias has, if anything, been accentuated in the 1970s, with a sprawling public sector (government and parastatal concerns) accounting for half the national total in salaried employment, and that half heavily concentrated around Dakar.[11] The capital city in this near catastrophic economic setting, with a population of over one million according to the most recent estimates,[12] offers the best available hope to much of the acutely distressed rural multitude.

Urbanization, and in particular the growth of the nation's capital, could provide the social basis for a serious threat to the established religious and political hegemony of the Sufi orders in Senegal. Religious precedent (in this century) to the north, in the Maghrib territories, suggests a possible incompatibility between the *tariqa* and the town, although there are notable exceptions (and even some urban Sufi success stories not far away, in Egypt[13]). Senegal's Sufi orders seem thus far to have made an effective adjustment to the urban setting, concentrating their spiritual activity on the *da'ira* (circle or association), which is devoted to religious singing, pilgrimage organization, and pious tribute to a local *shaykh*. Such circles have proliferated in all of Senegal's major towns, in proportion to the growth of the urban population.

In economic terms, the orders have followed different paths – in particular, the Tijaniyya and the Mourides. The Tijaniyya has dominated in wage employment, whether public or private, and the Mourides have secured a near monopoly in market trading (with some spectacular business successes). In political terms, this differentiation has taken on a partisan character in the towns, and the competition between the two orders would seem potentially dangerous. The capital city, as the centre of power, is effectively where the political succession is decided, whether by election, revolution, or *coup d'état*. On such an occasion, the capacity to mobilize the masses (in strike or riot) can be tactically decisive: the Sufi orders, increasingly, have that capacity.

The political authority of Senegal's Sufi leadership has thus far presented a united front only in a few crisis situations, when the *marabouts* could be seen to be acting at the behest of the government of the day: thus in 1958, on the occasion of De Gaulle's referendum on the independence issue, maraboutic appeals to the people helped to assure a heavy electoral majority for membership of the Communauté (*le 'oui' des marabouts*); and again ten years later, in 1968–9, as urban students and workers threatened by demonstrations and strikes to provoke the collapse of President Senghor's government, the rurally based Sufi leadership offered the reassurance of continuing mass support throughout the countryside.

Occasions of national crisis, when leaders of the different Sufi orders feel themselves to be collectively threatened by some form of revolutionary upheaval, call forth the conservative unity of a true establishment which is facing a common threat. Such occasions are exceptional. Factional strife, the competition within and between Sufi orders for material resources and spiritual clienteles, is the routine form of Sufi politics in calmer times. Sufi orders, now as in colonial times, thrive by acting as intermediaries between the government and the people, but they have yet to show much inclination to take over national government themselves. Although the saints have popular support, they lack the training, as well as any powerful inclination, to take over the often unpopular tasks of government. This preference for power without responsibility has been evident since colonial times. (Why act as gendarme or tax collector when the opposite path has so often led to power and prosperity?)

Recent developments in the wider world of Islam may foreshadow some new directions in Senegal's religious politics, although one hesitates to point with any precision. The Iranian revolution of 1979, notably, has had its echoes in Senegal as throughout the Islamic world, although the initial and most evident appeal of the Iranian example was to aspirant politicians rather than to men of religion. French-educated political opponents of the government, who had previously been of a secular outlook modelled on French ultra-left politics, discovered Islam as a hitherto unsuspected revolutionary resource. The realization that Islam could be equated with revolution and power, rather than as before with reaction and political impotence, offered these Westernized intellectuals a political incentive to attend to their Muslim roots. The previous decade (from 1968) had been that of the ascendant fashion of Parisian *gauchisme*, but those *gauchistes* who had a political career in mind had effectively cut themselves off from the masses to whom, at least in rhetoric, they appealed. As a result, even before the Iranian revolution, from 1975 onwards, *lycéens* and university students had begun to concern themselves with Muslim affairs. Political ambition lay behind some of this rediscovered spirituality: the pious vocabulary of Muslim piety usefully laid the basis for associations which could readily be turned to political account.

The initial appeal of Ayatullah Khumayni's example to the young Senegalese intelligentsia was also essentially political rather than religious. Any direct 'Khumayni effect', however, was to prove transitory, as Senegal's would-be revolutionaries discovered the difficulties of applying an Iranian model to their own circumstances. The revolutionary utility of Islam depended on an understanding of the character of the local Muslim community, and that understanding in radical student circles tended to be rather vague. Theological nuance had never been a strong point among Senegal's politicized youth, and, in any case, the fundamental division between Shi'i and Sunni Islam precluded any direct application of an Iranian example in a country where Shi'i Islam is virtually unknown. Senegal is broadly Sunni, with this doctrinal allegiance complicated by Sufi divisions and subdivisions, which have thus far made it impossible for a Muslim leader to rally all, or even most, Senegalese Muslims to a common programme. There was, in fact, one attempt to apply the Iranian lesson – that of Abdullah 'Khalifa' Niasse who, in Paris, proclaimed Senegal an Islamic republic in November 1979. But Niasse's Party of God (Hizbullahi) quickly proved to be a fiasco, since the aspirant caliph was disavowed by his own family (one of the country's three major Tijani branches). The party was then discredited by revelations that its sponsor had left Senegal after having misappropriated funds collected to pay air fares for the Pilgrimage to Mecca.[14]

Stubborn devotion to the long-established factions of the Muslim community was the main reason for the waning appeal of a 'Khumayni model'. Another reason was undoubtedly the development of the Iranian revolution itself, as locally reported through international news agencies. The astonishing manner of the Shah's overthrow first excited the imagination of those in Senegal who had some similar destiny in mind for their own president, but subsequent developments have led the Senegalese student elite to doubt the long-term expediency of a political alliance with Islamic dignitaries. In such a marriage of convenience, might not the men of religion get the upper hand?

The cultural gulf between the French-trained elite and the Muslim mass is again apparent when one turns to consider the style of government adopted in Senegal since independence. Rural administration in particular, now as in colonial days, still depends largely on the good will of Sufi intermediaries: this remains the case despite the steady growth in the number of civil servants and the improved formal training of officials at all levels. Bureaucratic modernizers find this dependence a constraint and even a humiliation; politicians and state planners resent the financial cost of maraboutic good will. Are not the *marabouts* an unproductive, parasitic feudal class? Do they not exploit the credulity of their Sufi disciples (*talibés*), turning the disciples' blind devotion to their own material advantage? When members of Senegal's ruling class ask such questions, as (at least privately) they do, it is logical that they should take some interest in fundamentalist Islam – whether that of *salafiyya* reformers or of *wahhabiyya* traditionalists – which denies the *marabouts* any place in a healthy expression of the faith.

An Islam reformed along fundamentalist lines might, in some people's view, become the natural ally of the state's expanding bureaucracy. The Algerian model seems pertinent here, as a case in which centralizing, state-sponsored modernization has worked with the effective complicity of the local *salafiyya* reform movement. State officials and reformist *'ulama* in this instance have worked together to undermine or destroy the prior hegemony of local Sufi *marabouts*.[15] It is at least tempting for the Senegalese government, in giving official encouragement to *salafiyya*-style Muslim reform, thereby to give an indirect warning to the *marabouts*. If the Sufi *marabouts* claim to address the state in the name of Islam, they should be reminded that theirs is not the only possible form of Muslim observance, and indeed that Sufi maraboutism has been successfully challenged by fundamentalists elsewhere in the Muslim world. The availability to the government of Arab financial and technical assistance over the past five years has underlined this reminder.

Inter-brotherhood rivalry

Senegal, however, is not an Arab state, and the effect of fundamentalist propaganda has not yet followed paths which Arab experience might suggest. The Sufi orders, in particular, appear to be as strong as ever. Yet although there has been a discernibly greater popular interest and involvement in Muslim affairs over the past five years, there has also been a sharpening of divisions and hostilities between Sufi orders: one major Sufi *shaykh* has publicly spoken of the eventual danger of a religious war, not between Sufis and fundamentalists, but between rival Sufi brotherhoods.[16]

An authentic urban fundamentalism has been present as a significant minority voice within Senegalese Islam ever since Shaykh Touré's foundation of the Union Culturelle Musulmane (UCM) in 1953. Fundamentalists in the style of the early UCM were in radical opposition to the Sufi orders – to their world of heresy, semi-pagan magical practice (*maraboutage*), worship of saints, and illegitimate division of the Muslim community.[17] The saints have survived this doctrinal assault and retained their spiritual authority, solidly reinforced as it is by economic and political power. The Sufi *zawiya* in local terms amounts to a Muslim welfare state, organizing not only devotional activity but also agricultural production and marketing, distribution of charity and hospitality, and representations to state authority. Against all this the urban reformists have had little to offer beyond pious aspirations, and although such aspirations may be shared by reformists and at least some *marabouts*, for example in encouraging Arabic learning and devotional assiduity, reformists and *marabouts* cannot agree on the desirable locus of power, sacred or profane.

Senegal's Sufi orders may usefully be differentiated by their response to recent attempts at reform, the most politically significant mark of difference being the extent to which Sufi disciples regard their *marabouts* as worldly masters (as well as spiritual initiators and guides). Worldly deference is weakest in the case of Qadiri disciples: the venerable Qadiriyya may in a sense be seen as already reformed, both in its emphasis on the total unity of Islam ('one book, one prophet') and in its restriction of the saintly role to initiation and spiritual guidance.

Political conflict within Senegalese Islam lies principally between Tijaniyya and the Mourides. Tijani *marabouts* present themselves as true heirs to an historic tradition of Muslim reform, harking back to their leading role in pre-colonial *jihad* movements, while also being men of current political and economic power.[18] Tijanis stress their doctrinal purity, their commitment to Arabic teaching, and their devotional rigour, by implicit contrast with Mouride laxity. A democratic communalist element may be discernible here, since the two orders appear to conflict less at the level of leadership than among disciples. At their annual pilgrimages in 1980, both Mouride and Tijani *khalifas* explicitly appealed for calm and Muslim unity after inter-brotherhood rivalries had been dramatically demonstrated by rioting in the Dakar area. This intercommunal rivalry is not in strict terms sectarian, but whereas in the past disciples of all Sufi orders have insisted on their commitment to a Muslim unity that transcends differences, since 1979 this insistence has lapsed. Mouride and Tijani disciples of late have freely accused each other of masking corporate political ambitions behind a screen of holy propaganda, of practising what one might typify as devotional imperialism.

Seen against this background of inter-brotherhood competition, state-sponsored, official Islamic reform can be taken as a veiled attack on the Mouride Brotherhood. The Union pour le Progrès Islamique au Sénégal and its affiliated organizations do not present themselves explicitly in such a light, with their bland appeals to Muslim solidarity and even to ecumenical tolerance. But when these reformists go on to condemn the general evils of fanaticism, superstition, and blind obedience to the *shaykh*, they are understood by Mourides to be directing an attack on the Mouride Brotherhood in particular. Deference to the *shaykh* is certainly at its strongest among Mouride disciples; superstitious belief in the magical prowess of holy men, although general to Senegalese Islam, is likewise ascribed particularly to Mourides; fanaticism, in the sense of an exclusivist corporate loyalty, is above all Mouride. These three 'evils' are indeed the very qualities that explain the continuing growth and power of the Mouride Brotherhood, a power that is resented and feared by other Senegalese Muslims. Tijani *marabouts* have been prominent members of the official reformist organizations, and Mourides tend to see official reform as sponsored by Tijaniyya for anti-Mouride purposes.

Competition between brotherhoods is above all a matter of political power. Mourides correctly believe themselves to be the best organized and most effectively unified brotherhood, in contrast with the Tijaniyya, which is divided into three lodges that recognize no overall leadership. Mourides, probably wrongly, also believe themselves to be the most numerous, 'advancing with a giant's step'. Since 1960 the government of Senegal has instructed its demographers not to gather census data on brotherhood membership, the question being regarded as politically explosive; the result is that one is left in a demographic vacuum. The Dakar census of 1956 suggested that there were then probably more than twice as many Tijanis as Mourides in the country as a whole, and it seems unlikely that Tijanis are now a national minority.[19] Without demographic verification one has to rely on impressionistic evidence, and this suggests that Mourides are present in growing numbers in Dakar and in Senegal's principal cities. The problem for an observer, as for civic peace in Senegal, is that *both* Tijanis and Mourides now believe themselves to constitute national majorities.

Demographic imponderables aside, it seems clear that Mourides are currently the most dynamic socio-political element in Senegalese Islam. They have, in particular, secured for themselves a dominant position in urban petty trade over the past decade.[20] This is an impressive adaptation to adverse circumstances – the decline of the groundnut trade, in which Mourides had specialized, and rural-urban migration, both caused by recurrent drought since 1965. Mouride proselytism in the towns appeals especially to young men, for whom the attraction of the Mouride Brotherhood is not doctrinal but political and economic: affiliation to the brotherhood provides a possibility of access to political patronage and financial credit, if at a heavy price. Such converts are predictably denounced as political opportunists, rather than true Muslims, by Tijani and Qadiri disciples.

Mouride proselytism takes aggressive forms, which tend to enflame resentments among Qadiri and especially Tijani disciples. The use of loudspeaker vans, with amplified religious chants invading non-Mouride neighbourhoods, is particularly resented. Mouride singing sessions are extremely noisy, and when held in mixed urban neighbourhoods they heighten tension between brotherhoods. This tension is evident both in the home (in mixed neighbourhoods) and at the work place (since markets have been virtually monopolized by Mouride traders, friction is particularly evident in Dakar factories[21]). Resentment has turned to riot with Mouride marches and demonstrations in Rufisque (1978) and Dakar (1980), when disciples armed with clubs stopped traffic and acted as an informal police force. The Tijani leadership's response to such provocation has been to warn – as at Tivouane in 1979 – of the eventual danger of civil war and to seek reconciliation between rival Tijani notables (effectively so far only within the Sy family of Tivouane). The Mouride leadership talks publicly – as at Touba in December 1980 – of the need to maintain Muslim unity, implying that this 'unity' is currently being threatened by popular enthusiasm.

The most striking and politically significant manifestations of Islamic renewal in Senegal are those emanating from the Mouride Brotherhood. It is understandable, given the charges of devotional laxity commonly levelled at Mouride disciples (superstition, fanaticism, blind obedience), that the brotherhood's leadership should seek to present a reforming and even puritanical image. Alcohol and cigarettes were banned from the brotherhood's capital in September 1980; failure to respect the ban means payment of a fine or a jail sentence, with these penalties being enforced by the state police. The Caliph-General has also made public his wish to see greater attention devoted both to study and to prayer among the Mouride faithful. A library, housing thousands of copies of the Qur'an and of the devotional poetry of the brotherhood's founder, Amadu Bamba, was completed in Touba in 1979, but it is not yet used for study. A university is also now under construction in Touba, covering a secondary cycle in Arabic. A Mouride primary school, with the prestigious name of Institut al-Azhar, has been teaching Arabic since 1975 with the help of Egyptian teachers.

In Senegal's principal towns, notably St Louis and Dakar, a new Mouride force has appeared in the form of a French-educated intelligentsia, bringing the brotherhood for the first time to the university and the *lycées*. An association of Mouride students and *lycéens*, the Da'ira des Etudiants et Elèves Mourides du Sénégal, has been active since 1977, making use of French translations of the founder's poetry and thus rendering his teaching accessible to those educated in the modern sector. Members of this association stress their pious concerns – religious singing, together with the translation and commentary of the founder's texts – and they deprecate the devotional excesses of the illiterate *talibés*.[22] In so doing, they lay the basis for what might become a Mouride fundamentalism. In the words of the association's leaders, 'Amadu Bamba's real miracles are his writings': this is a novel viewpoint in that popular enthusiasm credits the Mouride founder with a range of spectacular magical feats which this reformed view leaves to the belief of women and children. The founder's writings being in Sufi terms orthodox, although unintelligible to disciples who remain illiterate in Arabic, emphasis on comprehension and discussion of such texts is potentially a very significant reform.

Young men who are or who become Mourides, while being educated at secondary or tertiary level in French, now have access to a learning both sacred and profane, and thus to high status and to power. The association of Mouride students and *lycéens* is particularly encouraged by the brotherhood's leaders, no doubt in part because they regard it as opening the gate to a new arena of political power: whereas in the past Mourides have been marginal and unorganized within the state bureaucracy, they are unlikely to remain so with the ascendancy of this new generation. Non-Mourides suspect the association's members of seeking to use the brotherhood's power and patronage to secure for themselves reserved posts in the civil service. It is at least clear that the French-educated Mourides have brought open inter-brotherhood rivalry to the *lycée* and the university: a Tijani association, modelled on its Mouride predecessor, was established at Dakar University in 1980.

Rivalries between brotherhoods thus not only remain characteristic of Senegalese Islam, but have been reinforced by recent developments. The Tijaniyya leadership, and less significantly that of the Qadiriyya, have aligned themselves with the government and respect the secular state. The Mouride leadership presents itself as opposed to the government, and is so viewed by its own disciples. Tijanis and Qadiris with whom I spoke in January 1981 declared that under present conditions an Islamic republic could be translated into actuality only in the form of a Mouride state, and that, given the Mouride taint of heterodoxy, such a republic would not be truly Islamic. The Mourides are not yet sufficiently powerful to take over the state, although they do claim to speak for a 'national' Islam that does not have compromising links with the Arab world. Aggressive Mouride expansionism, a triumphalist mood of black Islam, could threaten civic peace in Senegal.

The resignation of Léopold Senghor from the Senegalese presidency on 31 December 1980, and the succession of Abdou Diouf with Habib

Thiam as the new prime minister, although a remarkably orderly transfer of power, suggest a potential for new problems in the communalist politics of religion. Now that the two principal offices of state are occupied by politicians at least nominally affiliated to the Tijaniyya Brotherhood, it remains to be seen whether the new president and prime minister can assert their authority without exciting further inter-Islamic jealousies. Léopold Senghor, a consummate politician, was able to play on factional and personal rivalries within the Islamic community, but for his successors this strategy might be more difficult. The ingredients of religious strife are certainly present, but Senegal's political leaders are no doubt well aware of the dangers involved and have had ample occasion to observe a master cook at work.

Notes

1. These precise figures may be delusory, given the fragility of Senegal's national statistics where religious matters are concerned, but they do represent a 'best guess' based on compilation of a wide range of demographic and sociological materials.
2. This estimate, undated, in Centre des Hautes Etudes Administratives sur l'Afrique et l'Asie Modernes (CHEAM), *Notes et études sur l'Islam en Afrique Noire* (Paris, Peyronnet, 1962), p. 196.
3. J. Abun Nasr, *The Tijaniyya: A Sufi Order in the Modern World* (London, Oxford University Press, 1965).
4. CHEAM, *Notes et études.*
5. *Ibid.* For more detailed figures, see Tables XXII, XXIV and XV in Donal B. Cruise O'Brien, *The Mourides of Senegal: The Political and Economic Organization of an Islamic Brotherhood* (Oxford, Clarendon Press, 1971), pp. 216, 242–3.
6. See Donal B. Cruise O'Brien, *Saints and Politicians: Essays in the Organisation of a Senegalese Peasant Society* (Cambridge, Cambridge University Press, 1975), pp. 85–111.
7. F. Quesnot, 'L'Influence du Mouridisme sur le Tidjanisme', in CHEAM, *Notes et études.*
8. See Christian Coulon, 'Les reformistes, les marabouts et l'état au Sénégal', to be published in *Année Africaine.* Generally, one should also see his *Le marabout et le prince: Islam et pouvoir au Sénégal* (Paris, Pedone, 1981).
9. Centre de Linguistique Appliquée de Dakar, *L'Expansion du Wolof au Sénégal* (n.d.). See also Donal B. Cruise O'Brien, 'Langue et nationalité au Sénégal: l'enjeu politique de la Wolofisation', in *Année Africaine* (1979), pp. 317–35.
10. International Bank for Reconstruction and Development, *Senegal: Tradition, Diversification and Economic Development* (Washington, DC, 1974), preface.
11. Cruise O'Brien, *Saints and Politicians*, pp. 131, 144.
12. Interview, Shaykh Mbacké, Bureau de la Statistique, Dakar, January 1981.
13. See M. Gilsenan, *Saint and Sufi in Modern Egypt: An Essay in the Sociology of Religion* (Oxford, Clarendon Press, 1973).
14. For the revelations, see *Le Soleil* (Dakar), January 1981.
15. B. Etienne, *Algérie, cultures et révolution* (Paris, Editions du Seuil, 1977).
16. Abdul Aziz Sy, *khalifa* of the Senegalese Tijaniyya, speaking at Tivouane at the end of Ramadan 1979. Cited in Momar Coumba Diop, 'La confrérie Mouride: organisation politique et mode d'implantation urbaine' (Ph.D. thesis, University

of Lyons, 1980), p. 191. This thesis, still unpublished, is an excellent source for developments over the years 1975–80.

17. See Cheikh Touré, *Afin que tu deviennes un croyant* (Dakar, Imprimerie Diop, 1953).
18. J. Abun Nasr, *The Tijaniyya*.
19. Haut Commissariat de l'Afrique Occidentale Française, *Recensement demographique de Dakar* (1955); also Cruise O'Brien, *The Mourides of Senegal*, p. 243.
20. Interview, Gerard Salem, currently doing research on this subject, ORSTOM, Dakar, December 1980.
21. Interview, Jean Copans, on the basis of his current research in Dakar factories, January 1981. See also his *Les Marabouts de l'Arachide* (Paris, Le Sycomore, 1980).
22. The association currently claims 400 members. Interviews, Saliou Mboup (president) and other bureau members, Dakar University, January 1981.

8   Religion and Politics in Modern Turkey

ŞERIF MARDIN

In the 1930s scholars who set out to describe the characteristics of Turkish society underlined the secularist reforms of the newly established Turkish republic. Since the 1950s the resurgence of Islam in Turkey has inverted this emphasis: today the deeply religious nature of the Turkish masses is stressed. Both of these findings are correct, but only as first approximations. To understand contemporary Turkish Islam one has to take into account certain details which are included in these broad interpretations, and which in some cases go back in history several centuries. One illustration will suffice. Early Ottoman Islam was deeply marked by the repercussions in Anatolia of the chaotic social history of the regions that lie to its north-east. Religious and social movements of great complexity that were taking shape in the regions of Ardabil, Tabriz, and Baku in the fifteenth century brought to Anatolian soil world-views whose effects are still discernible today.[1] The religious patterns, solidarity groups, and symbolic markers which emerged from such influences have been modified by time, but they are nevertheless important. For example, 'Haydar' (meaning 'the lion'), one title of the Caliph 'Ali as well as the name of one of the founders of the Safavid dynasty (1460–88), still has its echoes in the Turkish heterodox group known as the Alevi ('Alawi). These people are not in the mainstream of Twelver Shi'ism, but they certainly bear the stamp of Shi'i influences. The lament about Haydar which became a popular record in the 1960s was probably part of a conscious attempt of the Turkish left to politicize the Alevi minority of Turkey.

In some cases, students of Turkish religious history are handicapped by an inadequate conceptual apparatus. Much is made, for instance, of 'communications' and 'mass communications' these days, and this global process certainly affects local culture in Turkey, but a study of Turkish religious developments in the past century and a half indicates that there exists a specifically Islamic network of communications whose influence should be studied together with the effect of modern mass communications. The core of this system is the way in which Muslims, through the Pilgrimage, are concentrated in cities like Mecca and Medina. These cities function as communications 'nodes' and as communications 'exchanges'.[2] In Turkey, the *tarikat* (*tariqas*), or Sufi brotherhoods, functioned as sub-units in this vast communications network, and modern social movements with an Islamic background used these channels for their own ends. Two examples will illustrate my point. The first Ottoman reaction against the *Tanzimat* reforms of the mid-nineteenth century, on the grounds that they were new-fangled and alien, was initiated by a Nakşibendi leader, Şeyh Ahmed.[3] And today the Nakşibendi order is believed to be able to mobilize a portion of the votes which go to the Turkish 'clerical' party, the National Salvation Party.

The complex nature of Turkish Islam promises to provide the researcher with an inexhaustible source of important findings. However, one is filled with a sense of inadequacy when one investigates religion in Turkey. The following remarks, therefore, do not claim to be an explanation of the interrelation between politics and religion in that country, but are merely one version of the historical background, supplemented by a description of the social forces affecting religion in Turkey today.

The historical background

The traditional Ottoman bureaucracy

Ottoman bureaucrats who were trained in the 'palace' system rather than in the *medrese* (*madrasa*), or religious school, had an unusual view of the interrelation of politics and religion. Their outlook may be described as the primacy of *raison d'état*. The Ottoman bureaucrat saw as his duty the preservation of the integrity of the state and the promotion of Islam. This was expressed in the formula *din-ü devlet* (*din wa dawla*) or 'religion and state'.[4] But it was also understood that the viability of the state was essential for the preservation of religion. In the sense that the state was necessary to keep religion flourishing, it had priority over religion. The idea was not expressed as clearly as this; it was much more subtly interwoven into Ottoman culture. Nevertheless, the ability of the bureaucrats to separate religion as a personal commitment from religion as a means of collective cohesion is plain. It appears most strikingly in the controversies surrounding the application of secular codes of law and the tendency of bureaucrats to arrogate a large part of the Sultan's prerogative in criminal law.

Ottoman administrative practice was strongly marked by this bias. Because of the primacy that they accorded to the state, officials dealt severely with any religious manifestations that escaped their control. Charismatic leaders with wide popular appeal or unorthodox behaviour were not tolerated. 'In 1639 Murad IV executed a şeyh of the *nakşbendi* order of dervishes . . . who had grown too influential, and in Ilgin he put to death the Şeyh of Sakarya who had attracted some seven or eight thousand followers.'[5] Nor were ambitious *ulema* (*'ulama*) allowed to overstep certain boundaries. When, in 1703, the Şeyhülislam, or paramount religious official, tried to obtain for himself the position of Grand Vizier, he paid with his life for his presumption. In other Islamic states, there may well have been cases when differences between rulers and the *ulema* led to the latter being mistreated; under Ottoman rule, *raison d'état* was an actual system. However, the most effective aspect of the Ottoman government's control over the 'Learned Institution' – that is, the hierarchy of men of religious learning or *ilmiye* – was that the more important *ulema* became in effect part of the official class and were dependent upon the state for their emoluments.

The Ottoman official as reformer

For reasons which are not yet well understood, the Ottoman secular bureaucracy acquired increasing power during the eighteenth century in relation to the *ulema* and the military branch of Ottoman officialdom. But it is only in the context of the ideology of Ottoman officials, which gave priority to the preservation of the state above all other concerns, that we can understand how they could become sponsors of Westernization in the Ottoman Empire. For the policy of reforms that they inaugurated in the late 1830s (*Tanzimat*) amounted exactly to that. Bureaucratic ideology also explains the speed with which the secularization of Ottoman educational and judicial institutions proceeded during the nineteenth century. Already in the 1870s, Saffet Paşa, a Turkish Minister of Foreign Affairs who filled a number of key offices during the latter part of the *Tanzimat*, was arguing that there could be no half-way house to Westernization, which he equated with civilization.[6]

The attitude of Ottoman secular officials who saw Western-inspired reform as an answer to the decline of the Ottoman Empire was only one interpretation of the causes of this most disturbing phenomenon.

Ever since speculation about the empire's decline had been initiated, there existed a theory that had currency primarily in religious circles. This was the idea that the Ottomans had regressed because they had not observed their religious duties. During the nineteenth century, this theory, now reinforced by historicist elements, was transformed into one which argued that the religion and the culture of a people were one and that the Ottomans could not, therefore, devise social institutions which denied a role to Islam. The correct solution was to modernize the technological apparatus but to keep Islam as the central value-building core of Ottoman society. This argument was first advanced in full force by Ahmet Cevdet Paşa against those who wanted to translate the Code Napoléon for use in Ottoman society. Islam, stated Cevdet, was a principle of cohesion for the Ottomans, and the *Tanzimat* statesmen had undermined this element by their secularizing reforms in the judiciary.

Cevdet Paşa was arguing along similar lines to those of the first Ottoman constitutionalists, who had appeared on the scene at about the same time, even though he did not share their political views. It is interesting that Sultan Abdülhamid II, who had no sympathy for these so-called Young Ottomans, also seems to have agreed with them regarding Islam as an element of value in Ottoman society. For the Sultan, however, it was the cohesiveness of Ottoman society which was at stake: Islam had to be used as a flag to rally his Ottoman-Muslim citizens to a common cause. But the Sultan went further. He seems to have understood that the Western nation-state had acquired its peculiar impetus not only through its nationalist appeals but also by getting its citizens to take a more active part in supporting the causes that the state espoused. What was needed now was for the Ottomans to work for the active preservation of the empire.

The Young Ottomans had addressed themselves to Ottoman intellectuals in their call to action, but Sultan Abdülhamid had a much subtler – and it would seem more effective – method of harnessing the Ottomans to their new activist role. The Young Ottomans' approach was to create a new political machinery for participation: such participation would have of necessity involved only the elite, the literate population. Abdülhamid seems to have realized that it was the lower-class population which had to be sensitized. His use of Islam was consequently targeted to his humbler subjects. Professor Abu Manneh has described how the Sultan proceeded to this end: he used the *tarikat* as a means of reaching the people.[7] This was a brilliant move, and it is because the Sultan *was* able to communicate with his lower-class citizens with religious propaganda conducted through the *tarikat* and other channels that they (not the intellectuals) looked back on his reign with much warmth.[8]

The Turkish revolutions

The Young Turks, too, who were the sworn enemies of the Sultan, realized that they could not do away with Islam as long as the multi-ethnic Muslim composition of the empire endured. It was because the empire disappeared that Atatürk was able to carry out his own reforms. It is also clear that in a sense Atatürk took over the tradition of keeping the state free from the influence of *ulema* and *tarikat* leaders. In his thinking, however, the primacy of *devlet* or 'state' gave way to a new conception, that of the 'modern state', a concept which owed much of its inspiration to Durkheim. Like Durkheim, Atatürk believed that the modern state could be shored up by 'civic religion'. Here religion had only a secondary or marginal role to play; it was relegated to the role of a personal value. In order to engage the loyalty of the citizens of Turkey, one needed to create institutions which would encourage the growth of civic religion and promote the individual responsibility on which civic religion rests.[9] This is why Atatürk's secularization policy seems, in retrospect, to have consisted of creating a series of new institutions which were brought in wholesale from the West – something that neither the men of the *Tanzimat* nor the Young Turks had done.

What I want to point out here is that, from the time of the *Tanzimat* to that of the republic, there was an evolution which consisted not only in increasing the number of secular institutions, but – more important, perhaps – in developing an understanding of the ethical content of society. This content underlined the increasingly large responsibility that the individual citizen has to shoulder in a modern society. It is because he believed that Islam as a state religion denied such autonomy to the citizen that Atatürk secularized Turkey as drastically as he did. In this respect his ideas were radically different from those of the traditional bureaucratic elite to whose thinking he was an heir.

The measures in Atatürk's secularizing policy which are most often mentioned are the abolition of the caliphate, the adoption of the Swiss Civil Code, the adoption of the Latin alphabet, the disestablishment of Islam as the state religion, and the introduction of the principle of secularism in the Turkish constitution. What one hears less about is the simultaneous melting away of the 'Learned Institution'. On the day that the caliphate was abolished in 1924, the office of Şeyhulislam and the Ministry of Religious Affairs and Pious Foundations were abolished as well.[10] On that day, too, the Law on the Unification of Education, which made all education secular, was passed.[11] In April of the same year the Şer'i (*shari'a*) Courts were abolished.[12] The combined effect of these laws was virtually to wipe out the order of the *ilmiye*; only mosque personnel and some of the higher officials in the Directorate-General of Religious Affairs could still claim to be part of the *ilmiye*. Through the virtual disappearance of the *ulema*, the path to secularization had been prepared. It was thus easy to go on in 1928 to abrogate the clause of the Turkish constitution which made Islam a state religion. The principle of secularism or 'laicism', which, when debated in parliament for the first time in 1928, was defined as 'the separation of religion and worldly concerns',[13] was now made the paramount idea of Kemalism and became part of the Turkish constitution in 1937.

The next target for the secularists, after the cluster of secularizing laws in spring 1924, was the *tarikat*. The brotherhoods' role in opposition movements had been clearly demonstrated in the Şeyh Sait rebellion of 1925, when two Nakşibendi *şeyhs* (*shaykhs*) and leaders of the movement, Şeyh Sait and Şeyh Abdullah, organized the Zaza-speaking tribes of the Çapakçur–Lice–Palu area during the rebellion.[14] In consequence, in December 1925, all *tarikat* were abolished.

By erasing the *ilmiye* and driving the *tarikat* underground, the Republican People's Party (RPP) had, in effect, destroyed the two arms of religious power in Turkey. The state, however, still played a key role in the control of religion through the Directorate-General of Religious Affairs, an institution dependent on the Prime Minister's Office, to which all remaining religious personnel were attached. It is thus an ironic development that the impetus for the gradual reversal of this secular Jacobinism of the 1920s should have originated among the ranks of the Republican People's Party. This reversal occurred at the party's seventh congress, convened in 1947. A multi-party system had been given the green light since 1946, and the RPP realized that in the forthcoming elections it would have to face a rival party, the Democrat Party (DP), to which religious conservatives were rallying. But the reason why the RPP accorded such importance to the DP was that some leading RPP members were themselves feeling uneasy about the void created by the republican policy of secularization. Whether they saw this void, as they claimed, in the rootlessness of contemporary Turkish youth, or whether they projected onto Turkish youth their own deep *malaise*, is difficult to ascertain. Debates of the time show that some delegates were undoubtedly expressing their own feelings. In any case, delegates argued that the RPP had gone too far in erasing all traces of religious instruction and education.

In response to these views, the Ministry of Education reintroduced elective courses on religion into the programme of primary schools. It also established courses for the training of prayer leaders and preachers. (Through various swings of the pendulum, the net result of this initiative was that by 1980 these courses had been integrated into the curricula of no fewer than 506 secondary schools.) A number of further moves liberalizing the practice of religion followed the new attitude towards religious education inaugurated in 1947. In 1948 foreign exchange was allowed for the first time to persons who wanted to make the Pilgrimage to Mecca, and in 1949 the tombs of 'saints' were reopened for visitors.

Nevertheless, the policies following the victory of the Democrat Party at the polls in 1950 disappointed a number of Turks who had pinned their hopes on a return to a more Islamic Turkey. The Democrat Party bore down on maverick *tarikat* leaders, who were disturbing law and order, in a way that would have endeared it to Ottoman bureaucrats. The President of the republic, Celal Bayar, expressed his support for the general principle of secularism, and a law was passed by the Democrat-controlled parliament which expressly forbade the use of 'religion to obtain political or personal influence or gain'.[15] However, with time the temptation to use religious slogans against the RPP became overwhelming. During the 1957 electoral campaign the Democrat Party and the Nur sect cemented an alliance which up to then had been very tentative. The military coup of 27 May 1960, however, put an end to this alliance. Part of the motivation of the military in intervening in Turkish politics was its conviction that a number of Muslim 'fanatics', such as the leader of the Nur sect, Bediüzzaman Said Nursi, were about to turn Turkey back to what it perceived as a theocratic regime. The secularist principles of the Turkish republic were being undermined, and the generals felt they had to prevent this.

The titular successor to the Democrat Party, the Justice Party, reinstated the relaxed attitude towards Islam that had emerged at the end of World War II, but was extremely careful not to overstep the provisions of the new constitution of 1961 reaffirming the secular principles of the Turkish republic. The first new, politicized, dimension of Islam emerged only in the mid-1960s and came from an unexpected quarter. The alliance between the Democrat Party and religious interests had been an alliance of Sunni groups. Consequently, the crypto-Shi'i communities of the Alevi had felt the icy blast reminding them of their

former status as persecuted minorities under a Sunni Ottoman administration. The lay character of the early republic had constituted a
guarantee of tolerance for their way of life but, in the 1950s they felt
once more threatened. One of the results of the 1960 coup had been
an increase of tolerance for the Alevi as compared with the 1950s. By
now the Alevi were sharing in the general tendency which surfaced
in these years for ethnic groups to want to assert their separate identity.
This tendency, together with the renewed tolerance of the 1960s, resulted
in the formation of the Alevi political party in 1966, the Party of Union.
The party was unsuccessful at the polls, but the energy that went into
its formation was diverted to the support of other minority groups,
among whom groups of the Turkish left hold a prominent place. Con-
versely, there was a barefaced attempt by Turkish Marxists to exploit
some Alevi themes as general themes of rebellion and revolt. Alevi
religious dissent thus became an ambiguous mixture of radicalism and
support for minority rights.

In the light of this Alevi activity, it comes as no surprise that a Sunni
political party was established in 1970. This was the National Order
Party (NOP), founded by the present leader of the National Salvation
Party, Professor Necmettin Erbakan. At the time of its creation it was
stated that a major goal of the NOP was to 'revive the moral qualities
and the spiritual excellence dormant in the Turkish character so that
Turkish society can regain peace, order and social justice'.[16]

The NOP's assessment of Turkey's domestic problem was . . . divided into
two categories, the material and the spiritual. In the material field, the NOP's
criticism centred on (a) the dependence of the Turkish economy on foreign
markets and capital, and (b) on a low level of income per capita and an unjust
distribution of wealth . . . In the spiritual field it had fared no better: (a)
it was the only nation in the world where the educational system failed to
educate youth for national ends, and (b) its educational policy had centred
on the repudiation of its own history . . .[17]

The NOP was eventually dissolved because the Constitutional Court
decided that it had run foul of the provisions of the Law on Political
Parties. Nevertheless, another party, the National Salvation Party
(NSP), established in 1972, emerged. It competed in the elections of
1973, when it received 11 per cent of the electoral vote and was able
to appear in parliament with 48 deputies. In 1977 this figure was halved,
but from 1973 onwards the NSP has been strong enough to be a
candidate for coalition governments and to figure in more than one.

The contemporary situation

These signs of the emergence of a form of 'revitalized' Islam, aiming at providing a comprehensive economic, social, and political framework for Muslims, were not what experts had anticipated in their assessments of the future of Turkey. Yet, prompted by the events in Iran since 1978, the question of whether Turkey will 'go Muslim' is being asked increasingly frequently. The answer to this question has been partly obfuscated by the intervention of a group of the military in Turkish politics on 12 September 1980 and the interdict placed on the political activities of Turkish parliamentarians. Professor Erbakan, the leader of the National Salvation Party, was put in detention ostensibly for offences committed against the law on the use of Islam for political purposes, and the generals who took over are known for their determination to keep the secular foundations of modern Turkey intact. But the generals are also aware of the extent to which they have to accept new developments which have taken root in Turkey in the last three decades; their strong pragmatism guides them in that direction. In fact, Atatürk might be surprised if he came back to life to find out how many new developments which he would have rejected as counter to secularism have become routine aspects of daily life. One of these is the recent reinstatement of a course on Islam in the *lycées*.

It is doubtful, however, whether either the generals or the Turkish secular intelligentsia have a precise understanding of the admittedly diffuse and protoplasmic social forces which shape Turkish religion. One element which immediately comes to mind are the interest groups that can form around the dissemination of Islamic culture: books, counselling, spiritual guidance, and sermons on cassettes. I believe this inability on the part of secularists to gauge the cultural potential of religion is a weakness which might generate further unanticipated consequences and might lead to shocked disbelief. Among the military and the secular intelligentsia, for instance, sectarian strife between the Sunni and the Alevi is believed to be entirely an artificial creation. In fact, sectarian differences cut deep in Turkey. Moreover, they operate nowadays within the context of mass media, international exchange of information, and the financial support of rich Islamic states.

The following is an attempt to assess Islam's potential strength in contemporary Turkish society. The subject may be considered under four headings: the constitutional system, the political process, social change, and the role of Islam in 'reality construction', in the building of an outlook and a culture.

The constitutional system

The current Turkish constitution, which came into force in 1961, regulates religion both in its text and in its reference to a series of organic laws concerning secularization which have been part of the law of the land since the 1920s. The constitution expressly forbids these laws from being made the subject of judicial review; their amendment and modification are thus effectively blocked because they enshrine the principle of secularism. The laws thus protected are the following:

1. the law on the unification of education;
2. the law on the wearing of the hat;
3. the law on the abolition of the *tekke* and *zaviye* (*zawiya*, Sufi 'hostels')
4. the clause in the civil law pertaining to civil marriage;
5. the law on the adoption of international numerals;
6. the law on the Latin alphabet;
7. the law abolishing the titles of *efendi*, *bey*, *paşa*, and the like; and
8. the law forbidding certain clothes to be worn.

Not all the organic statutes of secularization were mentioned in the 1961 constitution. The abolition of the caliphate went unmentioned, as did the turning-over of the administration of religious institutions to the Directorate-General of Religious Affairs and the Directorate-General of Pious Foundations. Presumably the legislators of 1960–1 did not believe the caliphate could make a comeback. Whether the Directorate-General of Religious Affairs was considered an institution which could be eventually replaced by a Directorate of Cults in which Shi'is would be given a role is not clear. But the issue did arise in the 1960s, only to be put under wraps when confronted with strong Sunni protests.

It should also be noted that a number of organic statutes of secularization which are not mentioned in the constitution of 1961 had been already repealed. Among them were the statute 'Turkicizing' the call to prayer and the interdict on visiting the tombs of saints. In fact, these statutes were peripheral to the movement of secularization, and their repeal did not really undermine the practice of secularism as instituted in the Turkish republic. As one Turkish political scientist has said, it may be argued that some of the changes which in the 1950s pared down the Jacobin secularism of the early republic gave a new role to religion, that of a gauge of democratic control. As a consequence of this role, Islam ensures that Turkish citizens are granted what are considered to be fundamental religious rights in established democracies.[18] Undoubtedly, the fact that a municipal ordinance which once forbade the construction of more than one mosque within a radius of 500 metres is now a dead letter does underline that the ordinary Turkish citizen has more religious freedom than in the 1930s.

In Article 2, the Turkish constitution of 1961 proclaims that secularism is the foundation stone of the state. Article 19 reads: 'No individual can exploit religion with the aim of changing the social, economic, political, or legal structure of the state so as to promote religious principle, neither can he use religion to promote his personal or political interests.' The same article guarantees citizens their religious rights. Article 12 does the same for 'religious equality'. Article 57 states that political parties are required to conform to the principle of secularism, and Article 21 declares that religious education 'should proceed in accordance with the foundations of modern science and education'.

The Turkish Criminal Code provides for the implementation of these clauses through a catch-all article (Article 163). Two other articles of the code, Articles 241 and 242, deal also with prohibitions related to the exercise of religion. Article 241 makes it an offence for religious leaders to disapprove publicly of secularizing laws. Article 242 provides penalties for the use of an official religious title in provoking or encouraging civil disobedience against the government. The Law of Associations, another separate statute, outlaws organizations formed upon 'religious bases'. Article 163 has been used for prosecuting individuals or groups who were believed to endanger the principle of secularism. Today it is once more being invoked against 'religious extremism'. The law regulating the formation of political parties has similar strictures regarding the use of religion for political purposes.[19]

Islamic groups have been unable to challenge these principles directly, although they constantly stress the fact that social relations in Islamic society are subject to religious norms. Already in one case, that of the National Order Party, as noted, a court decision ruled that the party was illegal because it contravened the law. In 1980, despite the participation in a coalition government of the National Salvation Party, which was the successor of the NOP in all but name, Article 163 of the Criminal Code was still being applied by the courts. Since then the principle has been applied even more rigorously.

But the reason for the persistence of secularism must not be sought in the periodic intervention of the Turkish military to shore up Kemalist principles. Much more important are the set of positions that were created by the secular system. The occupants of these positions have had a vested interest in the preservation of secularism, and this is best understood in the framework of the Turkish Civil Code, one key organic

statute of the Turkish republic. Copied in 1926 – almost without change
– from the Swiss Civil Code, this code still constitutes the backbone
of Turkish private law, and as such it regulates an enormous volume
of legal transactions. Admittedly, it has not fitted the rural social
structure very well – for example, many rural marriages are not registered
as required – but, nevertheless, it stands like a rock in a sea of change.
The reason for this is that the intellectual elite, which is responsible
for its implementation, constitutes a powerful group in Turkish society
with access to and control over the mass media. This elite consists of
judges, public prosecutors, lawyers, professors, and administrators who
have been nurtured in the secular tradition now established around the
code.

The future of this group depends upon the perpetuation of the entire
lay system of which the Civil Code is only a segment. To impose an
Islamic order on such an establishment involves more than parliamentary
legitimation: it is because such an elite still wields power in Turkey
that the military has been able to intervene in Turkish politics on the
side of secularism without much opposition. Two more reasons exist
which explain the perpetuation of secularism. First, Turkey no longer
has an established corps of Doctors of Islamic Law, or higher independent religious authorities. Neither an official nor an unofficial group
of this type exists; only the somewhat unprestigious religious personnel
officiating in the mosques or the provincial *muftis* (canon lawyers)
attached to the Directorate-General of Religious Affairs could claim
such a status. In fact, they are salaried employees of the state who have
to follow instructions which are derived from state policy. It is on this
point that the situation in Iran was so different from that of Turkey.
Second, religion in Turkey is not the sole means whereby the political
opposition can obtain legitimation; there are other channels for the
shaping of political discontent (again in contrast with Iran, where
religious protest was the only existing mode for mass political participation). It is from this point – the importance that political participation
has acquired in Turkey in the past thirty years – that we move to an
analysis of Islam seen from the perspective of the Turkish political
process.

The political process

When multi-party politics was introduced in Turkey in 1946, the
accusation that Muslims had not been able to worship freely figures
prominently among the charges that were hurled against the political

party which had been in power for twenty-seven years, the Republican People's Party. These accusations came from a number of newly formed political parties with a thinly disguised Islamic ideology for a base. Among these were the Party of National Development, the Party of Social Justice, the Cultivator Peasant Party, the Party of Purification–Protection, the Party of Islamic Protection, and the Turkish Conservative Party.[20] What is interesting is that, after the elections of 1950 (the first free elections in Turkey), all of these parties had to disband, sooner or later, because it was seen that they had no electoral support. In other words, the appeal of the Islamic component of a party programme turned out to be less than that of other issues which the Democrat Party, the main rival of the RPP, underlined in its electoral and pre-electoral statements. The DP, though in tune with the demands for liberalization of worship, had many other things to offer. Possibly more important, it was so very cautious not to overstep the commitment to secularism that it was itself the subject of abuse in the days just before the elections and during its first term of office.

The polarization on which the DP capitalized was the somewhat more complex antinomy between 'centre' and 'periphery'. Arnold Leder has given us a clear picture of the pattern which made the centre–periphery polarization a key variable in modern Turkish politics:

> Western influence [after the *Tanzimat*] had considerable impact on the social relations and the life of the governmental elite, but it left the culture of local notables and peasants of the periphery largely untouched. Although the distinction between official and folk Islam had been an important part of the cultural divide between the centre and the periphery, general acceptance of Islam had also provided a link between the two. This link was broken when increasing dissatisfaction of the religious authorities with the secularist trend led many of them to condemn the centre while speaking out in favour of the traditional culture of the 'people' whose unorthodox Islamic beliefs and practices they had opposed. In the new cultural divide between centre and periphery, orthodox Islam found itself on the side of the periphery . . .[21]

Leder concludes, with regard to the politics of the 1950s:

> Although many of its founders at the national level were as much a part of the bureaucratic class as the CHP [initials of Turkish for Republican People's Party] leaders, within a short period of time, the DP became identified with the culture of the periphery. The DP became the first political party to recruit in the countryside and some CHP bureaucrats reacted to successful DP recruitment efforts by referring to DP members as 'hay seeds' and 'country bumpkins'. DP members quickly seized upon this as evidence of the party's 'folk character' and made every effort . . . to present themselves as champions of the periphery against the hated centre.[22]

The point of this argument is that political polarization had by 1950 developed to a point where it could coalesce around a new concept, that of the 'interests of the peasants', which was then supported by such policies as the abolition of income tax on agricultural produce, easy terms for agricultural credit, and road construction to facilitate the transportation of agricultural products. This policy stood in marked contrast with that of the RPP, which during its years of single-party rule had put forward the thesis 'the peasants are our overlords'; in fact, the peasants were able to see that in practice RPP policy meant that they were to pay for the infrastructural modernization of Turkey. The dialectic of economic interests had been successfully introduced into politics by the DP.

As Adnan Menderes, the DP Prime Minister, expressed it:

What will we do? . . . No roads? We will build them! We'll bring water and roads to the villages. The land is not fertile? We will find ways to make it fertile! We will give land to the landless villagers. No houses? No cement, factories, or food? We'll begin by building sugar refineries. Inadequate clothing? We'll expand and increase the textile factories . . .[23]

Despite the many convolutions through which Turkish politics has gone in the thirty-odd years since this speech, it is by such issues as touched upon by Menderes that Turkish politics is still shaped, and not primarily by religious issues. In 1966 Suleyman Demirel, the Prime Minister whose term was cut short by the military intervention of 1980, argued that 'declaring oneself a Muslim or invoking references to God' had been interpreted as the exploitation of religion for political purposes. Such declarations, he added, could not be labelled obscurantist: 'Every Muslim Turk can proudly announce that he is a Muslim.'[24] Yet although this mild and tolerant attitude towards Islam on the part of Demirel (who is known to be a practising Muslim) has been approved by over 40 per cent of the voters in almost all national elections, the truly 'clerical' party, the National Salvation Party, has not been able to muster more than 12 per cent of the national vote.

There is no doubt that the National Salvation Party stands for a re-Islamization of Turkish life. To what extent the party would attempt to make radical changes in the legal system by bringing back Islamic law is not clear, although this is certainly an accusation which it has had to face. But, in general, the legal system is not the most favourable area for the promotion of Muslim values, and the Salvation Party has not broached the issue. It is in its cultural stand that the National Salvation Party has been able to touch some sensitive – and responsive – areas of Turkish life. It is in these that we should expect it to achieve some success, but here too projections into the future are difficult.

The economic ideology of the National Salvation Party rests on the premise that Turkey has been prevented from developing by 'capitalist-Christian' interests in the West, and that it has to engage in sacrifices to make up for this backwardness. Turkey should not attempt to join the European Economic Community, since this would merely perpetuate its role as an economic underling of 'Western-Christian capitalism'. Turkey should industrialize by pulling itself up by its own bootstraps, and should try to achieve parity with the industrialized West by following Japan's example. This emphasis on gaining a position of strength in the industrial world has considerable appeal in Turkey, in particular, to those who are on the point of becoming industrialists, from having been successful small- or medium-range craftsmen. Necmettin Erbakan, the NSP leader, has something in common with such men. He too, after a successful career as a professor of engineering, tried his hand at small-scale industry by establishing the Sun Motor Industries, which were to produce water pumps but which had immense difficulties getting off the ground. The reason for these difficulties is still not very clear, but he has certainly acquired a deep dislike of banks. Indeed, much of the NSP's criticism of the Turkish economy has concentrated on the pattern of distribution of credit by banks. According to Erbakan, a certain group of Turks who live in Western Turkey have been favoured over small, would-be capitalists. He also seems to consider that the economic system should be made to function without interest being paid, although his thinking is rather vague here.

The National Salvation Party takes issue, too, against what it regards as the over-Westernization of the Turks of today. Dancing, the ballet, and Western theatre are 'new-fangled' innovations which do not sit easily with 'real' Turks. Erbakan is right to the extent that these cultural innovations were promoted by the republic with the aim of Westernizing Turkish culture. But there is a whole generation of people whose lives and careers are tied to the new cultural forms; they would hardly agree with the image of ballet schools as dens of iniquity. Again, the National Salvation Party believes that the Turkish family is disintegrating; the family should be based on respect for one's elders and separation of the sexes. Much is made of the respect that a Muslim should show towards women, who are thought of as 'roses'; beautiful and fragrant but fragile, they should be protected. In general, *ahlak* (morality) and *maneviyat* (spiritual values) are the central concepts around which society should be organized.

Who are the people who make up the leadership and the following of the National Salvation Party? The occupational breakdown of the party's leadership is much the same as that of the other political parties in Turkey. As for NSP support, although there is some correlation between NSP votes and economic underdevelopment, the provinces where the NSP is strongest are not the least economically developed. Its support is found in areas with incomes below the median, but also in the conservative quarters of large towns. To understand this phenomenon we have to take up the third dimension of our study, the analysis of the social changes which have changed Turkey so radically in the last thirty years.

Social change

In the 1960–78 period, Turkey's average annual rate of growth in per capita gross national product has been 3.6 per cent.[25] This is a success story by any standard. If one recalls that Turkey's population has increased from 17 million in 1940 to 46 million in 1980, one gets an idea of the extent to which the economic effort has been sustained. Moreover, the economic pattern has been complicated by a special demography. In 1935, Turkey was about 17 per cent urban; today this figure is 46 per cent.[26] Much of this growth is due to developments which occurred after 1960, when the urban population rose from 26 per cent to 46 per cent of the total population. Today Turkey is the only country in the Middle East (including Egypt, which follows closely behind) that has two of its largest cities growing at a rate of over 5 per cent a year. Taken together, these figures mean that large numbers of people have been propelled from a slot in society in which they were relatively immobile into a situation in which their lives are characterized by movement. They have been projected onto a new stage, regardless of whether this has involved an actual move or the expansion of the opportunities available to them.[27]

In the 1950s, Behice Boran, a Turkish sociologist (who has since had a political career as leader of a socialist party), found that villagers in Ankara were apprehensive of appearing not to know 'city ways' and values. Much of this awkwardness, however, is in the process of disappearing. For one thing, so many people have been suddenly propelled into positions of national prominence that they can hardly feel alone in their lack of preparation; for another, in all walks of life, Turks have begun to be more critical of the imitative process of Europeanization, which was one of the ideological underpinnings of Kemalism. In particular, people for whom traditional thought is still strong, either because of the speed with which they were torn from their moorings or because of their family backgrounds, have begun to compare the usefulness of this traditional component with the relative artificiality of Kemalism.

This dual source of Muslim traditionalism alerts us to two ways of looking at the development of traditionalism in Turkey today: one focuses on the mobilization of the masses, and the other on particular families, circles, or networks whose prestige has come from their guardianship of traditional values. Perhaps a third approach is from the demographic perspective. The overall rise in population has meant that there has been a marked increase in the number of towns with a population of between 50,000 and 100,000. Towns that were already in this category have been reinvigorated both by their role in politics and by economic development. But these are also the centres where tradition was kept alive by a literate Muslim elite, and the influence of cultural Kemalism had difficulty in making itself felt. Moreover, one of the interesting findings of the Turkish scholar Ahmet Yücekök has been that voluntary associations established for the support of religious culture, such as Qur'an courses approved by the Directorate-General of Religious Affairs and mosque-building associations, have constituted the foundation of religious revival in many parts of Turkey. These associations rose from 237 in 1951 to 2,510 in 1967, and they took root in small provincial towns. Although Yücekök does not make a point that is directly related to demographic statistics, he does argue that religion is used as a 'weapon' by 'small traders, craftsmen, and small farmers who are exploited by large-scale capital and who become alienated from a society which they could not adopt'.[28]

In my view, this work confirms that the root of Turkish religious conservatism is the provincial town. It is from this stratum that the NSP probably receives its strongest support. This also would explain why the NSP appears in relatively underdeveloped regions of Turkey, but does not have great strength in the most underdeveloped areas. The explanation, however, of why the conservative segment in large cities clings to Islamic values is extremely complex. Possibly one of the best ways of approaching this factor is through the study of 'reality construction'.

'Reality construction' and the force of Islam in Turkey

Our views of the world and our knowledge of it are not original creations of our individual minds; they are acquired in society and rest on an already elaborated culture. As Karl Mannheim put it:

Strictly speaking, it is incorrect to say that the single individual thinks. Rather, it is more correct to insist that he participates in thinking further what other men have thought before him. He finds himself in an inherited situation with patterns of thought that are appropriate to this situation and attempts to elaborate further the inherited modes of response or to substitute others for them in order to deal more adequately with the new challenges which have risen out of shifts and changes of his situation.[29]

If thinking is to 'participate in thinking further' what has been thought before, then radical discontinuities in the pattern of thought can become very disturbing. Kemalism, however, which took its cue from Western positivism, did have an Ottoman intellectual precedent: this was the pragmatism and relative secularism of the Ottoman official. It was this pragmatism which enabled Ottoman statesmen to understand that they needed a policy of reforms to strengthen the institutional foundations of the Ottoman Empire. It was the same background which made them introduce 'positive sciences' into the programme of military schools. These schools produced Atatürk and his generation. Atatürk then extended the pattern of secularization to all education and made 'positive sciences' the ideal form of knowledge which Turks should cultivate.

Before 1950, however, this ideal was far from being achieved. Secular education affected only a small part of the population because of the immense task of building a new school system. Today the lower reaches of this educational pyramid have been successfully completed. Over 90 per cent of children of primary school age are, in fact, in primary school. But, paradoxically, this has happened at a time when their chance of being inspired by the positivistic content of Kemalism, in its role as a philosophy of life, has diminished. Young men are being drawn into the world of science and technology because this will earn them a living, not because of an appreciation of positivistic views of the world. There is an acceptance of 'the facts of life', of 'the everyday world', among the younger generation in Turkey today, but it barely hides a deeper discontent and a pathetic hankering after absolutes. The change of intellectual climate that accompanied the military intervention of 1980 has left this generation in a state of disarray, which does not bode well for the future.

But then another factor, which actively *promotes* religious worldviews, is also at work. The inability of Atatürk's educational reforms to reach the rural masses left a blank in their understanding of social reality, which became critical as social change mobilized large numbers of them. Kemalism neither had an extensive explanation of how social justice was to be achieved nor did it provide a more general ethical underpinning of society by drawing its social principles out of a credible ideology. Turkish nationalism has been the only ideology of Kemalist origin to have had an unmitigated success. The republic created this ethical vacuum in a society where religious and ethical commands had been important – i.e., they constituted the core of the traditional social philosophy. The Ottoman middle classes – artisans, craftsmen, and merchants – saw society as an enterprise which had to be shaped by the commands of the Qur'an. Indeed, the ideal of a harmonized society was framed by religion. The inability of Kemalism to provide a social ethos that appealed to the heart as well as to the mind was more disorienting than would appear at first sight. This is also one of the reasons why Islam's chances in Turkey are not tied simply to the conservative leanings of the masses. There is an 'objective' side to the influence of Islam, which is extremely powerful although difficult to analyse, and this is its ability to marshal a rich store of symbols and ways of thinking about society.

We can see in the growth of the Nur sect some of the ways in which this cultural fund has influenced a considerable number of Turks from many walks of life (perhaps 200,000 to 300,000). 'Bediüzzaman'[30] Said Nursi (1873–1960), the founder of the sect, was brought up in eastern Turkey in the tradition of the mystic orders, such as the Nakşibendi and the Qadiri *tarikat*. He has been accused of having abetted Kurdish nationalism in his young days. However, although he had an understanding of the plight that tribal mountain groups had faced in being integrated into a newly centralistic Ottoman administration, he cannot be called a Kurdish nationalist. He worked with the Young Turks to promote pan-Islam during World War I. Later, after the Kurdish rebellion of 1925, he was singled out by the republican government as a dangerous focus of 'clerical' influence. He was exiled to a small village in western Turkey, where he wrote a number of Qur'anic commentaries. These commentaries provided a 'catechism' (in Turkish, not in Arabic, as are many of the 'orthodox' texts) for the many villagers and townspeople who lived in the vicinity, and it was to this population, which had been thoroughly confused by the Young Turks and later by the secularism of the republic, that he appealed. He stressed, in particular, that scientific knowledge is God's bounty to man and that modern technology should therefore be used rather than passively suffered.

These two aspects of his thought – the fact that he made Islamic theology accessible to the masses without robbing it of its mystic qualities, and his approval of technology and science as 'steeds that one should mount' and of progress as 'a train' that one should follow –

have made his teachings attractive to many Turks. Those who are attracted come especially from the middle classes of craftsmen and artisans and (rising) businessmen; recently, the Nur movement has also acquired an important contingent of professors. The sect publishes well-written popular manuals with such titles as *The Atom* and *Our Brain and Nervous System*, which suggest that God's presence is implied in the majesty of the system He has created. The Nur sect has taken a position in Turkish politics, but it is interesting that an alliance which it had formed with the National Salvation Party had dissolved in favour of its present support of the Justice Party. This seems to be a sign that the followers of this sect, too, though they take Islam extremely seriously, are more interested in Demirel's kind of national development than in Erbakan's more sectarian economics. The success of the Nur group, then, has to do with the fact that it has taken the need for a 'view of the world' seriously but has not made this view as directly related to the immediate establishment of a Muslim society as have Erbakan and the National Salvation Party.

Conclusion

I have tried to show that religion in Turkey is being shaped simultaneously by a number of social, political, and economic factors. Their complicated interaction has given rise to one idea that will continue to have an appeal – namely, social justice. It is because social justice *per se* is such a powerful concept in our time that the idea of *Islamic* social justice also has considerable attraction for the Turks. Nevertheless, in the last three decades the Turkish republic has been able to establish institutional channels for the expression of political preferences and social ideals which take the pressure in this matter away from religion. Indeed, the Turkish political system is one that has acquired widespread legitimacy. Trade unions, for instance, are a fact of Turkish life which cannot be eliminated.

It is this pluralistic system that Turkish 'anarchists', as they are described by Turks, have wanted to upset, and they have been partially successful. What will happen if anarchy is not taken out of the equation is anybody's guess. If, on the other hand, terrorism can be brought under control, and if, in addition, parliamentary institutions are placed back in operation, then an Islamic revival would take the form of a slow infiltration of Islamic world-views in Turkish society without much change in the legal system and in the present legal implementation of secularism. In any case, the numerous affiliations and ideologies which compete with religion in defining Turkish social and political life place it in a different category from that of religion in Iran. It is in this social structure that we have to search for answers as to whether, or to what extent, Turkey will 'go Muslim' in the future.

Notes

1. B. G. Martin, 'A Short History of the Khalwati Order of Dervishes', in Nikki R. Keddie (ed.), *Scholars, Saints, and Sufis: Muslim Religious Institutions in the Middle East Since 1500* (Berkeley and London, University of California Press, 1972), pp. 275–306.
2. Akbar S. Ahmad, *Millennium and Charisma Among the Pathans: A Critical Essay in Social Anthropology* (London, Routledge & Kegan Paul, 1980); Clifford Geertz, *Islam Observed: Religious Development in Morocco and Indonesia* (New Haven and London, Yale University Press, 1968).
3. Ahmet Cevdet, *Tezakir 13–20* (Ankara, Türk Tarih Kurumu, 1965), pp. 82–3.
4. Niyazi Berkes, *The Development of Secularism in Turkey* (Montreal, McGill University Press, 1964), pp. 9–10.
5. Halil Inalcik, *The Ottoman Empire: The Classical Age 1300–1600*, translated by Norman Itzkowitz and Colin Imber (London, Weidenfeld & Nicolson, 1973), p. 99.
6. Niyazi Berkes, *Türkiyede Çagdaşlaşma* (Istanbul, Istanbul Matbaası, 1978), p. 234.
7. B. Abu-Manneh, 'Sultan Abdulhamid II and Shaikh Abulhuda Al-Sayyadi', *Middle Eastern Studies*, 15 (1979), 131–53.
8. My source here is Professor Berkes who cannot be cited as a promoter of the Sultan's reputation.
9. I am indebted to Professor Donald Webster for sharing with me his perceptive account of Turkish civic religion in an unpublished manuscript.
10. See *Şer'iye ve Evkaf ve Erkan-t Harbiye-i Umumiye Vekaletlerinin Ilgasına Dair Kanun*, Kanun No. 429, 3 Mart 1340 (1924), *Düstur*, Tertip III, Cilt 5, p. 665.
11. See *Tevhid-i Tedrisat Kanunu*, Kanun No. 430, 3 Mart 1340 (1924), *Düstur*, Tertip III, Cilt 5, p. 667.
12. See *Mehakim-i Şer'iyenin Ilgasına ve Mehakimin Teşkilatına ait Ahkamı Muadil Kanun*, Kanun No. 469, 8 Nisan 1340 (1924), *Düstur*, Tertip III, Cilt 5, p. 794.
13. Çetin Özek, *Türkiyede Laiklik* (Istanbul, Baha Matbaası, 1962), p. 40.
14. M. M. van Bruinesson, *Agha, Shaikh and State: On the Social and Political Organization of Kurdistan* (Rijswik, Europrint, 1978), p. 403.
15. *Vicdan ve Toplanma Hürriyetinin Konunması Hakkındaki Kanun*, Kanun No. 6187, 29 July 1953.
16. Binnaz Sayari (Toprak), 'Türkiyede Dinin Denetim Işlevi', *Ankara Üniversitesi Siyasal Bilgiler Fakültesi Dergisi*, vol. 33, nos. 1–2 (1979), p. 174.
17. *Ibid.*, pp. 174–5.
18. *Ibid.*
19. Binnaz Sayari (Toprak), *Islam and Political Development in Turkey* (Leiden, E. J. Brill, 1981).
20. Sayari (Toprak), 'Türkiyede Dinin Denetim Işlevi', p. 181.
21. Arnold Leder, 'Party Competition in Rural Turkey: Agent of Change or Defender of Traditional Rule?', *Middle Eastern Studies*, 15 (1979), 82–3.
22. *Ibid.*, p. 84.
23. *Ibid.*, p. 86.
24. Suleyman Demirel, *Kongre Konuşmaları* (Ankara, Doguş Matbaacılık, 1967), p. 14.
25. William Hale, *The Political and Economic Development of Modern Turkey* (London, Croom Helm, 1981), p. 129.

26. Frederick Shorter and Belin Tekçe, 'The Demographic Determinants of Urbanization in Turkey, 1934–1970', in Peter Benedict, Erol Tümertekin, and Fatma Mansur (eds.), *Turkey: Geographical and Social Perspectives* (Leiden, E. J. Brill, 1974), pp. 281ff. Also see *The Economy of Turkey* (Istanbul, TUSIAD, 1981), p. 99.

27. The concept that explains the implications of this propelling ahead is that of 'empathy', the ability of a much larger population than was the case before these changes started to see themselves in the position of others who might be ahead of them in the social hierarchy. This concept, which we owe to Daniel Lerner, has recently been buried under the disapproval that his general findings have met among scholars of the Middle East, but it is an idea that needs disinterring. See his *The Passing of Traditional Society: Modernizing the Middle East* (Glencoe, Ill., The Free Press, 1958), pp. 49–50 *et passim*.

28. Ahmet N. Yücekök, *Türkiyede Orgütlenmiş Dinin Sosyo-Ekonomik Tabanı 1946–1968* (Ankara, Sevinç Matbaası, 1971), p. 235.

29. Karl Mannheim, *Ideology and Utopia* (London, Kegan Paul, 1936), p. 3.

30. Albert Hourani suggests this term is best translated as 'nonpareil of his time'.

9   Iran: Khumayni's Concept of the 'Guardianship of the Jurisconsult'

HAMID ENAYAT

The establishment of the Islamic republic following the revolution of 1978–9 was a unique event in Iran's long history. It is certainly possible to find precedents for the forging of a close alliance between religion and state, or attempts to legitimate political power by a religious ideology. In this respect, an obvious precursor to the Islamic republic is the Safavid state of the sixteenth and seventeenth centuries, with its avowed intention of making a particular vision of Islam (Twelver Shi'ism) the official creed of the Iranians, and its intricate panoply of offices and institutions designed to ensure the subordination of temporal rulers to spiritual authorities.[1] A bolder flight of fancy can take one even further back to pre-Islamic times – to the Sassanian Empire (AD 224–637), which is one of the closest parallels in ancient history to the modern ideological state.

But what distinguishes the regime set up by the Islamic revolution from all such antecedents is a notion related not so much to the nature of the political order, but to the person or persons considered to be solely qualified to act as ultimate rulers or arbiters of that political order. This notion has now come to be recognized by the phrase *wilayat-i faqih*, which can be translated as the 'guardianship (or rulership) of the jurisconsult' (and not 'of the theologian', as is sometimes suggested, for the simple reason that the theology and *fiqh*, or Islamic jurisprudence, are two different disciplines which can on occasions be at odds with each other). Although it has a long jurisprudential ancestry, it is a notion which is almost totally identified with the political outlook of Iran's religious leader, Ayatullah Ruhullah Khumayni.

Exponents of the 'guardianship of the jurisconsult' can be found among classical and medieval masters of the Shi'i *fiqh*, of whom perhaps the most influential was al-Karaki, known as al-Muhaqqiq al-Thani (d. 1534). This becomes more understandable when one remembers that as the Shaykh al-Islam (paramount religious leader) of Shah Tahmasp, al-Karaki was a powerful figure in the Safavid administration. His strong conviction on this issue[2] was in keeping with his other major theses, including his activist's perception of the principle of 'enjoining the good and prohibiting the evil' (al-amr bi'l-ma'ruf wa'l-nahy 'an al-munkar) as an unconditional duty incumbent on every individual Muslim – which means that no Muslim, even one who lacks proper knowledge of religious principles, is exonerated from the obligation to do all he can to secure the adherence of his fellow Muslims to those principles.[3]

But what makes Khumayni unique as a religious writer is his contention that a faqih should be not just one high official among the many who form the top echelon of the state administration, but its supreme overseer, judge, and guardian. And the significance of the Iranian revolution lies partly in the fact that it has – at least for the time being – fulfilled this old ambition of some ardent religionists. What is extraordinary is that this has come about in a moment of Iranian history when – for two main reasons – it was least expected: first, the process of modernization or Westernization, with all its aberrations, setbacks, and imbalances, seemed to have gone too far to allow the return to what many think of as an anachronism – that is, the subordination of politics to religious precepts; second, although religious thinking among Iranian Shi'is displayed an unusual vitality during the last decade of the Shah's era, it was far from reaching any consensus over the feasibility or advisability of faqihs' governing. There were, and still are, many prominent religious writers and jurists who adhere to the view stated by one of the greatest figures of Shi'i jurisprudential theory in the nineteenth century, Shaykh Murtada Ansari (d. 1864). That view must be stated here briefly in order to bring out part of the novelty of Khumayni's thesis.

Predecessors to Khumayni

Shaykh Ansari's main concern was to define the functions of the faqih, rather than to adumbrate the legitimating sources of his office. He enumerated these functions as: (1) ifta, the authority to issue legal opinions (fatwas) on 'subsidiary problems and deductive matters'; (2) hukuma, adjudication or arbitration for the settlement of disputes; and (3) wilayat al-tasarruf fi'l-amwal wa'l-anfus, guardianship for the 'disposal of properties and persons'. Ansari found no differences of opinion among the 'ulama on the first two functions and therefore did not dwell on them in any detail. But he considered the third function to be controversial enough to warrant a lengthy and particularly subtle discussion. He said that *wilaya*, or guardianship, can be conceived of in one of two forms: in the first, the guardian acts independently, regardless of the fact that the action of others depends on his permission, the reason being that 'his discretion is the cause (*sabab*) of his action'; in the second, the guardian himself does not act independently, but the action of others is dependent on his permission, the reason being that 'his discretion is the prerequisite (*shart*) of the action of others'. There can obviously be an overlap between the two. For instance, when a person is authorized by the ruler to administer endowments, in one sense he acts (as the ruler's deputy or agent) independently, and in another sense (as a person having no authority of his own) dependently.

Ansari had no doubt that in the first sense *wilaya* is the prerogative of the Prophet and of his successors to the leadership according to the Shi'i tradition, the Imams. This is so by virtue of the Qur'anic verses (4:59, for example) enjoining Muslims to obey God, the Prophet, and 'holders of authority' and of a saying in which the Prophet declares himself to be in charge of the faithful. According to Ansari, 'absolute authority' over the people in both temporal and spiritual matters falls within the jurisdiction of the Imams. But statutory and discretionary penalties (*hudud wa ta'zirat*), measures depriving people of their rights, and solutions to unforeseen events (*al-hawadith al-waqi'a*) are specifically delegated to the *faqihs* in the absence of the Imams. Thus, what remains for the *faqihs* is residual *wilaya*, in the sense that only certain kinds of power can be exercised and, then, only with regard to those Muslims who, for different reasons, are unable to administer their own affairs, such as the minor, the insane, the ailing, and the beneficiaries of public endowments.[4]

Two aspects of Shaykh Ansari's arguments are particularly important in view of the present debate in Iran over the compatibility of the *faqih*'s primacy with democracy: first is his attempt to demonstrate how absurd it is to reason that because the Imams should be obeyed in all temporal and spiritual matters, the *faqihs* are also entitled to such obedience; and second is his belief that in principle no individual, except the Prophet and the Imam, has the authority to exert *wilaya* over others.

Some polemical hints in Ansari's pronouncements indicate that views opposed to his, affirming the *faqihs*' competence to act as custodians of Muslims in matters far beyond those he was ready to accept, were already current in his time. This conjecture is supported by the fact that in his period the *'ulama* had just started to become actively involved

in arousing popular emotions against Russian and British encroach-
ments; it was also a period of vigorous jurisprudential and theological
debate. But it would be fair to assume that in the wake of Iran's defeats
at the hands of the Russians in 1828, for which the *'ulama* were regarded
as partly responsible, the exponents of *wilayat-i faqih* must have been
very much on the defensive.

The wider Islamic context

Although Khumayni's assertion of the right of the *faqih* to act as a full-
fledged political ruler cannot be strictly regarded as an innovation in
the history of Shi'i political theory, it does represent an unexpected
revival of an old, dormant theme. His arguments on this issue deserve
close study if one is to understand the ruling ideology of present-day
Iran. Although other sources have been consulted, my main source for
Khumayni's ideas has been a booklet published in his name in Tehran
in 1978, entitled *Namih-i az Imam Musawi Kashif al-Ghita (A Letter
from the Imam Musawi, the Dispeller of Obscurity)*, which was used by
his followers as the manifesto of the Islamic revolution. In the remainder
of this chapter, I will consider its contents in the context of modern
ecumenical trends in Islam, since this can explain the enormous appeal
of many of his ideas to large groups of Muslims, both Shi'i and Sunni,
inside and outside Iran.

One point can be disposed of quickly. In Khumayni's treatment of
the basic questions concerning the *wilaya*, all the nuances of Ansari's
discussions are reduced to a much simpler classification: *wilaya* is either
existential (*takwini*) or relative (*i'tibari*). The former is a spiritual pre-
eminence exclusive to the prophets and the Imams; the latter is the
social and political duty of the *faqihs* to 'administer and rule the state
and to implement the laws of the sacred path'.[5] One important consequence of this classification is that while it enhances the political status
of the *faqih*, it tries to dispel any impression of his 'supernaturalness'.
As such, Khumayni's thesis stands opposed to popular Shi'ism and
comes close to Sunnism. '*Wilaya*', he says, 'consists of government and
administration of the state and implementation of the laws of the sacred
path. This is a heavy and important duty, [but] not something which
would create a supernatural status for its holder, elevating him to a
position higher than that of an ordinary human being. In other words,
the *wilaya*, of which we are talking, means government and implementation. *Contrary to what many people might think*, it is not a privilege,
but a grave responsibility.'[6] This is meant to refute the conception,

held by some uninitiated Shi'is, as well as by their Western or Sunni critics, that as *ayatullahs* ('Signs of God') the leading *faqihs* are super-human, as if partaking of a quality almost tantamount to the Imams' infallibility. However, as will be noted later, the requirements of political power since 1978 have fostered a psychological environment which does accord extraordinary status to the *faqihs*.

The doctrine of the *wilayat-i faqih* is predicated on a belief in the Islamic state as the best form of government. This is a belief which has been advocated by many other fundamentalist Muslim thinkers in modern times, of whom the Syrian Rashid Rida, the Egyptian Muhammad al-Ghazzali, and the Pakistani Abu'l-A'la Maududi have been the most widely known.[7] Although, in contrast to them, Khumayni is a Shi'i *faqih*, there is nothing specifically Shi'i or sectarian about his case for the 'obligatoriness' of an Islamic state, based as it is on the same premises as those employed, say, by al-Ghazzali – namely, that the implementation of some of the most important religious injunctions, whether on defending the Muslim territory, collecting the alms-tax, or applying the penal system, is impossible without the creation of a state.[8] In agreement with all these authors, Khumayni maintains that the restoration of Muslim unity, either through recovering Muslim sovereignty from foreigners or removing internal lackeys, depends solely on the establishment of a government having the real interests of Muslims at heart.[9] He shares Maududi's conviction that such a government can only be born of a revolution,[10] but, unlike him, Khumayni does not give a systematic description of 'Islamic revolution'. However, his scattered remarks and statements make it clear that he does not share Maududi's idea of revolution as something purely spiritual, gradual, and peaceful, but that he sees it as political, brusque, and violent, even while its final goal is the spiritual regeneration of man. Although any regime which is corrupt or serves the interests of foreign powers would thus qualify as the target of such a revolution, monarchies in particular are singled out as being intrinsically anti-Islamic because they are considered to be in conflict with the most fundamental article of faith – the belief that sovereignty belongs only to God.[11]

But to the extent that Khumayni elaborates his arguments on all these points within the general framework of the *shari'a*, his political ideas, with their revolutionary tone, can be addressed to any Muslim audience without offending sectarian susceptibilities; in this respect, his thinking belongs to the mainstream of Islamic political thought. This statement applies particularly to the earlier stages of the Islamic revolution, when his ideas were less specific and when he used the general slogans of Muslim unity and authenticity. As, however, the revolution increasingly turned to violence and was rent with internal dissensions, Sunni criticisms of his ideas proliferated. But these were more political than religious, emphasizing some of the anti-democratic consequences of government by the *faqih*. The few religious criticisms that were published during 1979 concentrated on his intellectual formation as a Sh'i, and, therefore, as an advocate of the doctrines of the infallibility of the Imams, the occultation of the Twelfth Imam (*ghayba*), and the denial of the right of Abu Bakr, 'Umar, and 'Uthman to Muhammad's successorship – topics which have no direct bearing on Khumayni's notion of the Islamic state.[12] Such strictures might grow in scope and depth whenever there is a conflict of political interests between Iran and the Sunni Muslim regimes.

As was suggested before, Khumayni's most daring contribution to the modern debate on the Islamic state is his insistence that the essence of such a state is not so much its constitution, or the commitment of its rulers to complying with the *shari'a*, but the special quality of its leadership. He thinks that this special quality can be provided only by the *faqihs*. It is true that the position of the *faqih* assumes greater significance in Shi'ism than in Sunnism as the 'custodian' of the community in the absence of the Imam. It is also true that the canonical references used by Khumayni to prove his point are all taken from Shi'i sources. But the idea that only the *faqihs* can provide sound leadership for an Islamic state is not exclusive to the Shi'is. Among modern Muslim thinkers, Rashid Rida also has expressed this opinion in his treatise on the caliphate. In his outline of the Islamic state, the highest political position after that of the caliph (who is also himself a *mujtahid*, i.e. someone who exercises independent judgement or *ijtihad*) is allotted to a respected elite, *ahl al-hall wa'l-'aqd* ('the people who loose and bind'), who are the genuine representatives of the Muslims. After enumerating the qualities required of this elite, Rida deplores the decline in the political power of the *'ulama* in Egypt, Tunisia, India, and Turkey, thus revealing his wish to see them regain their paramount place in the administration of Muslim affairs. To drive his point further home, he contrasts the diminishing stature of the Sunni *'ulama* with the irrepressible popularity of the Shi'i *mujtahids*, and praises the political dynamism of the latter, as demonstrated in their leadership of the Tobacco Rebellion in Iran in 1892 and in the Iraqi revolt of 1920.[13]

Khumayni's vindication of the role of the *faqihs* is much more forceful, and his demands upon them much more explicit and exacting, than anything envisaged by Rida or Maududi. He wants to see the *faqihs* not simply as benign dispensers of advice and consent, but as real wielders of power. He knows that such a commanding position cannot be secured for them without making the *shari'a* the incontestable and unique law of the land. Thus, whereas Rida and Maududi were willing to make room for some secular legislation by permitting *ijtihad* and other accommodating devices, Khumayni unyieldingly holds that the *shari'a* must be the *only* law, and that human regulation is allowed only as a practical contrivance for the enforcement of the divine law.[14] This conception deprives all man-made laws, however wisely conceived and properly enacted, of any inherent binding force and subordinates them to the *faqih*'s approval.

This is an idea that is enshrined in the republican constitution of November 1979 (Principles 107–12), which confers vast powers on the leader (*rahbar*), or the 'guardian of affairs' (*waliy-yi amr*), who is 'a courageous, just, and knowledgeable *faqih*' enjoying 'the overwhelming support of the people'. (This position, now occupied by Khumayni, will probably be occupied after his death by Ayatullah Husayn 'Ali Muntaziri, or in the event of no agreement being reached on one person, by a Council of Leadership composed of three or five members to be nominated by 'popularly elected experts' – Principle 107.) Among the prerogatives of the leader is the appointment of a Council of Guardians, which is charged, among other things, with the monitoring of all the enactments of the Majlis (parliament) to ensure that these comply with the principles of Islam. Although only half the members of the Council are chosen by the leader from among the *faqihs* (the other half being elected by the Majlis, 'at the suggestion of the Supreme Judicial Council, from among Muslim jurists' – Principle 91),[15] it is evident that the Council cannot endorse any law against the wishes of the leaders.

None of these provisions clashes with any of the fundamental beliefs of the average Muslim, of whatever denomination, since no Muslim sect or rite has in principle prohibited the *'ulama*'s assumption of political leadership. Even the homage that Khumayni pays to such Shi'i symbols as 'Ashura, commemorating the martyrdom of Husayn, Imam (and Caliph) 'Ali's son, at Sunni hands,[16] and the anticipation of the Mahdi do not necessarily disqualify his blueprint in the eyes of Sunni Muslims. This is so because, first, these symbols and concepts are respected, if not adhered to, by many Sunnis as well, and, second, they do not impinge on the substance of Khumayni's proposed Islamic state. Ironically, if any canonical objection has been raised against his concept of the Islamic state, it has come, as we shall presently see, from some of the Shi'i *faqihs*, who have disagreed with his interpretation of the sacred sources.[17] Part of his argument amounts in fact to a historical criticism of the *'ulama*'s subservience to rulers, and their dereliction of duty and responsibility as guardians of the Muslim conscience,[18] with which no fair-minded religionist would disagree. But in addition to this criticism he quotes a number of *hadiths*, or sayings, from the Prophet Muhammad and the Imams, in which the *'ulama* have been described alternatively as 'the heirs of the prophets', 'the fortresses of Islam', and 'the trustees of the emissaries [of God]'. He also refers to the famous Qur'anic verse enjoining the Muslims to 'obey God and the Prophet and the holders of authority' (4:59), and to two *hadiths* (known as the 'narratives' of 'Umar Ibn Hanzala and Abu Khadija) attributed to the sixth Shi'i Imam, al-Sadiq, prohibiting the Shi'is from seeking redress from 'the unjust rulers of the age'.[19]

The conclusion he draws from all these and other quotations is that, with the obvious exception of the privilege of receiving the divine revelation, all the other responsibilities and powers of the Prophet have been devolved on the *'ulama* after the disappearance of the Twelfth Imam.[20] The two narratives of Ibn Hanzala and Abu Khadija have stark anti-Sunni connotations, but his interpretation of them and of other *hadiths* and his conclusion cannot be offensive to the Sunnis.

Shi'i criticism

Shi'i criticism of *wilayat-i faqih* has been conducted at various levels – religious and secular, right and left, scholarly and popular. But we need concern ourselves here only with that brand of criticism which shares at least some of the underlying assumptions of Khumayni's thesis, particularly dedication to Islam, belief in it as an all-encompassing system of morality, law, and government, and a combative spirit in the face of threats to the ethical and political integrity of Muslims. For only critics who share his assumptions will stand any chance of establishing a *rapport* with his disciples, and so of conducting a meaningful and sustained debate. Secularists or leftists who reject religion's relevance to modern politics, and conservatives who balk at the revolutionary overtones of Khumayni's teachings, merely provoke greater rigidity among his disciples, and ever more emphatic assertions of his doctrine.

A good example of benevolent Shi'i criticism of the concept of *wilayat-i faqih* can be found in a small but pithy book by Muhammad Jawad Maghniya, a prominent Lebanese writer and scholar whose works on Shi'i jurisprudence, exegesis, and political theory have enjoyed much influence among Iranian Shi'i intellectuals. His modernist formulation of the Shi'is' refusal throughout history to compromise with despotic rulers inspired many militant religious writers and preachers in their attacks on the *status quo ante* in Iran.[21]

Maghniya is full of admiration for Khumayni and the Iranian revolution. His view of Khumayni reaches metaphysical heights when he quotes a saying attributed to the seventh Shi'i Imam, Musa Ibn Ja'far (d. 799), predicting that 'a man will come out from Qum, summoning the people to the right. There will rally to him people resembling pieces of iron, not to be shaken by violent winds, indefatigable, unsparing [in their efforts], and relying upon God.'[22] He finds the Iranian revolution the symbol of the triumph of religious faith over military might. He pours scorn on the claim of some Arab nationalists that the Iranians, by instituting the revolutionary regime on the basis of religion, have given another weapon to the Zionists who justify the state of Israel in terms of Judaism: according to him, this Arab nationalist argument is like saying that Muslims should desist from upholding the right, lest their action tempts their adversaries to preach evil and falsehood.[23] He also refutes the arguments of some secularist or semi-secularist Muslims who deny the obligatoriness of the Islamic state by quoting, for instance, the verse of the Qur'an (88:22) which warns the Prophet not to act as the 'overlord' of Muslims. His explanation is that this verse belongs to the Meccan period of revelation when the Prophet had not yet achieved political power and, therefore, had to act cautiously.[24]

Nevertheless, having said all this, Maghniya is opposed to the doctrine of *wilayat-i faqih*, which in his view equates the position of the jurisconsult, an ordinary mortal, with that of the infallible Imam (*ma'sum*). His arguments can be summarized as follows: in principle, no human being should have rulership or custodianship over another, except by virtue of an explicit Qur'anic injunction or authenticated tradition. The function of the *faqih* is to extract religious rulings from the sources and formulate them in a form comprehensible to the people. A *faqih* can infer new rulings from the sources only for new events – that is, happenings which could not have been observed by his predecessor. This does not imply that he has any superiority over his predecessor: it only means that each of them lives in a world different from that of the other. The sixth Imam, al-Sadiq, is quoted as saying, 'Science [or knowledge] is something which materializes day and night, day by day, and hour by hour; there is no affair over which two people differ and for which there is not a principle in the Book of God, but the intellects of men cannot perceive it.'[25] Every religious scholar, therefore, excels in the rulings appropriate to a particular time and place.

In saying this, Maghniya is merely asserting a well-known tenet of the Usuli school of Twelver Shi'ism, which enjoins the believers to imitate only the living *mujtahids*. In his view, the issue becomes clearer when the position of the *faqih* is compared with that of the infallible Imam. The latter has custodianship over all human beings, whether learned or ignorant, and his pronouncements have the same authority as divine revelation. But, being a mortal himself, a *faqih* is liable to be conceited, forgetful, or mistaken. He may be swayed by his personal feelings, and his judgements are inevitably shaped by the environment and the socio-economic circumstances of his time. Thus, although he has the competence and the duty to act as the guardian of certain areas of social life (e.g., public endowments) and of certain categories of Muslims (e.g., the legally incompetent and those who die without heirs), he cannot be the guardian of all areas of social life and all categories of Muslims. As we saw, this was the view of Shaykh Murtada Ansari, but, as Maghniya reminds us, it was shared by many other eminent scholars, such as Sayyid Muhammad Bahr al-'Ulum and Mirza-yi Na'ini.[26]

In addition to critics like Maghniya, there have been some Shi'i writers who think that if the *'ulama* have inherited any part of the Prophet's spiritual and political burden, they have inherited the spiritual component only. These writers admit that the narratives of Ibn Hanzala and Abu Khadija confirm the *'ulama*'s competence, as well as obligation, to act as judges. They also agree that in times of crisis, or when there has been a breakdown of law and order, the *'ulama* have a duty to step into the breach and lead the community out of chaos. But they believe that in ordinary circumstances the religious officials should avoid direct involvement in political administration; if they do not, they will surely incur the opprobrium of the temporal power-holders, and may even incur unfair blame for any failure of the regime.[27]

Khumayni's activism

Khumayni has anticipated such objections in his treatises, as well as doubts concerning the *'ulama*'s technical expertise and professional acumen in managing governmental affairs. His answer to all of them, which is couched very much in the style of classical dialectics, is that it would be absurd to acknowledge the *'ulama* as the inheritors and successors of the Prophet without recognizing their authority and duty as political leaders as well. He dismisses the argument that they lack technocratic expertise and administrative ability by turning it on their detractors and pointing to the mediocrity and incompetence of Muslim rulers both in the present and in the past: 'Which one of them', he asks, 'is more qualified than an ordinary person? Many of them are not educated at all. Where has the ruler of the Hijaz [i.e., Sa'udi Arabia] received his education? Riza Khan [the founder of the Pahlavi dynasty] was not even literate ... It has been the same in history. Many autocratic and over-weening rulers were devoid of the competence to administer the society and lead the nation, as well as of knowledge and virtue.' By way of contrast, the *faqih* has learned, through his comprehensive training, what is necessary for the supreme control and administration of the country and for promoting justice among people. Sciences and techniques are required only for executive and administrative affairs, and the *faqihs* can always call on the services of those who are well-versed in them.[28]

Running through all these arguments is the conviction that no amount of opposition to the thesis of 'government by the *faqih*' can outweigh the compelling need for a vigorous intervention by the *'ulama* to save Islam from the dual challenge of Western aggressiveness and the internal dissolution of religious values. 'Protecting Islam is a more imperative duty than uttering the prayers, or fasting,' he says in denigration of the ritual and theological niceties obstructing the politicization of the religious leadership.[29] On one occasion, in condemning the attitude of Shurayh, a judge in Kufa at the time of the 'rightly-guided' caliphs (AD 632–61), he uses the word *akhund* to describe him (a generic Persian term which was formerly used to refer to a Shi'i *mulla* but now has a derogatory meaning, referring to a hide-bound 'clergyman'). In this way, he denotes his contempt for the traditional type of religious leaders who either are devoted to an aloofness from politics or allow themselves to be used by the rulers.[30]

This predominance of politics in his religious thinking differentiates Khumayni from most Shi'i religious leaders of the recent past and present.[31] 'It is, of course, essential for you', he says, addressing the Shi'i *faqihs*, 'to teach ritual matters. But what is important are the political, economic, and legal problems of Islam. This has always been, and still ought to be, the pivot of [our] activity.' He also says: 'Many of the ritual rules of Islam are the source of social and political services. Ritual acts in Islam are as a rule bound up with politics and administration of society. The congregational prayer, for instance, and the Pilgrimage have political, as well as moral and doctrinal, implications. Islam has provided for these gatherings so that ... its followers may find solutions to their social and political problems.'[32]

These manifestations of activism are striking, not so much because they come from a spiritual figure but because they collide with

Khumayni's own background: he was a teacher of Islamic philosophy, a discipline well-known for its sublime detachment from politics. Equally conspicuous has been his penchant for Sufism,[33] and for a highly theosophical understanding of Islam, which surfaces in his attacks on materialism and on those of his critics who worry that preoccupation with religion might hinder Muslims' economic and technological development.

But his activism stands out most sharply against the background of his intellectual formation, which is deeply rooted in solid, traditional scholarship. As a revolutionary, he has been uncompromising in his appeal for the punishment of all those who had cooperated politically, administratively, or culturally with the old regime. But as an authority on Shi'i jurisprudence he offers a different image: keeping well within the bounds set by the great masters of the past, he adheres to a juridical logic which, when fully developed in the realm of Islamic penal law, often protects the individual against unfair accusations. This emerges most clearly in his scholarly discussion of the problem of 'accepting office from unjust rulers' – an old irritant in Shi'i political theory. Although as the 'leader of the Islamic revolution and the founder of the Islamic republic', his name has often been invoked by various revolutionary officials in blanket condemnation of all the associates of the Pahlavi regime, he is often highly meticulous and discriminating in his assessment of what can be regarded as right or wrong by Shi'i jurisconsults. Instead of issuing a single, sweeping rule for all those who 'accept office from unjust rulers', he classifies them according to their motives: (1) those who do this to enhance the honour and save the liberty of the faithful; (2) those who do it both for this reason and to secure their own livelihood; (3) those who do it purely to secure their own livelihood; and (4) those who do it to assist and strengthen the rulers. Whereas the first three types are pardonable, the fourth is guilty of a grave offence, as are all who in any form aid and abet tyrants.[34]

But Khumayni does something more: he shows that even the term 'unjust' (*zalim, ja'ir*) is ambiguous and must be clarified before judgement can be passed on those described as such. Four groups of people, he says, can be regarded as unjust: (*a*) ordinary criminals, such as thieves and bandits; (*b*) kings and rulers violating the norms of justice; (*c*) those claiming the successorship to the Prophet; and (*d*) usurpers of the rulership of the righteous Imam – namely, the Sunni dynasties, the Umayyads and 'Abbasids. He has no doubt about prohibiting people from working for groups (*a*), (*c*), and (*d*). He elaborates on group (*d*) in order to bring out the complexity of the issues involved: in addition to the question of motive, one should take account of the possibility that the rulers are Shi'is. Distinction should also be made between low and high officials: obviously petty officials can be excused, but even the conduct of high-ranking administrators should be scrutinized before any judgement is made on them.[35]

While the content of Khumayni's teachings is thus largely traditional, the methods he has employed for propagating his views, both before and after achieving power, are populistic and revolutionary. This is seen in his direct appeal to the masses, his emphasis on the necessity of observing the people's wishes, and his fearless, uncompromising attitude towards those whom he considers to be the enemies of Islam. In so far as his denunciations of American imperialism and of Zionism and his attacks on capitalists and plutocrats can be considered substantive rather than rhetorical, his ideology also should be regarded as revolutionary; as such it has captured the imagination of many Muslims outside Iran. Moreover, his declarations in favour of political activism and against excessive concentration on ritual matters have delighted militants, who regard it as a warrant for subordinating canonical niceties to the demands of high politics. This accounts for the behaviour of many radical but self-avowed Muslims in Iran for whom solidarity with the people of El Salvador is more important than solidarity with the people of Afghanistan, since fighting American imperialism takes precedence over the fear of Soviet expansionism.

Despite all his diatribes against despots and his revolutionary language, it is quite clear that the system of government that Khumayni proposes is no more democratic than Maududi's Islamic state. Although it is meant to be government for the people, it is certainly not government by the people. This goes to show the coherence of Khumayni's political thought, because it is in the nature of any hieratic government to be patriarchal in spirit, if not in form, thus precluding any conception of the national interest other than that defined by, or enjoying the approval of, the rulers. 'The *faqih*'s guardianship [of the people],' he says, 'is a subjective, rational notion which does not materialize except through designation, similar to the appointment of a custodian for minors. From the viewpoint of its duty and position, the custodianship of the nation is no different from that of minors.'[36] But according to his plan, there are two important safeguards against the *faqihs'* abuse of their power once they attain political office: one is their own moral integrity, which, in addition to religious knowledge, constitutes one of the two prerequisites of rulership; the other is the proviso, in accord with the legitimacy of many beliefs inside Shi'ism, that no *faqih* can have 'absolute custodianship' over other *faqihs*, nor can he appoint or dismiss them: 'There is no hierarchy [among the *faqihs*] so that one may be higher than the other ones, or one may be more a custodian than the other ones.'[37]

This principle proved extremely difficult to put into practice after the creation of the Islamic republic. It is one thing to disagree with a *faqih*, by virture of the permissibility of difference of opinion on secondary matters, while he is a mere religious dignitary among his peers; it is quite another to oppose his views when he is acting as head of state. This is a point on which the Persian and the Arabic versions of Khumayni's writing differ. The Arabic version, *Kitab al-bay'* (*Book of Sale*), which was written about a decade before the revolution, clearly asserts the superiority of the *faqih* who has acquired the status of political ruler (*hakim*) over the others.[38]

According to the devoted interpreters of Khumayni's doctrine, the commands of such a ruler are of two types. The first type purports merely to state a well-established canonical notion or a religious precept, without requiring Muslims to do something which had not been required of them before; such a command is called *al-hukm al-kashif*, an order which simply indicates a religious rule. The second type is issued on the basis of the ruler's personal discretion and his understanding of what is expedient or beneficial for Muslims, even if there is no religious warrant or precedent for such a command; this command is called *al-hukm al-wilayati*, custodial order. An example of the first type is a ruler's pronouncement on 'the vision of the crescent of the moon' to determine the beginning of the lunar month; an example of the second type is the fixing of commodity prices. Commands of the first type are not binding on other *faqihs*, if these choose to dissent from the ruler; however, he does make exception of the ruler's legal orders for the settlement of disputes, since otherwise disputes would never end. But commands of the second type are binding at all times: here the dissenting *faqihs* must submit to the ruler's will for the sake of preserving Muslim unity and public order.[39]

On the whole, Khumayni's arguments in favour of the subordination of non-ruling or 'apolitical' *faqihs* to the ruling *faqih* are pragmatic rather than purely juristic or derived from traditional texts. Moreover, if there is anything novel or unprecedented in his views on *wilaya*, it is not so much the concept of the government by the *faqih* as this requirement of the superiority of one *faqih* over the others.

Political leadership in the Islamic republic has been organized along the lines prescribed by Khumayni in *Kitab al-bay'*. Although the *marja'iyya*, or religious authority of the principal *faqihs* of the land, such as Sayyid Kazim Shari'at-madari, Sayyid Muhammad Riza Gulpayigani, and Sayyid Shihab al-Din Najafi Mar'shi in Qum or Sayyid Hasan Qumi and Sayyid 'Abdullah Shirazi in Mashhad, has remained intact, in political matters it is the 'custodial commands' of Khumayni that often prevail. The emerging system is thus an autocracy, which cannot possibly be reconciled with republicanism or democracy as understood in the West. But the duality that Khumayni has introduced into the institution of *marja'iyya*, dividing it into a religious and a political variety, has enabled the system to accommodate that principle of juristic pluralism which has always been a hallmark of Shi'ism. However, as the legal system of the Islamic republic becomes gradually Islamized in conformity with Khumayni's, or his disciples', perception of Islam, the strains on this duality are bound to increase: there will be more and more pressure on the independent religious authorities to refrain from dissent in order to safeguard the 'consensus of the *umma* (community of the faithful)'.

Khumayni's thesis also has certain theological implications that are not entirely free of political significance. One of them is the weakening, if not the outright rejection, of a major tenet of popular (but by no means classical) Shi'ism – the anticipation of the Mahdi (*intizar*). As is well known, not only the critics, but even some of the more enlightened defenders, of Shi'ism regard this tenet as one of the main causes of the notorious political passivity of its adherents during the greater part of their history. *Intizar* is often understood by ordinary Shi'is to signify that the fulfilment of real justice, whether in its cosmic or in its socio-juridical sense, is conditional only upon the return of the Hidden Imam, and that such an apocalyptic redress can take place only after the world is 'filled with injustice'. While never relinquishing his faith in the doctrine of Mahdism, Khumayni tries to denude it of its negative political content by summoning the Shi'is to set up an Islamic state, and by openly pouring scorn on the popular belief that justice cannot prevail until injustice engulfs the whole universe.[40]

Taken together, Khumayni's main political ideas thus obliterate some of the most important differences between the Sunnis and the Shi'is. He minimizes the extent of the rift by stating that the essence of the Shi'i case is nothing other than a legitimate objection to the failure of the first three caliphs to fulfil one of the main preconditions of rulership – *'ilm* (religious knowledge). But his appeal to the Shi'is to revolt against injustice and to install an Islamic state indicates his denunciation of the practice of expedient concealment of one's convictions (*taqiyya*), as well as criticism of the popular conception of anticipation; he thus attacks two Shi'i practices that have become staple themes of Sunni polemics against Shi'ism.

The successful convergence of Sunni and Shi'i thought depends, in part, on whether these ideas are developed in the writings of future Sunni and Shi'i thinkers. But, in the light of the Islamic experience in Iran, it also depends, perhaps to an equal degree, on non-theoretical, concrete social and political realities – on the conflict between Arab and Iranian nationalisms, between the 'Alawi minority regime in Syria and its Sunni opponents (notwithstanding some major differences between the Syrian 'Alawi and the Twelver versions of Shi'ism), and between the 'disinherited' Shi'i masses and the Sunni feudal lords in the Lebanon.

From theory to practice

In spite of his staunch, theoretical anti-communism, there is nothing in Khumayni's description of the Islamic state, in contrast to that of Maududi, to indicate economic conservatism. On the contrary, in so far as there is even the barest outline of an economic theory in his writings, it is of an Islamic socialism of sorts, with a vigorous defence of the rights and interests of the oppressed and disinherited. But being opposed to any 'Islamic eclecticism' (*Islam-i iltiqati*), he has avoided translating his general condemnations of profligacy, corruption, and class differences into a scheme of systematic reforms, since this would have involved him in reconciling Islam with modern economic ideas.

The same, however, cannot be said about his social outlook, especially on female rights, which is identical with, and even more conservative than, that of Maududi. But Khumayni's social conservatism is seen most clearly with regard to the Islamic penalties (*hudud*). If al-Ghazzali and Maududi argued for suspending the divinely ordained punishments until all the prerequisites of an Islamic state had fully materialized, Khumayni does not endorse, or his Islamic republic allow, any such respite for wrongdoers. It is true that the penal philosophy of the Islamic republic has been determined largely by the demands of a revolutionary situation, in which the combination of growing internal dissent and external animosity has seemed to threaten the very survival of a young regime. It has also been determined by the unavoidable accompaniment of every revolution – a desire for revenge. This was at first directed against former high officials – ministers, generals, organizers of mass media – but, in violation of Khumayni's earlier teachings, it was soon turned on even

the lowest ranks in the *ancien régime* – policemen, soldiers, petty administrators – until it permeated Iranian social life in its entirety. In this
political and psychological atmosphere, it has been possible to implement
a deliberate policy of Islamizing the legal system by dispensing with
Westernized procedures and concepts of justice.

Here again Khumayni's influence has been paramount. As early as
1941, he expressed his utter contempt for the secular method of administering justice, with its slow-moving, time-wasting procedures and with
what he held to be its often ineffectual sanctions and penalties. 'If the
Islamic law of *qisas* [retribution]', he said, '*diyat* [blood money], and
hudud [punishments] were put into practice even for a single year, the
seeds of injustice, theft, and unchasteness would be eliminated from
the country. Anybody wanting to extirpate theft from the world must
cut off the thief's hands; otherwise imprisonments [such as those
imposed by secular courts] will merely help the thieves and promote
larceny.'[41]

The full rigour of this certainty, of this belief in the self-sufficiency
of the traditional religious concept of justice, has made itself felt since
the revolution. Hundreds of people have been executed on the orders
of revolutionary tribunals, whose verdicts have often invoked a famous
Qur'anic verse (5:33), stating that the punishment of 'those who fight
God and his emissary' and 'cause corruption on the earth' is 'that they
shall be slain or crucified, have alternate hands and feet cut off, or be
banished from the land'. In the past, commentators have understood
this verse to refer to bandits and highway robbers, but the tribunals,
resorting to the loosest possible interpretation of the terms, have used
it as a warrant for capital punishment against a wide variety of offenders,
ranging from former high officials, torturers, and embezzlers to political
'conspirators' and ordinary criminals.[42]

The principal authority for the application of the verse to specific
alleged offences is again the *faqih* acting as the revolutionary prosecutor.
And it is not, of course, only penal matters which are determined in
accordance with the doctrine of *wilayat-i faqih*: all the major legislative,
judicial, and educational institutions of the Islamic republic are expected
to take their shape under its direct influence. On the legislative side,
I have already mentioned the Council of Guardians, and more important,
the Majlis, which despite its occasional internal differences (and except-
ing its non-Muslim members) is united in its unswerving loyalty to
Khumayni's teachings. The main judicial organ of the state, the Supreme
Judicial Council, is composed of five members, of whom three 'should
be religious and just judges, to be elected by [all] the judges of the

country', the other two being the president of the Supreme Court and the public prosecutor (Principle 158). In practice, the two latter have been nominated from among the *faqihs*. The functions of the council consist of instituting the necessary judicial organizations in the country, preparing bills 'appropriate to the Islamic republic', and recruiting competent judges – including religious judges.[43] The educational life of the nation has been brought under the surveillance of the Council of Cultural Revolution, composed mostly of 'committed and doctrinaire (*maktabi*)' Muslims, charged with restructuring all aspects of culture and education along Islamic lines.[44] Its most significant measure has been the closure of the universities, with the intention of overhauling the academic curricula, rewriting textbooks, and purging the teaching staff of 'anti-Islamic elements'.

On the more practical plane, there are numerous bodies, both formal and informal, which directly or indirectly seek to ensure the continued rulership of the *faqih*: the Revolutionary Guards, who have practically taken over the functions of the police but also assist the army; the Hizbullahis ('the Party of God'), amorphous groups organized to counter threats to the revolution; and the Islamic *anjumans* (associations), which act as the 'party-cells' of the more radical supporters of the Islamic republic in all governmental and non-governmental departments and agencies.[45] There also are three organizations entrusted with the task of mobilizing the masses for urgent political, economic, and educational causes: the Jihad of Construction, the Jihad of the Universities, and the Mobilization of the Oppressed. Last but not least, there is the Islamic Republic Party, which is supposedly the chief ideological and organizational force behind the state apparatus.

One must note in conclusion that the doctrine of *wilayat-i faqih* does contain an attribute of *formal* democracy in that the *faqih* achieves his status not through the decision of his superiors or in the conclave of his peers, but by virture of his longstanding reputation as a man whom the public can trust in financial matters and in the just settlement of their disputes. This democratic ingredient has been strengthened since the revolution by some of the opportunities which have been created for the expression of popular will, such as the referendum on the establishment of the Islamic republic, and the elections for the Assembly of Experts (charged with the drawing up of the constitution) as well as for the presidency and the Majlis. But, however generous one may be in pointing to such signs of democratic tendencies, one must also note the counter-evidence provided by the functions of the *faqih*. These functions presuppose powers far superior to those of any modern ruler, since they now involve not only sweeping political powers but also, contrary to what Khumayni initially wanted or declared, spiritual prerogatives.[46]

Notes

1. See *Tadhkirat al-muluk* (*A Manual of Safavid Administration*), translated and explained by V. Minorsky (London, Luzac, 1943), pp. 41–3; Jean Aubin, 'Etudes Safavides I, Şah Isma'il et les notables de l'Iraq persan', *Journal of the Economic and Social History of the Orient*, 2 (1959), esp. 180–6.
2. 'Ali Ibn 'Abd al-'Ali al-Karaki, 'Qati'at al-lidjaj fi hill al-kharaj', in *Kalimat al-rida 'iyyat wa'l-kharajiyyat* (Tehran, 1313 [1895]); Cf. Sayyid Husayn Modarresi Tabataba'i, *Ashna'i ba chand nuskhih-yi khatti* (Qum, 1396 [1976]), p. 274; for Karaki's administrative involvement, see Wilfred Madelung, 'Shiite Discussions on the Legality of the Kharaj', in Rudolph Peters (ed.), *Proceedings of the Ninth Congress of the Union Européenne des Arabisants et Islamisants* (Leiden, E. J. Brill, 1981), pp. 193–202.
3. For a modernist interpretation of Karaki's view on this issue, see Sayyid Ahmad Tayyibi Shabastari, *Taqiyya, amr bi-ma'ruf wa nahy az munkar* (Tehran, 1350 [1971]), p. 101.
4. Shaykh Murtada Ansari, *Kitab al-makasib* (Tabriz, 1375 [1955]), pp. 155–6.
5. This classification also has a long odyssey, apparently going back to the teachings of the Illuminationist school (*ishraqi*) of Islamic philosophy, in which Iranians have played a prominent part. Some contemporary *faqihs* have used the same classification, and with a slightly different terminology: *wilaya*, according to them, is also of two kinds: (1) *takwini* (existential) and (2) *tashri'i* (legislative) or *shar'i* (canonical); the first is exclusive to the prophets and the Imams, and the second is the duty of the *faqihs*. See Muhammad Muqimi (ed.), *Wilayat az did-gah-i marja'iyyat-i Shi'a* (Tehran, n.d.). This book contains brief statements by most of the Iranian Shi'i leaders on the question of *wilayat*. Also see Ruhullah Musawi al-Khumayni, *Misbah al-hidaya ila'l-khilafa wa'l-wilaya*, translated from Arabic by Sayyid Ahmad Fahri (Tehran, Payam-i Azadi, 1360 [1981]).
6. Ruhullah Musawi Khumayni, *Namih-i az Imam Musawi Kashif al-Ghita* (Tehran, 1356 [1976]), pp. 64–5. Italics are mine. A more widely publicized edition of this book is entitled *Hukumat-i islami*, or *The Government of Islam*.
7. For an analysis of the views of these thinkers on the Islamic government, see my *Modern Islamic Political Thought* (London, Macmillan, 1982).
8. See Muhammad al-Ghazzali, *Min huna na'lam* (Cairo, n.d.), pp. 55–9; English translation, *Our Beginning in Wisdom* by Isma'il R. el-Faruqi (New York, Octagon Books, 1975), pp. 25–8.
9. Khumayni, *Namih-i az Imam*, pp. 41–2.
10. *Ibid.*, p. 39. Cf. Sayyid Abulala Maudoodi, *The Process of Islamic Revolution* (Lahore, Maktaba Jama'at-e-Islam, 1955).
11. Khumayni, *Namih-i az Imam*, pp. 55–6, 204–7. While in this work Khumayni declares the illegitimacy of any form of cooperation with monarchs, in an earlier book, *Kashf al-asrar* (see n. 41 below), he quotes numerous Shi'i authorities of the past in recommendation of 'accepting office' from temporal rulers, even the unjust, with the intention of reforming political systems from within (pp. 227–8).
12. See, *inter alia*, the tract of Al-Ikhwan Al-Jumhuriyyun (Republican Brothers of the Sudan), entitled *Al-Khumayni yu'akhkhir 'aqarib al-sa'a* (Omdurman, December 1979), especially pp. 36–7; also *Fitna Iran* (April 1979).

13. Muhammad Rashid Rida, *Al-khilafa wa'l-imama al-'uzma* (Cairo, 1341 [1922]), p. 60.
14. Khumayni, *Namih-i az Imam*, p. 53.
15. 'Matn-i kamil-i qanun-i asasi-i Iran' ('Full Text of the Constitution of Iran'), *Ettela'at* (Tehran), 26 Aban 1358 (17 Nov. 1979). Cf. 'Constitution of the Islamic Republic of Iran', *The Middle East Journal*, 34 (1980), 184–204.
16. Khumayni, *Namih-i az Imam*, p. 181.
17. For a summary of such objections in Iran, see Nasir Katuziyan, *Piyami bi-Majlis-i Khubrigan* (*A Message to the Assembly of Experts*), Publication No. 2 (Tehran, The Commission of Education, Junbish, n.d.), esp. pp. 12–16.
18. Khumayni, *Namih-i az Imam*, pp. 11, 23.
19. *Ibid.*, pp. 74–143.
20. *Ibid.*, p. 160ff., also p. 30.
21. Examples of Maghniya's political works translated into Persian are: *In ast a'in-i wahhabiyyat* (*This is the Doctrine of Wahhabism*), translated by Sayyid Ibrahim 'Alavi (1351[1971]), and *Shi'a wa zamam-daran-i khud-sar* (*The Shi'is and Despotic Rulers*), translated by Mustafa Zamani (1343 [1966]).
22. Muhammad Jawad Maghniya, *Al-Khumayni wa'l-dawla al-islamiyya* (Beirut, Dar al-'Ilm li'l-Malayin, 1979), p. 38. This prediction has been mentioned by some of Khumayni's followers in Iran as well; see Muhammad Rida Hakimi, *Tafsir-i aftab* (Tehran, 1358? [1978]), p. 437.
23. Maghniya, *Al-Khumayni wa'l-dawla al-islamiyya*, pp. 33–4.
24. *Ibid.*, pp. 13–14.
25. *Ibid.*, pp. 52–3.
26. *Ibid.*, pp. 62–4. Some of Maghniya's arguments are more subtle than those presented here, but they cannot be quoted or discussed within the space of this chapter. His main concern about the government by the *faqih* is that if it turns out to be unjust it would be even worse than the regime of a 'just atheist' (pp. 72–3). Cf. his *Fiqh al-Imam Ja'far al-Sadiq* (Beirut, Dar al-'Ilm li'l-Malayin, 1966), vol. 5, p. 237.
27. Statements to this effect have been made by a number of religious leaders, especially those who took part in the early stages of the revolution, such as Sayyid Mahmud Taliqani, Sayyid Kazim Shari'at-madari, and Sayyid Abu'l-Fadl Zanjani. On Taliqani and Shari'at-madari, see Maghniya, *Al-Khumayni wa'l-dawla al-islamiyya*, pp. 74–5, 112–17.
28. Khumayni, *Namih-i az Imam*, p. 189.
29. *Ibid.*, p. 87; cf. p. 174.
30. *Ibid.*, p. 23.
31. Sayyid Jamal al-Din Asad-abadi or al-Afghani (d. 1897), one of the founders of Islamic modernism, and Sayyid Abul'l-Qasim Kashani (d. 1962), the principal religious leader in the oil nationalization movement in Iran (1951–3), can be mentioned as the forerunners of political activism in modern Shi'ism. However, Afghani was not an *'alim* in the strict sense, and Kashani did not attain the same scholarly status as Khumayni.
32. Khumayni, *Namih-i az Imam*, pp. 174, 179.
33. See, for instance, his 'Mi'raj as-salikin wa salat al-'arifin', in 'Abd al-Karim Surush (ed.), *Yad-namih-yi ustad-i shahid Murtada Mutahhari* (Tehran, 1360 [1981]); Khumayni is also known to have written treatises on the 'mysteries of praying', and a commentary on Ibn'Arabi's *Fusus al-hikam*.
34. Ruhullah Musawi Khumayni, *Al-makasib al-muharrama* (Qum, 1381 [1961]), vol. 2, p. 124ff.; also p. 137.
35. *Ibid.*, p. 106. On the definition of 'unjust', see p. 93.
36. Khumayni, *Namih-i az Imam*, p. 65.
37. *Ibid.*, p. 66.

38. Ruhullah Musawi al-Khumayni, *Kitab al-bay'* (Qum, Mihr Press, n.d.), vol. 2, p. 466.
39. Our main source here is the appendix of Sayyid Kazim Ha'iri, *Asas al-hukuma al-islamiyya* (Beirut, 1979), esp. pp. 189ff., which incorporates the relevant sections of Khumayni's *Kitab al-bay'*.
40. Khumayni, *Namih-i az Imam*, pp. 63, 87.
41. Khumayni, *Kashf al-asrar* (Tehran, 1360 [1941]), p. 274; cf. Khumayni, *Tahrir al-wasila* (Najaf, 1392 [1972]), vol. 2, pp. 509–52.
42. For further discussion of this issue, see my *Modern Islamic Political Thought*, pp. 91–5.
43. Cf. the statement by Ayatullah Muhammad Bihishti concerning the Supreme Judicial Council, in *Ettela'at*, No. 16242, 27 Shahrivar 1359 (18 Sept. 1980).
44. See, *inter alia*, *Ettela'at*, No. 16202, 7 Murdad 1359 (29 July 1980).
45. *Ettela'at*, No. 16201, 6 Murdad 1359 (28 July 1980).
46. This interpretation has been confirmed by the trend of events since the dismissal of the first president of the Islamic republic, Abu'l-Hasan Bani Sadr, in the summer of 1981. Various officials of the republic have since stressed the illegality of any challenge to the position of the *faqih* as a revolt against 'divine sovereignty'. See the statement by Hujjat al-Islam Sani'i, member of the Council of Guardians, in *Ettela'at*, No. 16540, 9 Murdad 1360 (31 July 1981).

10 The Politics of Islam and Islamization in Pakistan

DAVID TAYLOR

To the regime headed by General Zia ul-Haq, the programme of Islamization which it initiated in Pakistan in 1978 was the direct, necessary, and much-delayed outcome of the country's foundation in 1947 as a homeland for the Muslims of the Indian subcontinent. The opportunity that had been missed in the early years of independence had been re-created at a time when Muslims world-wide were asserting the validity of the original formulas of Islam. Only if the moment was seized would Pakistan's prolonged difficulties be resolved. To those who are sceptical about the regime's proclaimed intentions, however, the Islamization programme seems unlikely to lead to stability and renewed political confidence; further, the programme itself appears to be concerned only with the husk and not the core of Islam. The compulsion to move beyond the simple acceptance that the population of Pakistan is overwhelmingly Muslim and that Islamic values are widely accepted appears to be a symptom of the very malaise it is intended to cure.

It would indeed be possible to treat Islam as a purely contingent factor in a prolonged crisis brought about by lop-sided development and un-resolved regional tensions, but such an analysis would be incomplete. Bhutto himself, whose personal vision was entirely secular, was well aware of the ideological significance of Islam and, even before his pathetic efforts during his last weeks in power to play the religious card, took care to use Islamic symbolism wherever possible. General Zia has succeeded in evoking a response to his imposition of various measures that are intended to Islamize the country's institutions. But while Bhutto was not taken seriously by the guardians of Islamic orthodoxy, General Zia has not been rewarded for his endeavours by an extension of his political constituency beyond the armed forces and a restricted section of the middle class.

Pakistan has so far failed to achieve a stable political structure based upon Islamic values, whether these are treated as prescriptive or indicative. This in itself can hardly be taken as proof that the idea of a separate state for South Asia's Muslims was misconceived, even though it provides yet another example of the difficulties that there have always been in achieving a consensus on the nature of an Islamic political order. The thesis of this chapter, however, is that Pakistan's problem is not primarily exegetical or philosophical. Rather, it has been and continues to be the task of reconciling and integrating a set of not always fully consistent ideological perspectives with the political legacies of the past and the constraints of the present. It will be argued in particular that developments before and after the creation of Pakistan in 1947 can only be understood in terms of the extremely complex interrelationship in South Asia between Islam and political power.

Islam in South Asia

The Muslims of the Indian subcontinent today number more than 200 million. A substantial, although not overwhelming, majority of them are Sunnis, almost wholly of the Hanafi school. However, even without regard to the multiplicity of Shi'i groups, some of which are locally important, South Asia's Muslims seem distinguished by their diversity rather than their unity. This can partly be explained in terms of geographical distribution. Although today two-thirds of them are contained within the mainly Muslim states of Pakistan and Bangladesh, it is often forgotten both that there are still as many Muslims scattered throughout India as there are in Pakistan and that, before the population transfers that accompanied independence, Muslims had almost everywhere lived interspersed with Hindu and Sikh neighbours, the only significant exceptions being in the western border areas. These demographic facts point in turn to the crucial importance of conversion. Only a minority of South Asia's Muslims were of immigrant stock, coming over the centuries either as invaders or to serve existing Muslim-ruled states. The remainder were indigenous converts. Although individual conversions were not uncommon, in most of the subcontinent, especially in Bengal and the Punjab, some sections of Hindu society became Muslim more or less wholesale. Coercion was rarely used, and Sufi influence was particularly important.[1]

Two major consequences flow from all this. First, among the mass of converted Muslims, change of religious allegiance did not necessarily entail a total transformation of life-style. Linguistically, for example, most continued to speak the regional language rather than the Persian or Urdu associated with the Muslim courts. While over much of northern India Urdu functioned as a *lingua franca* and could easily be learnt as a second language, elsewhere this was not the case. More generally, assumptions about social organization were carried over from the regional tradition. Personal law often followed local custom rather than the *shari'a*, and marriage relations continued to be organized within much smaller units than the whole Muslim community.[2] It would be misleading to argue that South Asian Muslim society is simply Hindu society writ small, not least because whatever people's subterranean beliefs it lacks the overt commitment of Hinduism to social compartmentalization; indeed, many converts were probably originally attracted to Islam because it lacked a formal hierarchy, but clearly it would be difficult to argue that before 1947 the two societies were entirely distinct. In the rural areas they were often fused into one. In the towns, by contrast, they more usually operated along parallel tracks, and there was often considerable occupational and residential segregation at the local level, thus creating an environment in which political tensions in the late nineteenth and twentieth centuries could all too easily degenerate into intercommunal violence. Even today, many similarities in social organization remain, although there is now a much greater awareness of an overriding Muslim identity.[3]

The second consequence has been that upper-class Muslims, although they have always been clear about their distinct religious and social identity, have generally defined their political position in terms of existing power relations within the subcontinent rather than in terms of an ideal Islamic community. This in itself is hardly unique to South Asia, but under the Mughals, and earlier also, Muslim-ruled states were essentially dynastic entities operating within a largely non-Muslim environment. While Muslims naturally predominated at court, important officials were often Hindu, and in the countryside what mattered most in the eyes of the government were the resources available to the individual and not his religious faith. The effect was to produce a greater sense of distance than might otherwise have existed between the Muslim masses and the upper class.[4] This sense of distance was often expressed in terms of the distinction between *ashraf* and *ajlaf*. While the latter referred to the low-born, the former category defined an elite group which embraced those who could make a claim, however fictive, to foreign origin, spoke Urdu and appreciated Persian culture, owned land, and had a tradition of service to the government in responsible positions.[5] Their practice of Islam, while it did not have to be too zealous, followed orthodox lines. It was not entirely a closed category, but clearly access to it would have been difficult. It was also a category in which those Hindus who shared a similar relationship with political power could, as it were, obtain associate or honorary membership, although the ultimate privilege of intermarriage was always ruled out. It should be noted that although the *ashraf* elite extended throughout India, its heartland was in the northern plains, particularly in what was then the United Provinces (UP), and its headquarters were in such cities as Delhi and Lucknow, although in the region as a whole Muslims were in a minority.

While the Muslims of South Asia were often regarded by others as forming a distinct community, it was at most a highly fractured and localized one. The exercise of political power by Muslim dynasties within a predominantly non-Muslim society had done nothing to change this situation and had in some ways reinforced it. The activities of the *'ulama* and the Sufi shrines bridged the gap in that they catered to different sections of society, and the principal centres of learning preserved the central core of Islamic doctrine, but they did little to challenge the social and political pre-eminence of the *ashraf* elite.[6] Thus it was hardly surprising that it was the difficulties faced by this elite which provided the spur to formal political organization and led eventually to the demand for Pakistan.[7]

The colonial period

The demand for a sovereign Muslim state within the Indian subcontinent emerged only in the 1930s, but it was the culmination of a series of efforts, both political and intellectual, on the part of the elite to adapt to changing circumstances. Once the reality of Mughal power had crumbled in the eighteenth century and the East India Company began to consolidate its position, many Muslim families lost the secure status they had previously enjoyed, but others managed to survive and prosper. Once the trauma of the 1857 revolt, in which Muslim 'fanaticism' had been seen as an element, had been overcome,[8] the British went out of their way to encourage the *ashraf* elite, a group which they saw as one of their natural allies. One particularly important manifestation of this policy was the support given to Sayyid Ahmad Khan's activities in the 1860s and 1870s in establishing educational institutions at Aligarh, where the sons of the elite could prepare themselves for appropriate careers, principally in government service. The atmosphere Sayyid Ahmad sought to create was one which would encourage the qualities the British required in their senior Indian lieutenants while insulating them from dangerous currents of thought outside.[9]

In their early years the Aligarh institutions received support from Hindus as well as Muslims, but they soon became the exclusive property of the latter. In 1906 the Aligarh movement was closely associated with the events which led to the establishment of the Muslim League. The League was in effect a pressure group on behalf of the *ashraf*; it was established to respond to the gradual transformation in the second half of the nineteenth century in the terms on which the government dealt with its subjects. The elaboration of the administrative and legal systems, the introduction of a limited degree of representation, particularly in the local boards, the rapid growth of the universities, all affected the interests of Muslim families who had earlier enjoyed a more direct and flexible relationship with the government. Above all, public employment was now regulated through entrance examinations and fixed norms for promotion. Even those who were not directly affected were concerned that the officials who dealt with their landholdings and taxes should be men of a similar background. It was not that the government had changed its basic assessment of the character of the *ashraf* elite, and, as several writers have shown, Muslims in northern India continued to occupy a disproportionate share of senior positions, but that the general situation was becoming progressively more restrictive.[10] The efforts by some Hindus in northern India to have Hindi adopted as the language of lower-level administration, rather than or alongside Urdu, indicated the difficulties that might lie ahead, as in a more general sense did the increasing level of Hindu self-consciousness.

The growth of such organizations as the Arya Samaj in the last quarter of the nineteenth century, however, accompanied rather than preceded the equivalent process among the Muslims, and it must still be asked what other factors may have led the Urdu-speaking elite to redefine itself in terms of an exclusivistic religious denominator. To some extent it was encouraged to do so by the government. As mentioned earlier, there had been official patronage of the Aligarh movement, and the government had played some part in the moves which led up to the formation of the Muslim League. The British, however, were concerned to protect the *status quo*, and were as anxious to foster intercommunal landlord bodies such as the British Indian Association. One has also to look at the intellectual currents of the period. Even in the eighteenth century, the influential Shah Waliullah of Delhi had stressed the need for renewed *ijtihad* (independent judgement), a theme that was to play a major part in the work of Sayyid Ahmad. Of equal importance were the writings of such authors as Shibli, Hali, and Ameer Ali who reminded South Asia's Muslims of the wider Islamic world and stressed the past glories of Islamic civilization.[11] Thoroughgoing modernists like Sayyid Ahmad, who believed in the total compatibility of religion and positive science, were rare, but in a rather looser sense modernist ideas came to enjoy a wide currency among the elite. Of course, they did not bring about a wholesale transformation of basic attitudes, even among the university-educated, nor did such ideas all point in the same direction; nevertheless, the overall result was to create a climate in which at the same time the inherited essence of an individual's faith could be reaffirmed and its social and political implications re-examined.

The Muslim League's claim to represent the interests of all South Asia's Muslims, despite its primary concern with the problems of the elite, reflected the new forms of communal consciousness that were developing. Its initial approach had been to stress Muslim loyalty to the British Empire, but after a few years it came under the control of what has been dubbed the 'Young Party' among the Aligarh graduates.[12] This group was much less favourably disposed towards the government and was anxious to promote the cause of pan-Islam. In 1916 the League joined forces with the largely Hindu Indian National Congress to present a joint demand for constitutional reform. This meant the abandonment of what had seemed to the original leaders of the League to be the sensible policy of collaboration, but the rift in the Muslim elite was far from total. Many of the Old Party, for example, were concerned about the fate of Turkey, while the radicals were very far from identifying their future with the Congress. Indeed, the 1916 agreement was extremely advantageous to the elite on two counts. First, the Congress sanctioned the system of separate Hindu and Muslim electorates for the legislative councils, which it had initially opposed on its introduction in 1909. Second, the Muslims of the northern heartlands were given seats in the legislative councils in a proportion considerably in excess of their population, whereas in Bengal and the Punjab the situation was reversed. The ratios established in 1916 were broadly incorporated into the post-war Montagu-Chelmsford reforms, so that the Muslim elite could feel that its position was recognized both by the British and, with whatever reservations, by the majority of Indian political leaders.

Within a very few years of the 1916 agreement, however, the face of Muslim politics, as of Indian politics generally, had changed completely. Constitutional requests for reform were temporarily forgotten as a wave of agitation swept the country. For the Muslims, the immediate issue was the post-war fate of Turkey and the caliphate.[13] This must have seemed a quixotic enterprise from the very beginning, for the Turks had been defeated in the war, and the British clearly had enough military force to contain whatever unrest was generated in India; nevertheless, it inspired a country-wide fervour only previously seen in much more localized movements.

The leadership of the Khilafat movement, which supported Turkey against the European powers, was divided between radicals from the elite such as the Ali brothers and sections of the 'ulama. For the former, their long-standing concern with pan-Islamic issues merged with an anti-British feeling that had become more intense during the war. The 'ulama had always been divided in their approach to the colonial power.[14] Attitudes had ranged from grudging toleration to total rejection, and 'ulama had been involved in several of the early resistance movements against British rule. After the failure of the 1857 uprising, however, withdrawal rather than outright hostility became the dominant mode. For some this continued to be so, but for others, particularly those associated with the seminaries at Farangi Mahal and Deoband, an awareness of changes both in the Muslim world as a whole and within South Asia led them to search for forms of political action beyond the traditional.

In that search, the leaders of the Khilafat movement were willing, even anxious, to join hands with Gandhi and a Congress that had itself suddenly widened its base of support. Indeed, until the end of 1920 when Gandhi finally gained control of Congress (a victory which owed much to his Muslim allies) the non-cooperation campaign that he had launched centred on the Khilafat issue.[15] For a brief period, the fusion of Congress and Muslim political organizations was very much greater than it had been in 1916. When one asks, however, how far there was a fusion of long-term objectives, the position is rather different. M. A. Ansari, for example, one of the Khilafatist leaders who remained close to Congress throughout, expressed his position in 1918 in this way: 'While anxious to fight for the common rights of the two communities, the Musalman is determined to maintain his position in this country and will jealously guard all his legitimate rights'.[16] While Gandhi and Congress could give their consent to this formula in the euphoria of the non-cooperation movement, it was hardly a recipe for permanent harmony. In practical terms, the radicals clung to the rock of separate electorates, while the 'ulama were not prepared to yield an inch on the principle that Muslim social and religious practices should not be subject to control by a secular state.[17]

Once the non-cooperation campaign had collapsed in 1922, Congress and Khilafatists drifted apart remarkably quickly, until in 1928 the findings of the Nehru Committee, which had been charged with producing a constitutional scheme acceptable to all major Indian political groups, were rejected by virtually every Muslim leader. Just as seriously, a wave of Hindu–Muslim riots occurred in many major cities, and in 1926 Swami Shraddhanand, who had preached in Delhi's Jama Masjid in 1919, was assassinated for his part in a campaign to reconvert Muslims to Hinduism.[18]

Meanwhile, the unity of the Muslim leadership had also dissolved. The Khilafat Committee soon degenerated into a mere shell, while the Muslim League, which had effectively been in abeyance at the height of the non-cooperation movement, was revived but failed to make a major impact. The only viable focus for Muslim political activity appeared to be at the provincial level. In the United Provinces Muslims had to manoeuvre in the cross-currents created by Congress and government, but in the Punjab Fazli Husain succeeded in creating in the Unionist Party an organization that was Muslim-led but based upon the support of rural magnates and yeoman peasantry of all communities. In Bengal, too, several Muslim politicians, notably Fazlul Huq, played an important role in provincial politics.

The Punjab pattern, with its symbiotic links to British power and its assumption of the priority of the province, was not suitable for UP, and in any case it was soon undermined by developments at the all-India level. Except in the north-west frontier areas, many fewer Muslims participated in the civil disobedience movements of 1930 than had in the non-cooperation movement, but they took part in the major reformulation of British policy that took place at the same time. Although under the 1935 Government of India Act Muslim interests in the Punjab and Bengal were fairly well looked after, and after the 1937 elections Muslim-led ministries were formed in both provinces, it was clear that under the new conditions of provincial autonomy it would be difficult for the Muslims to retain the privileged position they had enjoyed in UP. It was also clear that if the all-India federation envisaged under the Act came into being, the Muslims would be dependent on the goodwill either of Congress or of the British. While this was acceptable to some, particularly in the Muslim-majority provinces, to others it served as a catalyst to a total rethinking of the political shape of the Muslim community.

In March 1940 the Muslim League formalized its views by calling in the Lahore resolution for separate statehood for Muslim-majority areas. It is beyond the scope of this chapter to analyse in detail how and why this was achieved within seven and a half years, but certain points need to be emphasized. The Pakistan movement brought together the same broad coalition of forces among Muslims that had been seen during the Khilafat period. It had, however, an apparently much more clearly defined goal, and it was therefore possible for the League to be controlled, at least at the national level, by one man, M. A. Jinnah. Jinnah could not be called a typical representative of the northern elite, not least because of his Gujarat and Bombay origins, but he was close to its leading members. Like them he sought to protect the interests of those Muslims who owned property or who came from educated backgrounds, but to an extent shared by few he saw the potentiality of mobilizing the whole Muslim community on the basis of secular ambition. He thus linked the ideal of Pakistan with the general uplift of the Muslim masses and, more concretely, with the encouragement of new forms of Muslim business enterprise.[19]

Jinnah and the Muslim League welcomed the support of the 'ulama, but this had now to be at a subordinate level. Not unnaturally, many were unprepared to accept their downgrading, and throughout the Pakistan movement Jinnah faced bitter criticism from some of the leading 'ulama, who claimed, quite correctly, that the League's Pakistan would never be a truly Islamic state. Their alternative, however, which depended on what one writer has aptly described as the 'mental partition' of India, seemed obscure and pallid in comparison with the apparent simplicity of a territorial homeland, quite apart from the obvious fact that it was doubtful whether an independent India under Nehru would provide the necessary conditions.[20] At least in the short term, the Muslim League was able to get the best of both worlds. Members of the 'ulama helped it to secure a massive popular vote in the 1946 elections, while at the same time the obvious disarray in their ranks prevented a united challenge to the League's ideology.[21]

The leading provincial politicians showed a somewhat similar ambivalence towards Jinnah and the League. Some continued to attempt to defend their provincial bailiwicks to the end, relying where necessary on Congress support; others, often for distinctly expedient reasons, chose to switch to the League. While retaining control of negotiations with the Congress and the British, Jinnah was willing to accept influential latecomers and to give them positions of respect.

The League's most enthusiastic supporters, however, were students. Along with the 'ulama, they were responsible for spreading the League's message and mobilizing popular support for Pakistan, particularly during the 1946 election campaign.[22] For some of them, no doubt, Pakistan was seen primarily in terms of self-interest, but to many its main appeal was the opportunity that it appeared to offer to create a new relationship between personal belief and political action. For almost all, it was a means to transcend problems that in various forms had vexed the Muslim elite for most of the preceding century.

The material interests of members of the elite and their religious concerns intertwined to form a continuous thread of development from Sayyid Ahmad's earliest endeavours to the hectic decade after 1937. Pakistan was created to serve their needs, but it would not have come into existence without the involvement of much wider sections of society. Here, too, religious fervour and material interests interacted, although because mass involvement was much more episodic and was often expressed through local issues, it is hard to generalize.[23] What was clear, however, was that other groups outside the elite would have demands to make on the new state of Pakistan.

Pakistan: Islamic state or Muslim homeland?

The problems faced by the state that came into existence on 14 August 1947 were enormous. After centuries in which there had been only one centre of ultimate authority in the subcontinent, there were now to be two. Even at the practical level of administration there were major difficulties. Most senior Indian government officials before 1947 had been non-Muslim and chose to serve India; the new capital, Karachi, was isolated from the other main population centres of the country and was, in any case, no more than a medium-sized provincial city; the main industrial centres of the subcontinent were all in India.

The political difficulties were as great. The League, despite its success in creating Pakistan, lacked a well-developed organization that could span the provinces and link the localities to the centre. Jinnah himself died in September 1948. His successor, Liaqat Ali Khan, although able to take over the reins of power smoothly, lacked the personal authority that Jinnah had had. Moreover, there was the regional question. Liaqat, like other senior League leaders, had come from what was now India, but it was clear that the indigenous inhabitants of Pakistan, particularly in Bengal and the Punjab, many of whose political leaders had accepted the idea of Pakistan only at the last moment, had to be given an assured place within the nation. There was the further complication that whereas the capital and political centre of gravity were in the western half of the country, the majority of the population, albeit a slight one, lived in the eastern. Beyond all these was the question of how to give effect to the country's destiny as a Muslim-ruled state.

It was in fact to take two constituent assemblies and nine years to produce a constitution, and that too was abrogated by the 1958 coup

before it came fully into effect. But the specific question of Islam did
not appear to its framers to be a major problem. Most members of the
constituent assembly were happy with a declaration in the preamble
that sovereignty belongs to God. There was also a provision that no
law repugnant to Islam should be passed, but there was no mechanism
by which the elected legislature could be overriden.[24] Like Jinnah, whose
name was constantly evoked by successive governments, the political
leadership believed that if Pakistan was to become a shining example
of a twentieth-century Muslim-ruled state, it would do so through the
hard work of its citizens as much as by its rigid adherence to the forms
of the past.

The leadership's essentially modernist consensus on the place of Islam
was challenged from two directions. There was most directly the claim
that Pakistan should be a more overtly Islamic state. As well as the
'ulama, who felt that their support of the League had been betrayed,
a new fundamentalism had begun to stir in the interwar period, particularly in the urban areas. The Khaksars, for example, whose founder
Mashriqi had received his education in England rather than in the
madrasa, saw themselves as the shock-troops of a new Islamic order.[25]
Since independence, the most important group has been the Jama'at-i-
Islami, under the leadership of the late Maulana Maududi.[26] Maududi
had originally been associated with the Jam'iyyat-ul-'Ulama-i-Hind, and
like many of its members he had been opposed to the creation of
Pakistan. After the event, however, he set out to examine from first
principles the question of how Islam could be the basis of a contemporary state. Through his writings and through the activities of the
Jama'at, which is organized along more disciplined and hierarchical lines
than most other political parties in the country, he succeeded in creating
a political alternative to the modernist consensus.[27] In contrast with
the orthodox *'ulama*, Maududi and the Jama'at evolved a programme
which blends the discipline of religion with individual responsibility in
a way that appeals to a wide section of the urban middle and lower-
middle classes. A particularly active student wing has been influential
in the universities and colleges.

The potentiality of an alliance between *'ulama* and fundamentalist
leaders was demonstrated in 1953 when serious rioting broke out in
Lahore over the question of whether the members of the Ahmadi sect
should officially be regarded as a non-Islamic minority. The issue was
of particular importance because of the presence of Ahmadis in senior
government positions. Although the unrest was serious enough for
martial law to be used, it was nevertheless the only occasion on which

a specifically religious issue has been responsible for large-scale protest.[28] In 1961, for example, even though the wide-ranging Family Laws Ordinance aroused considerable antagonism among the *'ulama*, it did not provoke coordinated protest.

The absence of direct confrontation indicates not so much the weakness of overtly Islamic forces as, on the one hand, their recognition of the tactical advantages of working through the system and, on the other, a willingness to concede the sincerity of many of those in the modernist camp. The genealogies of modernists and fundamentalists do indeed contain quite a few common ancestors, while the *'ulama* have always had an ambivalent attitude towards the holders of power. Those in power at a particular moment could reinforce these feelings by appropriate manipulation of Islamic symbols. Thus Ayub Khan, for example, despite his Family Laws Ordinance, used the same formulas in his 1962 constitution as had appeared in 1956. He did in fact go further by providing for a council of scholars, one of whose main functions would be to advise on how far legislation was in line with Islamic principles. There was, however, no means for the council to implement its findings, and in addition the power of appointment was retained in the government's hands.[29]

Two further factors may have been important. First, the Kashmir issue, and associated problems in relations with India, inevitably cast any regnant party or individual in the role of protector of the country's right to exist as a Muslim state. Second, the compulsions of domestic politics, particularly the problem of relations between the two wings, led to a short-term convergence of interest between the government, which was always dominated by West Pakistanis, and the Jama'at, for whom it is axiomatic that an Islamic state should not recognize internal ethnic differences. Throughout the 1950s and 1960s the Islamic parties continued to criticize government policy, but for the most part it was low-key. The 1968-9 agitation that led to the downfall of Ayub was concerned with secular issues. The disturbances occurred in both parts of the country, but they were more widespread in Bengal, where the only issue was the Awami League's demand for a degree of autonomy that amounted to virtual independence.

That such a demand should have been made, and should have been shown by the elections of 1970 to be the overwhelming desire of the Bengali citizens of Pakistan, points to the second general challenge that faced the country's leadership after independence. Broadly speaking, it had to demonstrate that its view of Islam provided an adequate ground for the development of a national identity. Very soon after independence, events showed that this would be a difficult task. In 1948 there were demonstrations in Bengal against the use of Urdu as the sole national language. Whereas the Muslim League had seen this as the natural consequence of the language's historic role in the subcontinent, the nascent Bengali middle class saw it as a means of perpetuating their subordinate position. Developments in the 1950s showed that while a limited accommodation of Bengali politicians was possible, the western wing of the country was not prepared to accept their domination.[30] Policies of both more and less centralization were put forward as alternatives to the rather piecemeal approach of the government. Neither was given a chance, but despite the reassessment of the past that has recently taken place in Bangladesh one may doubt whether anything would have overcome the inherent contradictions between the material interests of east and west. In so far as religion was a factor, it operated in a negative manner, in that Bengalis saw it as a means for the westerners to justify their exploitation of Bengal.

The relationship with Bengal is no longer a live issue, but the Pakistani leadership continues to wrestle with somewhat similar problems within its present territory. Although the refugees from India, whose principal centre became the burgeoning industrial and commercial city of Karachi, and the Punjabi landlords and traders soon adjusted to each other, important elements within the minority provinces of Sind, North-West Frontier Province, and Baluchistan have often felt that the common bond of Islam has not led the national leaders to take their problems seriously enough. There is, however, an important difference from the earlier position in Bengal, in that within the western provinces the Islamic parties, particularly the Jam'iyyat-ul-'Ulama-i-Islam, have significant support.[31]

The end of 1971 marked the start of a new era in Pakistan, not simply because of the forcible detachment of Bengal but because the same traumatic experience brought to power Zulfikar Ali Bhutto, the first politician since Jinnah to have both the will and the opportunity to mobilize mass support for a political programme. In the 1970 elections he had won a substantial majority of the seats in the western wing, with the remainder divided unequally between the National Awami Party and the Muslim League on the one hand, and the three overtly Islamic parties on the other – two of them *ulama*-supported and the third the Jama'at. The manifesto of the Pakistan People's Party (PPP) had been deliberately radical in its promises for the reorganization of economic relations.[32] Yet despite its essentially secular concerns, Bhutto chose to describe his party's objective as Islamic socialism. Again, despite his obvious determination to devise a system of government that would allow the fullest freedom of action to whoever held power in Islamabad, the 1973 constitution was rather similar to its predecessors in the seemingly generous, but in fact emasculated, provisions for review of legislation by a council of scholars.[33] Another important aspect of Bhutto's period in power was the emphasis he laid on Pakistan's relations with the Arab countries and with the Islamic world in general. There were of course sound economic and strategic reasons for such a policy, but it could hardly fail to include an Islamic dimension.

Bhutto and Jinnah diverged widely in their styles of leadership, but their views on the role of Islam in Pakistan's political life were similar. They both appreciated that Islam was central to most Pakistanis' lives. They believed that if properly respected, Islam could be a source of strength, but that if its traditional requirements were taken too literally, or its professional exponents allowed an independent role, then it would be likely to hinder healthy national development.

Developments since 1977

Despite the high hopes of 1970, when Bhutto demonstrated the appeal that a radical party could exercise, his regime came to a disastrous end in July 1977. Having alienated many of those who had originally supported him, he also managed to provoke an otherwise highly fragmented opposition to form a united front for the elections of March 1977. When the front failed – in its own view because of widespread interference by the government – to achieve a majority, it launched a mass agitation that paralysed the country and gave the army under General Zia ul-Haq the opportunity to intervene.

General Zia's initial justification for the army's action was that Bhutto had lost his moral right to rule. Not only had the army a duty to intervene to prevent further disorder and to ensure fresh elections; it also had an obligation to bring the Bhutto government to account. During this long-drawn process, which culminated with Bhutto's execution in April 1979, a rather different version of the army's duty emerged. It was now to ensure a return, not to the multi-party democracy envisaged under the 1973 constitution, but to a form of democracy that was truly Islamic. Even before the re-establishment of civilian rule, an event postponed indefinitely in October 1979, the martial law government considered that it could legitimately make far-reaching changes in every aspect of Pakistan's institutional structure, whether judicial, political, or economic.

General Zia considered that he was justified in his actions because no sincere Muslim could doubt that they were in line with the Islamic principles on which Pakistan had been founded. Thus in September 1980, in a speech on the anniversary of Jinnah's death, he stated that 'the measures which are being initiated today to establish an Islamic social order in Pakistan are the true manifestation of [Jinnah's] dreams.'[34] Jinnah, who if he had not led the Pakistan movement might still be remembered as one of the most outstanding Indian lawyers, would perhaps have had qualms about the shape that Pakistan has today assumed. Nevertheless, one must still ask whether the elite's consistent emphasis on Islamic modernism has not perhaps concealed and suppressed the people's yearning for a simpler past. Taking a more analytical perspective, one might ask whether social and intellectual changes during the past decade or so not only have rendered obsolete the consensus of the 1950s and 1960s, a consensus whose viability had in any case never fully been demonstrated, but have also created the conditions in which some form of Islamization might work. Increased links with the Middle East, both at government level and through large-scale migration of labour, as well as the example of events in Iran and elsewhere, have certainly led to a greater awareness of the possible options.

The debate on these questions has mostly been conducted at the ideological level, and such empirical evidence as exists is difficult to interpret. The 1977 agitation, for example, was presented by General Zia as indicating the Islamic sentiment of the people, and it is certainly true that calls for *nizam-i-mustafa*, or a state based on the Prophet's teachings, were much in evidence.[35] But the people who used such slogans were very often those who had been affected by Bhutto's nationalization policies or by some other aspect of his authoritarian style of rule. Overall, the agitation could just as plausibly be represented as a generalized protest against oppressive rule, in many ways similar to the events of 1968–9.[36] At the elections, the Islamic parties had been only one section of the united front, which, even if there had been no bending of the rules, would probably still not have secured a majority.

It is equally difficult to assess the likely appeal of a programme of Islamization by looking simply at the experience of the Zia period. Although the regime has lasted longer than many predicted, it is clear that its political base remains very narrow and that its institutional reforms have attracted little committed support. It survives in power partly because of the disunity of the opposition and partly because of the complications introduced by the Soviet intervention in Afghanistan. This may simply indicate, however, that those in Pakistan who are anxious to establish an Islamic form of state do not consider a military regime a suitable vehicle. Either because of inherent mistrust of the army's *bona fides* or as a result of political calculation, the Islamic parties (including the Jama'at, to which General Zia has personal as well as ideological connections) have been careful not to become closely identified with the regime.

There are doubts also about whether General Zia, for all his reliance on scholarly authority both in Pakistan and elsewhere in the Islamic world, has really formulated an adequate programme of change. Not only has he seemed to concentrate too much on the punitive aspects (in other words, advocating the application of the traditional penalties of Islamic law); there has also been little attempt to create a sense of popular involvement. Far-reaching pronouncements on the need for an interest-free banking system, for example, have in fact been implemented very cautiously. All in all, the values that General Zia is enforcing seem rather similar to the traditional military values of loyalty and discipline, an impression reinforced by his belief that local councillors elected in party-free elections are more representative of the people's wishes than political leaders.[37]

General Zia has attempted to impose his version of an Islamic political and social order from a position of great political weakness. By so doing he has damaged his own cause, and it is unlikely that a successor government will continue his efforts, at least in their present form. The complexities of the domestic and international situation are such that it would be hard to predict the general direction of change, let alone the precise approach that will be taken as regards the place of Islam. Pakistan's citizens are anxious to achieve both stability and a form of government that sits comfortably with their religious and cultural values. In the long run, the two can hardly be achieved separately, but the means by which stability is achieved will determine which aspects of Pakistan's Islamic heritage predominate.

Notes

1. For general accounts, see M. Mujeeb, *The Indian Muslims* (London, Allen & Unwin, 1967), and I. H. Qureshi, *The Muslim Community of the Indo-Pakistan Subcontinent (610–1967)* (The Hague, Mouton, 1962). A valuable historiographical survey of the literature on conversion can be found in P. Hardy, 'Modern European and Muslim Explanations of Conversion to Islam: A Preliminary Survey of the Literature', *Journal of the Royal Asiatic Society*, no. 2 (1977), pp. 177–206.
2. Imtiaz Ahmad (ed.), *Family, Kinship and Marriage Among Muslims in India* (Delhi, Manohar Book Service, 1976), *passim*; and Imtiaz Ahmad (ed.), *Caste and Social Stratification among Muslims in India* (Delhi, Manohar Book Service, 2nd edn, 1978).

3. For a relevant case study, see P. C. Aggarwal, *Caste, Religion and Power: An Indian Case Study* (New Delhi, Shri Ram Centre, 1971).

4. Hardy observes that before the first census was taken in 1872, most British officials estimated the number of Muslims in India to be less than half the actual figure; in other words, they identified Muslims with the upper and urban classes: 'Modern European and Muslim Explanations', pp. 179–81.

5. An excellent description of the life-style of this group can be found in David Lelyveld, *Aligarh's First Generation* (Princeton, Princeton University Press, 1979), ch. 2. See also Francis Robinson, *Separatism Among Indian Muslims* (London, Cambridge University Press, 1974), p. 31.

6. There were, of course, close links between the political and the religious elites, with the latter often controlling considerable quantities of land. See, for example, David Gilmartin, 'Religious Leadership and the Pakistan Movement in the Punjab', *Modern Asian Studies*, 13 (1979), 485–93.

7. This is not to imply that non-elite Muslims were always passive, but government repression ensured that their activities were limited in time and place.

8. For the reality of the revolt in one district of northern India, see Eric Stokes, *The Peasant and the Raj* (London, Cambridge University Press, 1978), ch. 6. See also ch. 8.

9. Lelyveld, *Aligarh's First Generation*, passim.

10. Robinson, *Separatism Among Indian Muslims*, ch. 2. See also Paul Brass, *Language, Religion and Politics in North India* (London, Cambridge University Press, 1974).

11. See Aziz Ahmad, *Islamic Modernism in India and Pakistan, 1857–1964* (London, Oxford University Press, 1967).

12. Robinson, *Separatism Among Indian Muslims*, p. 6.

13. See A. C. Niemeijer, *The Khilafat Movement in India* (The Hague, Martinus Nijhoff, 1972).

14. Much research needs to be done on both the social and the religious position of the *'ulama*. See, however, I. H. Qureshi, *Ulema in Politics* (Karachi, Ma'aref, 1972); Mushirul Hasan, 'Religion and Politics', *Economic and Political Weekly* (Bombay), 16 May 1981; M. Naeem Qureshi, 'The "Ulama" of British India and the Hijrat of 1920', *Modern Asian Studies*, 13 (1979), 41–59.

15. Richard Gordon, 'Non-Cooperation and Council Entry, 1919–1920', *Modern Asian Studies*, 7 (1973), 443–73.

16. Mushirul Hasan (ed.), *Muslims and the Congress* (Delhi, Manohar Book Service, 1979), p. 278.

17. For the *'ulama's* position, see P. Hardy, *The Muslims of British India* (London, Cambridge University Press, 1972), pp. 193–5.

18. J. T. F. Jordens, *Swami Shraddhananda: His Life and Causes* (Delhi, Oxford University Press, 1981).

19. Z. H. Zaidi, 'Aspects of Muslim League Policy, 1937–47', in C. H. Philips and M. D. Wainwright (eds.), *The Partition of India: Policies and Perspectives* (London, Allen & Unwin, 1970), pp. 268–9; Jamil-ud-Din Ahmad (ed.), *Some Recent Speeches and Writings of Mr Jinnah* (Lahore, Sh. Muhammad Ashraf, 1943), pp. 482–3 and 505–6.

20. Hardy, *The Muslims of British India*, p. 195.

21. *Ibid.*, pp. 238 and 242–6.

22. The students of Aligarh were naturally particularly active, but there were other important centres: Mahmud Husain, 'Dacca University and the Pakistan Movement', in Philips and Wainwright, *The Partition of India*, p. 372.

23. The Moplah rebellion in the extreme south of India was a particularly striking example: Robert L. Hardgrave Jr., 'The Mappilla Rebellion, 1921: Peasant Revolt in Malabar', *Modern Asian Studies*, 11 (1972), 57–99.

24. Khalid B. Sayeed, *The Political System of Pakistan* (Boston, Houghton Mifflin, 1967), p. 82.
25. See Wilfred Cantwell Smith, *Modern Islam in India* (London, Gollancz, 1946), pp. 235–45.
26. For Maududi's political thought in general, see Sayed Riaz Ahmad, *Maulana Maududi and the Islamic State* (Lahore, People's Publishing House, 1976).
27. Charles J. Adams, 'The Ideology of Mawlana Mawdudi', in D. E. Smith (ed.), *South Asian Politics and Religion* (Princeton, Princeton University Press, 1966), pp. 371–97.
28. The official *Report of the Court of Inquiry into the Punjab Disturbances of 1953* (Lahore, 1954), commonly known as the Munir report, offers an articulate statement of the official position on the place of Islam in Pakistan.
29. Mushtaq Ahmad, *Government and Politics in Pakistan* (Karachi, Pakistan Publishing House, 2nd edn, 1963), pp. 266–7.
30. Rounaq Jahan, *Pakistan: Failure in National Integration* (New York, Columbia University Press, 1972), ch. 2.
31. For the position in 1970, see Craig Baxter, 'Pakistan Votes – 1970', *Asian Survey*, 11 (1971), 211.
32. See S. J. Burki, *Pakistan under Bhutto, 1971–1977* (London, Macmillan, 1980), ch. 3.
33. Fazlur Rahman, 'Islam and the New Constitution of Pakistan', in J. Henry Korson (ed.), *Contemporary Problems of Pakistan* (Leiden, E. J. Brill, 1974), pp. 38–44. The author stresses the concessions that Bhutto was prepared to make in order to ensure a consensus for the new constitution in the National Assembly.
34. *Dawn*, 11 Sept. 1980.
35. *Ibid.*, 22 Aug. 1980, speech by General Zia.
36. See, for example, Khalid B. Sayeed, *Politics in Pakistan: The Nature and Direction of Change* (New York, Praeger, 1980), pp. 157–61.
37. *Dawn*, 7 Mar. 1980, speech by General Zia.

11 Faith as the Outsider: Islam in Indonesian Politics

RUTH McVEY

They have treated us, said the Muslim leader Muhammad Natsir, like cats with ringworm.[1] Indeed, Indonesia's military rulers have not been kind to the spokesmen for Islam, however much they called on the religion's forces during their seizure of power in 1965–6. At first slowly and through the voices of lesser commanders, then ever more clearly in the presidential name, demands were made and measures taken which not only limited the political expression of Islam but attacked some of its fundamental institutions. By the mid-1970s it was clear that the rightist regime of Suharto's New Order was going much farther towards restricting the political and social role of Islam than the preceding leftist government of Sukarno had dared. The religion's political role has itself changed from being the hammer of the left into the major perceived threat to military rule.

The restriction of Islam under the New Order reflects, on the one hand, the proclivities of state leaders influenced by both technocratic and pre-Islamic ideas and fearful of any institutions they do not control. It also, however, continues the experience of Indonesian Islam over a far longer time: politically, the religion has characteristically been on the defensive, and since the 1945–9 war of independence it has fought for an ever-narrowing range of claims on the state.

Yet Islam was the first basis on which Indonesia established a modern political organization which attracted mass support. No state had governed all the ethnically and linguistically diverse islands of the archipelago before colonial rule, so that there was no historical or cultural basis for national consciousness; but over 90 per cent of the population were at least nominal Muslims, and it was on this ground that they first conceived their unity against the colonial order. The Dutch had been keenly aware of the threat that Islamic political consciousness posed to their domination, and the architect of their policy on Muslim affairs, the orientalist C. Snouck Hurgronje, had urged tolerance of Islamic social and spiritual endeavours combined with the discouragement of any involvement of religion in politics. In the end the Dutch could not prevent it: from 1913 to 1923 the Sarekat Islam (Islamic Union) formed the centre of the Indonesian national awakening. Since then, however, leadership has lain in the hands of overtly secular forces.

One problem was that if nothing united Indonesia like Islam, neither does anything divide it so deeply. The fissures are of two main kinds, so far as their political effect is concerned: one is based on the extent to which the religion itself is regarded as a valid motive force, and the other on the division between 'modernist' and 'traditionalist' interpretations of it. In spite of the high nominal adherence to Islam, the first of these divisions is the more important. The process of Islamization of the archipelago, which began in earnest in the fourteenth century, is still far from complete.[2] By and large the religion penetrated from the coasts to the interior, its spread reflecting trading networks, the rivalry between coastal and interior states, and the competition of different cultural groups. Thus the ethnic Indonesian merchant class is overwhelmingly strongly Muslim; so is the population of Java's north coast, as opposed to its interior. In islands where inland peoples differ from those on the coast it is common to find the littoral cultures strongly Muslim and the hill folk 'animists', Christians, or at best nominal adherents of Islam. In some cases – most notably on Java, the most populous and politically central island – nominal followers of Islam are sufficiently conscious of separateness that in many respects they think of themselves essentially as a different belief group. Javanese nominal Muslims – usually called *abangan*, as opposed to strict Muslim *santri* – may, at the extreme, refer to themselves jestingly as *Islam statistik* (statistical Muslims) and hold their own practices, strongly influenced by pre-Islamic Hindu-Buddhist mysticism, as constituting a distinct *agama Jawa* (religion of Java).[3]

For all the overwhelming number of Islam's formal adherents in Indonesia, which makes it on paper the world's largest Muslim nation, unambiguous Islam is a minority religion. Yet it remains the belief system with which most Indonesians identify themselves, and between those for whom it is everything and those for whom it is merely an uncomfortable label there are many who adhere to it positively but are unsure of the extent to which its claims should impinge on their lives. Depending on the circumstances – for our purposes, the juxta-position of religious activists, the state, and social conditions – such people may see in Islam the central symbol of their identity, discover in it a voice of protest, or resent the sectarian demands of its zealots. The ambiguity of Islam's political strength and role has been mirrored in the ambivalence of Indonesia's rulers towards it; by and large, while trying to use it as a source of legitimacy, they have held it at arm's length.

In the interior states which formed the great pre-colonial centres of Java, whose culture still heavily influences Indonesian political style, the relationship of Islam to royal power was always ambivalent. Rulers adopted the new religion as a means of adding to their spiritual armoury; it did not mean discarding older beliefs, though individual princes might become strong *santri*. The *kauman*, the quarter of the capital inhabited by pious Muslims, most of them traders and artisans, typically nestled close by the royal palace but was in appearance and atmosphere a very different world. This already marked contrast was greatly intensified in the nineteenth century under colonial rule, when the Netherlands East Indies authorities deliberately set out to estrange the Javanese administrative elite, the *priyayi*, from strict Islam in an effort to remove that religion as a motivational force for their resistance and/ or alliance with the masses. A Javanese official who was too punctilious in his religious observance was less likely to win a favourable posting, and *priyayi* patronage of religious leaders was discouraged.

At the same time the increasing influence of Islamic orthodoxy – particularly after the coming of the steamship and opening of the Suez Canal brought a rapid rise in the number of Indonesians making the Pilgrimage and studying religion abroad – meant there was growing pressure on the faithful to purify their practices from those legitimating the royal courts and old social order. Moreover, the late nineteenth century saw social strains caused by the population pressure and impoverishment which followed the penetration of a cash economy and the development of plantation agriculture. This, together with the decline in popular regard for *priyayi* leadership resulting from the colonial cooptation of the traditional elite, meant that common people began to look for new sources of meaning and support. Some – particularly among those parts of the population where acceptance of Islam was relatively unequivocal – found this in religious leadership and a stricter insistence on the centrality of Islam to their lives; ultimately, as religious parties arose, they identified with these. This stricter observance provided them with a sense of community and purpose, but at the same time that it shut out the colonial power and its collaborators it also built a wall between the *santri* and those who could not accept so unequivocal a religious commitment. Such people sought leadership, ultimately, in secular parties, and party competition helped to fix and intensify communal barriers. Rural *santri* and *abangan* were, often enough, segregated from each other in separate villages or hamlets; they dressed somewhat differently, played different music, observed different feasts. By the mid-twentieth century this cultural apartheid became sufficiently serious for communal feeling to dominate popular choice of political allegiances. In 1948, at the time of a short-lived leftist rebellion against the government of the revolutionary republic, the divisive potential of this cultural-political separation was bloodily revealed through communal killings in rural areas, in which political adherence was clearly less important than religious identification.[4]

Out of this process came the tie between religious and political partisanship that was to dominate the parliamentary democracy of the 1950s – *santri* loyalties going to the modernist Masyumi Party or, especially in rural Central and East Java, the traditionalist Nahdatul Ulama (NU); and *abangan* support being given to the *priyayi*-oriented Partai Nasional Indonesia (PNI) or the lower-class Partai Komunis Indonesia (PKI). This religious-political identification was particularly important because the decay of indigenous institutions coupled with the colonial propping up of traditional social forms had ideologically emptied large segments of rural society, especially on Java, and in the post-colonial period political movements flowed into the resulting vacuum to provide organization and meaning to people's lives.[5] For many ordinary Indonesians, political-religious identification thus became part of their sense of self. It also meant that, as economic decline brought social tension, there was renewed danger that political competition would bring communal violence. The unity of nationalist, religious, and communist forces (Nasakom), which was a major principle of Sukarno's Guided Democracy rule of 1959–65, was not simply a device for manipulating Indonesian politics but was also aimed at overcoming this widening breach in social solidarity.[6]

The military leadership under General Suharto took advantage of the religious contrast in seizing power from Sukarno in 1965, encouraging popular anti-communist violence which in rural Java assumed the form of *santri* attack on *abangan* and resulted in one of the great massacres of our time. The killing thoroughly intimidated that part of the population which had been the PKI's greatest strength, but it also widened the gulf between *santri* and *abangan* on Java and, in the rest of the archipelago (the 'Outer Islands'), between cultural groups which were strongly identified with Islam and those which were not. They enhanced the already common image of strict Muslims as aggressive and intolerant – *Islam fanatik* against *Islam statistik*. Some *abangan* Muslims, no longer able to accept a religion that they had come to see as fundamentally intolerant, turned to mystical *kebatinan* sects as their primary spiritual identification. Hinduism and Buddhism, dead in Java for centuries, began to revive as small but significantly growing religious minorities, and the small Christian population experienced a rapid rise in numbers.[7] Leaders of Suharto's New Order, themselves overwhelmingly of *abangan* cultural origins and *priyayi* social pretensions, were not only concerned to reduce Islamic militancy once their regime was established but strove to increase the autonomy of the *abangan* religious variant as a political counterbalance. In 1973 they went so far as to recognize *kebatinan* as a separate religious orientation, in the face of fierce opposition by the Muslim orthodox, to whom this appeared as an attempt to encourage *abangan* Muslims away from the faith entirely.[8]

Although the *abangan* and secular aspects of the New Order's cultural orientation are particularly pronounced, they have been generally characteristic of the mainstream of Indonesian political leadership. Socially, this has drawn its principal support from what has been called Indonesia's 'metropolitan superculture', the semi-Western life-style that developed among the class of modern-educated, middle-class Indonesians that emerged in the great colonial cities of Indonesia in the early part of this century.[9] In addition to a colonial-derived Western style, they adopted much of the *priyayi* outlook, both because part of the new elite came from the lower ranks of that class and because it was congenial to the bureaucratic, clerkly, and professional roles in which they engaged. The group contained an important Christian element, since although the Christians were a small portion of the population their relatively advanced education and preferment under colonialism give them a disproportionately high representation in the modern elite. In addition to the check this imposed on an Islamic commitment for the new elite, European ideas of modernity inclined its members to view religion as something peripheral if not hostile to progress. Religion seemed to them in practice all too often the codification of rural superstitions or else narrow disputation on religious law that seemed irrelevant to the needs of the time.

The *santri* themselves had little to do with this new elite. In so far as they were urban they were largely engaged in independent trade and artisanry and had very different values and life-styles from the new bureaucratic-professional class. The proponents of Islam within the new elite consisted largely of Outer Islanders from population groups where Islam had penetrated more uniformly and deeply than in Java (most notably the small but influential Minangkabau population of West Sumatra) and Javanese of *santri* families who had – usually by achieving a measure of advanced secular education – acculturated sufficiently to the modern, *priyayi*-tinged style to communicate effectively with *abangan* and Christian elements.

From the mid-1920s adherents of the 'metropolitan superculture', which was to become the life-style of the national elite, dominated the independence movement. In spite of the fact that they were an extremely small group, their ideological hegemony met no effective Muslim challenge – political, administrative, or social. It was not simply the centrality of the new elite that determined this, but also the development of contradictions within the broad movement that had constituted the Sarekat Islam (SI). In the early 1920s the Netherlands Indies government had begun to take strong measures against the political and economic demands being put forward by the mass organization, and its more conservative leaders sought to avoid repression by turning attention towards religious affairs. This resulted, however, in a considerable contraction of the SI's appeal. A large number of Sarekat Islam adherents had joined precisely because of its political and economic challenge to the *status quo*; these drifted away in disappointment or else adhered to the communist party, which had developed within it and captured most of the association's local branches when it was expelled from the mother organization in 1923. The new emphasis also meant the loss of those who were quite happy to accept the religion as a general label but not as the specific object of their activity.

Even among the religiously concerned, the new stress meant schism, for it involved the question of Islamic orthodoxy. Those who led the association were modernists, who looked to Middle Eastern reformism for doctrinal inspiration and wished to see Indonesia free of colonial domination but otherwise retaining the Western-derived institutions of economic and political modernity. The efforts of the purged Sarekat Islam to present itself as the spokesman for Indonesian Muslims in political affairs persuaded the traditionalist *ulama* (*'ulama*) of East and Central Java that they must also organize, if only in order to prevent the modernists from obtaining state authority to impose their vision. They therefore established the Nahdatul Ulama in 1926, and thenceforth – save for an uneasy and superficial amalgamation between 1937 and

1952 – Indonesian Islam was represented by two competing major movements.

For most of the traditionalists, the question of reshaping the state according to Islamic beliefs did not arise. Colonial or post-colonial, the state was something too alien and too powerful to be converted. It therefore had to be accommodated, and the political task of the religiously concerned was to see that it impinged as little as possible on the life of the *santri* community. This could be achieved by a combination of the carrot and the stick: the carrot of political support in return for autonomy and patronage, the stick of threatened or actual riot under the cry of Islam endangered. Thus in spite of its fundamental conservatism the Nahdatul Ulama provided the religious mainstay of Sukarno's leftist regime, which took care to place patronage over religious affairs in NU hands. Gradually, however, the provincial religious notables who formed the backbone of the party became convinced that growing communist strength within the system formed a danger to the material support and spiritual values of the *santri* community, most particularly as a result of the PKI's efforts to press land reform. In 1964–5 they helped unleash rural anti-communist violence which, after the coup of October 1965, became a major element in the massacre of the left.[10]

Although militant Islam formed a major initial source of support for the subsequent New Order regime, relations soon foundered on the desire of Suharto and his *abangan* associates to limit the political claims of the Muslims, on the regime's general imperviousness to non-elite civilian opinion, and on military reluctance to rehabilitate groups – most notably the Masyumi Party – thought to have sympathized with the regional and religious rebellions which had plagued Indonesia's first post-revolutionary decade. By 1968 tension between government and Islam was openly acknowledged; from then on, religious parties and activists appeared ever more clearly in opposition, and with the general election of 1971 Islam established itself as the chief popular voice against the regime. It is not the Muslim modernists who led this protest, however, but the hitherto reluctantly political traditionalists. Their opposition does not simply reflect the reaction of rural obscurantism; to the contrary, 'traditional' Islam has increasingly become the voice of younger-generation, urban protest against the *status quo*, thus confounding assumptions of a one-to-one relationship between religious modernism and political modernity and between urbanism and secularism.

The radicalism of tradition

In part, the role of spokesman against the regime fell by default to traditional Islam (we shall continue to use the adjective in spite of its clear present inappropriateness, for the other labels applied to this religious wing – 'conservative' and 'orthodox' – are at least equally misleading).[11] No other politically organized group was in a position to form a coherent opposition. The communists had been violently eliminated in 1965, and under the military-controlled regime no leftist movements were tolerated. The nationalists, shorn of their populist aspect by the fall of Sukarno and the post-coup purges, were too identified with the bureaucratic elite and too dependent on state patronage to play an effective oppositional role. The religious modernists, whose Masyumi Party had been banned in the Guided Democracy period, were allowed to re-emerge as the Parmusi (Partai Muslimin Indonesia, Indonesian Muslim Party) only after heavy inter- ference that ensured political servility. On the other hand, the traditionalist NU had largely escaped the attention of the authorities before the 1971 election campaign, in good part because of its past record of anti-communism and political pliability. It also did not depend on the state apparatus for cadres or financial backing and so could mount a credible independent campaign, in the course of which it attracted popular support (and also official harassment) as the only out- spoken competitor to the government-sponsored organization Golkar.[12] That this role was not simply a matter of historical accident was made clear, however, by the fact that the traditionalists thereafter maintained a critical stance in spite of very heavy pressure from the authorities, to whom militant Islam now appears as the principal threat to security.

One reason why this has been possible is that the institutions of traditional Islam are relatively inaccessible to official interference. In a sense, the religion's past uninvolvement in the state has promoted its present involvement in politics. We have already noted its ambivalent relationship with the rulers of pre-colonial Java; under the colonial regime relations between Islam and political authority moved towards clear hostility. The Dutch concentrated, however, on alienating traditional ruling elites from religious leadership and on limiting the possibilities for the political organization of Islam.[13] Partly to avoid provoking a Muslim reaction and partly to reassure politically powerful Christian sensibilities in the metropolis, the authorities refrained from otherwise interfering in religious affairs, restricting themselves to appointing *penghulu* (officials who administered religious justice) as supervisors of religious affairs at territorial levels. Since these officials' power derived from their relationship to the colonial administration, they were, except in the few cases when persons of religious distinction accepted the role, unable to act as an effective bridge between Islam and the state.

Similarly, though the Dutch preserved the system of religious courts that had administered justice in pre-colonial Indonesia, they progressively limited their competence and subordinated them to the claims of both European and *adat* (customary) law, so that they came to represent, from the state's viewpoint, a peripheral and anachronistic aspect of the colonial system. The poorly valued and rewarded *penghulu* were scarcely a positive link between Islam and the state; if anything, they were points of disaffection.[14] But perhaps more important than the weakness of bonds through formal office was the contrast in style and perception between the Islamic world and the colonial one. The emerging Indonesian national elite, adopting many of the Europeans' attitudes (including, in the case of the lawyers, advocacy of Dutch and *adat* law at the expense of Islamic jurisprudence), was culturally more distant from the Muslim community than the already ambivalent pre-colonial *priyayi* had been, which increased the sense of unease that had already marked *santri–priyayi* relations in pre-colonial Java.

With independence, the *penghulu* system was replaced by a full-fledged Ministry of Religion, but until the end of the Sukarno period this was less a means for the state to control religion than for political Islam to gain patronage and ensure freedom from outside interference. The first republican Minister of Religion, and the architect of that ministry's policies, was K.H. (Kiyayi Haji) Wahid Hasyim, leader of the Nahdatul Ulama Party and son of K.H. Hasyim Asyari, head of the great East Java religious school of Tebuireng. The ministry was undisputedly an NU fief until after Sukarno's fall: it was only under Suharto's New Order that steps were taken to bring religion more closely under state control.

Once it had consolidated its power the New Order moved to increase bureaucratic leverage over Islam. In 1972 it appointed as Minister of Religion Professor Mukti Ali, who was both a modernist and a strong accommodationist as far as relations with the state were concerned. His appointment was intended not only to free the ministry of traditionalist influence but to point Muslim leadership towards cooperation with government authorities for the purpose of 'national development'. Mukti Ali had pursued advanced education in Islamic studies not in a Muslim institution but at McGill University, as had a handful of other modernists of elite families before 1965. The New Order has strongly encouraged Muslim scholars to obtain higher training at Western centres of study, both because of the regime's general admiration for the Western, technocratic approach and from a desire to urge Muslim intellectuals towards a more 'objective' view of religion's role and an appreciation of the need to accommodate it to a secularized modern world.[15]

In doing this, New Order policy-makers have tried to bridge the gap between the *santri* community and the state by providing Islam with spokesmen who can communicate easily with the regime and share its general perceptions. The question is whether people who are culturally (and often economically) so distant from the run of the *santri* community and who lack religious prestige that is recognizable in traditional terms will act as links, or whether they will simply ensure that the religious bureaucracy is a state enclave with no real purchase on the *santri* world. The problem is compounded by the fact that the regime has not contented itself with installing a more like-minded leadership in the Islamic bureaucracy but, as elsewhere, has worked to ensure direct military control. An army colonel was appointed as secretary-general to Mukti Ali's ministry; later, the professor was himself replaced by General Alamsyah, a close adviser to President Suharto.

The personnel and patronage changes that followed the transfer of power in the Ministry of Religion affected the perquisites enjoyed by Muslim institutions and leaders, though not as much as might be imagined, for – owing in part to the relative undesirability for university graduates of a career in the Ministry of Religion – the bulk of its bureaucracy has thus far remained in old hands.[16] But these changes did not seriously increase the state's control of Islam, since its resources, communications, and prestige systems were largely independent of the state. We can see the bureaucrats' ineffectiveness in this respect through their continued search for more effective instruments of control and their failure to gain acceptance of any but the most cautious innovations. Thus an effort by the Ministry of Religion in 1970 to establish a national *fatwa* commission in order to provide a central source of authoritative rulings on religious law was rejected by the conference of *ulama* called to endorse it, with the polite argument that such an institution could endanger Islam if ever there should be a government unfavourable to the religion. In 1975, the government succeeded in creating a hierarchy of consultative councils, headed by a national

Majlis Ulama, which it hoped would form a bridge between religious leadership and the state. However, the *ulama* who accepted membership in the councils have been acutely aware of the danger both to religious independence and to their own personal standing in the Muslim community of becoming too closely identified with the state, and the system has thus far had little real impact on the affairs of the Islamic community.[17]

Institutionally, Islam's ability to escape government authority has rested largely on the network of traditional religious schools (*pesantren*) and their headteachers (*kiyayi*). The schools, in their classical form, are completely outside state support and control. They come into existence by the decision of a religiously learned man to set himself up as a teacher; if he attracts a following, youths seeking religious knowledge will settle around his house, and will stay there as long as they wish to lead a religious life and find their search for knowledge served. The typical minor *kiyayi* engages in farming to make ends meet, and those who study with him may contribute their labour, but this is normally not a large source of income. The students' families and other admirers of the teacher make gifts, but the *kiyayi* is expected to ask no fees for his teaching or other services to the community. Though the life of the lesser *kiyayi* can be economically very uncertain, leaders of the great *pesantren* are often rich, through the gifts of the faithful and investment in land and commerce. Consequently, it has not been easy for governments, colonial or independent, to attack the *kiyayi*'s position at its financial source. State pressure on religion leads all too easily to greater solidarity and mutual aid among religious leaders, and to increased popular support for the Muslim teachers as champions against oppressive authority.

The traditional *pesantren* of Indonesia are typically not *wakaf* (*waqfs*), or religious foundations, but the property of the *kiyayi* or his family; depending heavily on the individual teacher's learning and charisma, they often decay soon after his death. Such stability as the *pesantren* enjoy is due largely to the regard for heredity, for the importance of a *kiyayi* is judged not only by his religious learning, his piety, and the number of his followers, but by his family relationship to other great religious teachers. Therefore, although Indonesian Muslim theology follows Sunni doctrine in providing no basis for hereditary charisma, there is a strong tendency for religious leadership to concentrate in certain families. Intermarriage between families of religious note creates a complex of relationships which both reinforces the solidarity of *santri* leadership and expresses the hierarchy within it, a source of recognition which is peculiarly invulnerable to manipulation by the state.[18]

Communication and mobilization by the religious leadership has run traditionally – and still does to a marked extent – through the network of *kiyayi* relationships. It also follows the pattern of connections and pupil–teacher loyalties established by movement from one *pesantren* to another. The serious *santri* student will not stay exclusively with one teacher but travels in order to exchange ideas and further his knowledge. Though this contact is not, in principle, secret, it has an association with rejection of the things of this world (and thus avoidance of non-religious authority) which lends it easily to clandestine communication. Traditional Indonesian Islam is heavily influenced by Sufi mysticism, and in times past Sufi *tarekat* (*tariqas*, brotherhoods) played an important role in the life of the *pesantren* and in organizing popular support during social crises. Since much of the advanced learning transferred from a *kiyayi* to his pupils is mystical knowledge, the teacher–student relationship is typically characterized by initiation into ever more secret layers of meaning. Those who are not yet ready to understand are kept from the knowledge, while shared familiarity with a particular teaching forms a strong bond among adepts. Needless to say, this can be applied to politics and forms a basis for communication that is relatively impervious to government penetration and control.

The government's evident inability to manage the institutions of traditional Islam enhanced the Nahdatul Ulama's popularity and led to a trend which became more marked as the 1970s progressed: the detachment of the NU from an identification with social conservatism and rural Java. The movement began to draw support from a broader geographic base and to appeal to urban as well as rural discontent. Some young urban intellectuals began to see in it a more positive force than the mainstream of Islamic modernism, which appeared disunited, politically cowed, and absorbed in legalistic debate. The NU's refusal to accept unquestioningly modern ways began to seem not backward but sensible to a generation sceptical of the country's course. The identification of the NU with rural reaction has been further blurred by agrarian changes accompanying the spreading capitalist transformation of agriculture and investment in land by the urban elite: rural religious notables began to appear less as exploiters of the village poor and more as fellow victims of an urban, capitalist assault on peasant livelihood and values. The ferment resulting from such reorientation not only enhanced the image of religion as socially and politically relevant but blurred the distinction between traditional and modern in Indonesian Islam – a process which was also furthered inadvertently by the government's decision in 1972 to amalgamate all Muslim parties into a single bloc.

The attraction of the institutions of Islam for the younger generation of intellectuals lies precisely in their otherness to what is seen as the corruption and cultural betrayal of Indonesia's current rulers, the social costs of capitalist development, and the materialism of the West. They see them as being closer to the common people than are the institutions of the modern state – correctly so, for they are culturally more familiar and physically more accessible to the population at large. The religious courts, for example, do not want for cases in spite of their lowly status and limited competence. They cost little for people to use and do not emphasize their difference from common folk in their ambience, procedure, or language; they tend to base judgements on compromise, which is more compatible with their clientele's inherited ideas of justice than is the determination of right and wrong through the examination of evidence.[19] What matter, then, that in the eyes of state authorities their judges are poorly trained, their judgements unsoundly based, and their application of Islamic law incompatible with the needs of the time? To people seeking an alternative to the state's behemoth, efficiency and modernity may not be what counts. Similarly, the failure of the *pesantren* to provide adequate skills or career opportunities for the modern world may seem less relevant than the fact that its education emphasizes the whole person and that it seeks to produce not successful man but moral man.[20]

Such sentiments give rise to two problems, however. One is that, like it or not, Indonesia exists in the modern world and unless a fundamental rejection of outside contact is contemplated – so far not the position of Muslim militants – the country must have institutions capable of responding to its international technological, economic, and political environment. The second is that institutions which distinguish Islam from an unacceptable modernity may also be, for important segments of the Muslim community, symbols of an equally unacceptable backwardness or fanaticism. This greatly limits the extent to which Islam in any of its previously familiar forms can serve as a shorthand for feelings of social discontent and cultural alienation. In spite of its prominent oppositional role, Islam is not the automatic orientation for younger Indonesians troubled by the problems of the day; there are too many problems in presenting it as an alternative ideology, too many memories of religious violence, too many historically (if not now openly) available secular models of social protest.

The paradoxes of modernism

From the beginning the religious modernists took a much more positive attitude towards the relationship between religion and the state than did the traditionalists, in line with their belief that Islam can and must relate to the modern world. They have, however, not been able to agree on the extent to which non-Islamic institutions and ideas should be accommodated, and their ambivalence has greatly weakened their ability to act effectively as a political force. Two characteristics of Indonesian Islamic modernism are particularly relevant here. First of all, it accepts a world dominated by industrial economies and their accompanying technology; the problem for religion is to respond to this environment, by purifying itself of 'feudal' accretions which have tied it to limited and outmoded ways of thinking and by modifying the community's institutions so as to respond to the new social, economic, and political needs.[21] Secondly, modernist Indonesian Islam has generally accepted the primacy of the goal of national independence.[22]

Acceptance of modernity naturally raises the question of what can be adopted from an essentially Western-derived culture without sacrificing religious content. It thus compounds the nationalists' problem of defining an Indonesian identity that is not simply a product of the colonial experience and irrelevant to current social and political needs. The modernists' inclination has been to assert that purified religious doctrine fits the needs of all times, and the problem is only to determine where the knife must be applied. The result is a strong emphasis on the search for original authority in the Qur'an and early traditions of Islam – scripturalism, as it has been pointed out, is perhaps more appropriate than modernism to describe its approach.[23] This has led the mainstream of Indonesian modernism to something of a dead end, centring on rigorous interpretation of religious law as the basis for deciding what is properly Islamic and what is not. But the interpretation of the law is strongly affected by the need to accord with acceptance of modernity and the primacy of the nation-state. Thus, modernist Indonesian Islam has been defensive not only towards the larger modern world but also to the categories established by the ideological hegemony of Indonesian secular nationalism. Much intellectual energy has gone to asserting the national character of the religion, its contribution to the independence struggle, and its centrality to Indonesia's hopes for future strength and prosperity. It has meant that those cases in which segments of Indonesian Islam chose a different road from that taken by the nationalist-controlled state have been judged not by their spiritual or social qualities, but by categories proposed by the secular nationalist elite.[24]

One way in which to escape from the subordination to a secular elite which acceptance of the nation-state generally implies is to demand an Islamic state. Very few Indonesian modernists carried their claims so far, however: they have demanded, rather more nebulously, a 'state based on the tenets of Islam' (*negara yang berdasarkan Islam*, as opposed to *negara Islam*); and even in this they have had little success. The question of the relationship between religion and an Indonesian state became immediate with the defeat of Dutch power by the Japanese in 1942, and acute when Japan's surrender in 1945 brought the collapse of all effective authority. In some regions local Muslim leaders responded to popular revolutionary pressures and their own concepts of Islam's political role by seizing power, but these were short-lived and spontaneous efforts which showed little real vision of an Islamic state. They were put down by a revolutionary government concerned to prevent social upheaval in order both to consolidate the power of the secular nationalist elite and to win the international recognition deemed essential to the republic's survival.[25]

The major Muslim political leaders accepted this as part of their general acquiescence in the nationalists' hegemony; in any event, they had not the armed strength to take another course. The Japanese-trained paramilitary force which became the nucleus of the republican army had been drawn from the same social sources as the secular nationalist elite; late in the war the Japanese had formed a Muslim militia, the Hizbullah, but the main effect of this was to institutionalize the segregation of religious and secular armed forces, with the latter achieving legitimacy and power as the national army. Though some prominent officers were known as pious Muslims, the army was strongly united on the idea of the secular state, and the most powerful cultural element in it was *abangan* Javanese. This was reinforced by the army's role during the 1950s and early 1960s in suppressing Muslim and regional revolts, which discouraged *santri* and non-Javanese recruitment. As a technocratic orientation became stronger in the post-revolutionary officer corps, ideas of a modern, 'scientific' military establishment further reduced the possibility of religious attachment.

The only serious attempt to establish a Muslim alternative to the secular nationalist state came late in the revolution, amidst a general crisis of confidence in the republic's leadership. In 1948 the Darul Islam movement, formed around a cadre of Hizbullah forces under the conservative modernist religious leader Sekarmaji Kartosuwiryo, set up a liberated area in Sundanese-speaking West Java, where it proclaimed the Indonesian Islamic State (Negara Islam Indonesia). The movement also established itself under local leadership in Aceh, the northernmost part of Sumatra, and in southern Sulawesi (Celebes), and carried out a stubborn guerrilla struggle until the early 1960s. The considerable strength of the Darul Islam rested on objections by local populations which had been mobilized by wartime and revolutionary experiences to the consolidation of power in the hands of an alien and ideologically unsympathetic ruling elite – the Javanese-dominated nationalist administration. They were, however, unable to gain the commitment of *santri* populations elsewhere or to persuade important Muslim religious leaders and politicians to proclaim for them, so that after the early 1950s the movement's struggle was essentially local and defensive.[26] Nonetheless, many Muslim spokesmen felt varying degrees of sympathy for the Darul Islam, and the modernist Masyumi Party was a strong advocate of a mediated settlement with it. This, plus the involvement of Masyumi sympathizers in the Outer Islands regional rebellion in the late 1950s, helped to make modernist Islam suspect in nationalist eyes. The Suharto regime used this sentiment in a carefully developed campaign to prevent the reappearance of the best-known Masyumi leaders in any political role and generally to reduce religion's claims to a voice in public affairs. The net result of efforts to establish an Islamic state was thus to push Islam further to the fringes of the Indonesian polity and to increase the defensiveness of the community's established leaders.

The mainstream of Indonesian Muslim political leadership was willing to settle for a good deal less than an Islamic state and accepted, on the eve of the revolution, a formula which included an acknowledgement of religion as essential to Indonesian nationhood and the requirement that all Indonesian Muslims be subject to *shari'a* law (although the extent to which the state was bound to enforce this remained vague). This principle, contained in the Jakarta Charter agreed by the major political leaders in June 1945, was abandoned only a few months later by the revolutionary government in a revision which transformed the charter into the preamble to the republic's first constitution. In the Five Principles (Panca Sila) proclaimed as the new state's ideological basis, 'Belief in the One God' was declared an essential attribute of Indonesian identity, but no specific place was ascribed to Islam or to the need for the Muslim community to follow the *shari'a*. The subsequent history of efforts to revive the constitutional recognition of Islam ended with the defeat of post-coup efforts to restore the Jakarta Charter in the People's Consultative Assembly session of 1968; the military was a leading source of opposition to it.

The battle thereafter turned to the interpretation of the religious principle of the Panca Sila, and here the New Order has gone much further than the old in asserting an interpretation that minimizes the role of Islam. The meaning of religion was broadened until, as we have seen, *kebatinan* was recognized as a distinct religious category. General Ali Murtopo, a principal ideologue and policy-maker of the Suharto regime, put forward the argument that 'belief in the One God', properly understood, did not imply any formal religious belief but rather a broad 'democratic theism'.[27]

The weakness of the modernists' position and the failure of their demands on the state result in part from their very modernity. For one thing, the challenge they present is more immediately obvious: their actions are on roughly the same wavelength as those of the political power-holders and are therefore more easily perceived by them. It was only with the NU's rather involuntary emergence as the focus of overt political opposition that the New Order leaders became alert to the challenge that traditional religious institutions might pose. The modernists' threat has also been easier for secular authorities to deal with. They lack the informal networks that make traditional Islam so elusive: modern schools, associations for education and social welfare like the Muhammadiyah, youth and student groups, and so on are much more vulnerable to state control. Modern communication methods can reach a wide audience quickly, but they can also be censored easily. Modern institutions nearly always find themselves in a close relationship with regulatory authorities; a habit of cooperation arises, and the regulators acquire a fairly intimate knowledge of what goes on inside them.

Thus the *madrasah* (*madrasa*, Islamic school), with its formal curriculum, its inclusion of secular subjects, and its acceptance of state-run examinations, is far more vulnerable to government interference than the classical *pesantren*. The *madrasah* teacher is more an intellectual specialist and less a charismatic figure than the *kiyayi*; his students can rarely be expected to commit themselves morally to him. His livelihood depends on his continued acceptability to the school's leaders, and they will be conscious of their need for recognition by the state. At the upper levels of the system, the state has itself moved into the field of religious education through developing a series of State Institutes for Islam (Institut Agama Islam Negeri, IAIN) which accept graduates of both the *madrasah* and the state school systems and are aimed at providing religious teachers with modern qualifications and attitudes as well as an opportunity for students in the religious school system to compete for bureaucratic and professional positions. Needless to say, the creation of an advanced level of religious teaching directly dependent on the state does much towards bringing the whole system under bureaucratic control.[28]

Adopting modern organizational forms means confronting the modern state on its own grounds. The problem does not apply only to the religious modernists: all parts of the *umma* have been touched by the modernization of institutions. The 1926 decision by religious tradition- alists to organize the Nahdatul Ulama was itself a modernizing step, in spite of its anti-modernist purpose. NU leaders were also among the early proponents of *madrasah* education, realizing that the classical *pesantren*, with its emphasis solely on religious learning, could not provide the literacy and mathematical skills necessary to cope with the world in which the *santri* would increasingly find themselves. The *pesantren* is typically located in the countryside and emphasizes its alienation from the everyday world; the *madrasah*, built in town, is open to the urban life which it prepares its students to enter. With the increasing penetration of urban values, commerce, and bureaucratic requirements into the countryside, the *pesantren* becomes an esoteric institution, and this in turn threatens the system of communication, mobilization, and authority which makes traditional Islam so difficult for the state to control.

One way of confronting the vulnerability of organizations is, of course, not to organize. There is in fact a significant movement within the better-educated younger generation of modernist Muslims which urges that Islam cease to segregate itself by insisting on its own social, education, and political associations. In a radical reinterpretation of modernist thought, the Gerakan Pembaharuan (Renewal Movement) led by Nurcholish Madjid had urged that the religion express itself socially not through formal institutions but through the light of individual consciences.[29] The rise during the 1970s of this movement, which represents a tiny if intellectually significant and growing part of the Muslim community, reflects not only the frustration of modernist efforts on the basis of existing institutions but also a blurring of the boundary between *santri* and secularist at the upper end of the social and educational scale. Young graduates of the religious school system find themselves trained for white-collar positions that they are unable to obtain because they are not as well qualified and connected as their counterparts from government schools; this and the pervasiveness of secular values in the contemporary urban middle class cause them to question *santri* self-segregation. At the same time young middle-class

Indonesians of non-*santri* families, offended by the gross materialism of the New Order life-style but also partaking of the individualism which Indonesia's capitalist transformation has encouraged, show an increased interest in Islam as a *pegangan* (ideological handhold) which can provide a personal sense of identity and moral direction.

The abandoning of institutional expression also offers a possibility of overcoming one of the principal drawbacks to Islam as an ideology of resistance: the fact that, as we have seen, the formal expression of identity by one part of the Muslim community may arouse hostility on the part of another. At the same time, it should be noted that the formal institutions of Islam serve a need within the community that is if anything more necessary today. The growing number of lower middle-class and working-class urban dwellers, denied the family and neighbourhood support still available in villages and in need of aid, a sense of belonging, and a moral and economic discipline to help them survive in the harsh world of Indonesia's great cities, can find this in such institutions as the modernist educational and social welfare association Muhammadiyah.[30] The upper bourgeois Muslim may find himself constrained by such organizations, but the struggling may find them the only source of hope and protection. Thus, at the same time that younger-generation members of the urban elite attempt to blur the boundaries between the *santri* and secular modernity, their poorer co-believers may look to those forms and institutions which set the pious off from others. This could easily lead to a situation where Muslim intellectuals of the Pembaharuan ilk would find themselves forced to choose between supporting a fundamentalist and intolerant popular Islam with whose political aims and prospects they had little sympathy, or making a tacit alliance with secularist modernizers with whom, when all is said and done, they have a great deal more in common.

The vulnerability of Islam's modern organizational forms to state control has been most evident in the case of political parties. The Suharto government is far stronger than was Sukarno's in terms of being able to impose its will by force, and after an initial period of consolidation it moved strongly in the direction of reducing the level of political mobilization among the population. In the process all parties have been subjected to manipulation and pressure, but the modernist Muslims have been most greatly affected. Parmusi, the Masyumi's pallid epigone, was not allowed to grant any of the major modernist political spokesmen a prominent role and was forced to accept a chairman, H.M. Mintareja, who was imposed by Suharto's personal intervention. Islam's political role was still more restricted by the 1972 'simplification' of the parties into three blocs: the government's Golkar (Golongan Karya, Functional Groups), the Muslim PPP (Partai Persatuan Pembangunan, Party for Unity and Development), and an Indonesian Democratic Party (Partai Demokrat Indonesia, PDI) consisting of former nationalist and Christian parties. The Islamic group was not allowed to refer to Islam in its title, though as a sop it was permitted to portray the Ka'ba (the sacred shrine in Mecca) on its emblem; party rights to organization and agitation were restricted, and the government's power to manipulate the choice of leaders ensured the continuing command of accommodationalists.[31]

One result of the restriction of political parties has been to turn Muslim leaders away from formal political activity. Thus the modernist Muhammadiyah reaffirmed its role as exclusively one of *dakwah* (*da'wa*, missionary activity) through non-political social welfare and educational work, and the Nahdatul Ulama rediscovered its roots in a generalized desire to further the cause of Islam. But this has not really meant depoliticization – rather removal of Muslim political activity from the vulnerable and by now pointless arena of party politics to the more salient one of broad social action. The fact that New Order leaders have proclaimed the principle of the 'floating mass', by which the populace is to be protected from political involvement, has not taken away the reasons why religious-political adherence became so important to the Indonesian masses in the first place. On the contrary, the quickened pace of economic and cultural change under the New Order has greatly increased the rate of decay of older social institutions, and the restoration of local elites and customs which the regime has promoted echoes in spirit and futility the late colonial effort to shore up *priyayi* and *adat* authority. This is of great importance, for – inspired to some extent by the Islamic revival elsewhere but largely propelled by Indonesian circumstances – a religious militancy has been developing which radically challenges the socio-economic and cultural assumptions of the established Indonesian order and appears as the spokesman for the common man against an exploiting elite.

Religion and social protest

The sources of Islam's modern role as defender of the populace go back to the nineteenth century, when Dutch cooptation of the *priyayi* elite into the native sector of its colonial administrative corps greatly increased the distance between that class and the mass of the population. *Abangan* court culture and Dutch encouragement meant that *priyayi* officials were not strongly identified with Islam, and, as people began to view the *priyayi* not as their natural chiefs but as instruments of oppressive rule, they turned to religious notables as an alternative source of leadership. This occurred most markedly in those parts of Java where Islam was deeply established; the first significant popular rising against Dutch rule, which was also a peasant rejection of *priyayi* domination, took place in the former sultanate of Banten in West Java in 1888.[32] In the Outer Islands, Dutch anti-Islamic policies and cooptation of local power-holders brought the development of strong Muslim movements against social hierarchies made grossly irrelevant by the pace of change. Kept in place only by colonial favour, these 'feudal' elites found themselves the victims of local social revolutions in the early stages of Indonesia's 1945–9 war of independence, most notably and bloodily in Aceh and North Sumatra.

In this role, Islam appears as the champion of the people and the challenger of established order, not opposed to social revolution but advocating it. Indeed, until 1923 the Communist Party developed within the Sarekat Islam, and the P K I-led anti-colonial rebellion of 1926–7 took place in two of the most fervently Muslim areas of Indonesia, Banten and West Sumatra.[33] Although growing hostility between Muslim and communist leaderships and the identification of political parties with the *santri–abangan* split meant that during the post-colonial period there has been little serious chance of a religious–communist alliance, Islam's potential for organizing popular resistance to the *status quo* remains very significant. It has not been simply the *abangan* and secularist proclivities of the Suharto regime that have caused it to react against Islam, but also its appreciation of the fact that the forces which impelled Muslim violence against the communists and Sukarno's establishment could also rally popular feeling against its own order.

The New Order represents the culmination of the struggle for power by the new urban elite whose values were reflected in the 'metropolitan superculture'. Liberated, by the defeat of the communists and by the participation of the military, from the need to make concessions to other economic and cultural segments of the population, it has given full play to its own ambitions and preferences, and the result has been a rich mixture of Western consumptionism, *abangan* mysticism, damn-the-public capitalism, technocratic elitism, and bureaucratic politics. Culturally, politically, and economically, the New Order elite is considerably more distant from the mass of the population than were its indigenous predecessors. Its alienation is enhanced by the effective abandonment of a nationalist appeal through its close association with foreign countries, particularly the United States and Japan, and by the public reliance of key leaders on the advice and economic patronage of members of Indonesia's Chinese minority, who form much of the country's independent bourgeoisie and are widely viewed, particularly by the *santri*, as economic and cultural enemies.

Very few *santri* participate in the New Order elite, and its style is totally different from that associated with pious Islam. Its materialism, cosmopolitanism, and emphasis on things modern incline its members to look on the devout as anachronistic and backward, while the otherness of the *santri*-style and the elite's uncertainty of its hold on the masses have magnified its concern at Islam's revolutionary potential. Attacks on Muslim institutions in the name of modernization have been one way of expressing the contempt and fear that has resulted. Thus far such efforts have made little headway; indeed, serious riot resulted from an attempt in 1973 to abolish the difference between Muslim and non-Muslim communities with regard to marriage and divorce through a law which sought to impose rules considered appropriate by the Westernized urban elite. Shaken, state leaders have not since attempted to challenge Islam so directly, though, given the regime's inclinations and the Muslims' long experience of retreat, the latter have good reason to fear the ultimate encroachment of secular law on their institutions.

The affair of the marriage law did much to bring together the divided forces of Islam and to convince them that the regime was fundamentally hostile to religion. This belief, together with the forced union of the Muslim parties, has probably united Indonesian Islam more than it has been in a very long time. Indeed, the historical experience of repression has not served Indonesian Islam badly. It has been remarked that colonial pressure on the religion ultimately enhanced its position by increasing its unity and popular appeal.[34] The same may be true of its present situation, the more so since there is a marked similarity between the colonial regime and the New Order, not only in their treatment of Islam but in the general relationship of a culturally and economically distant elite administering a subservient, 'backward' mass. It is interesting to note in this connection that the main impact of the Iranian revolution on Indonesian opinion appears to have lain not in its prescriptions for social order or for the role of religious leadership – concerning which Indonesian Muslim feelings are decidedly mixed – but in its demonstration that popular will united under the banner of Islam could overcome a despotism backed by military might and Western favour.[35]

So far, however, there has been little sign of a religiously oriented revolutionary movement. Such non-defensive violence as has occurred has not provided very convincing evidence of a trend in this direction.[36] We have seen that there are great difficulties in Islam becoming a general ideology of revolt: it is in important respects a minority commitment, and its leadership is deeply divided. Its strength rests on institutions that are historically obsolescent, for in spite of the rejuvenation of traditional Islam the long-term trend seems to be away from older forms and towards a general acceptance of urban-dominated modernity.

In the end the emergence of revolutionary Islam depends largely on the ability of Indonesia's ruling elite to respond to challenge. Alleviating the country's great socio-economic problems and providing the mass of the population with more reason to obey than force is one – undoubtedly very difficult – way to approach this. Far easier, and with more historical precedent, would be to divide the Muslim community and to separate off its socially more conservative elements by discarding those features of the New Order least acceptable to the *santri* and claiming, under challenge, that the regime acted in the name of religion. This may be a declining possibility, however. The cultural alienation of the ruling elite from the Muslim mass of the population and its dependence on non-Muslim foreign and domestic allies already make the credible adoption of piety a very awkward proposition. It would not be the first time an elite was trapped by its own perception of modernity into a course that destroyed its ability to rule.

Notes

1. At a meeting of reformist Muslim leaders on 1 June 1972; from the minutes as quoted in Muhammad Kamal Hassan, *Muslim Intellectual Responses to 'New Order' Modernization in Indonesia* (Kuala Lumpur, Dewan Bahasa dan Pustaka Kementerian Pelajaran Malaysia, 1980), p. 125.
2. For a succinct account of Islam's penetration and role in Indonesian society, see M. C. Ricklefs, 'Six Centuries of Islamization in Java', in Nehemia Levtzion (ed.), *Conversion to Islam* (New York and London, Holmes & Meier, 1979), pp. 100–28.
3. The variants of Javanese Islam and their social significance are described in Clifford Geertz, *The Religion of Java* (Glencoe, Ill., The Free Press, 1960).
4. For the religious aspect of the Madiun Affair, see Robert Jay, *Religion and Politics in Rural Central Java* (New Haven and London, Yale University Southeast Asia Studies, 1963), pp. 28–9, 70–6. A vivid account is also provided in Pramudya Ananta Tur's novella *Dia Jang Menjerah* (Jakarta, Pustaka Rakjat, 1950).
5. For this process, see Clifford Geertz, *The Social History of an Indonesian Town* (Cambridge, Mass., MIT Press, 1965), especially pp. 119–52; also Jay, *Religion and Politics*. For a general treatment of religion in the pre-1965 political system, see B. J. Boland, *The Struggle of Islam in Modern Indonesia* (The Hague, Martinus Nijhoff, 1971), pp. 45–105.

6. For further discussion of this, see Ruth McVey, 'The Management of Ideological Conflict in Indonesia', introduction to Soekarno, *Nationalism, Islam and Marxism* (Ithaca, Cornell Modern Indonesia Project, 1969), pp. 1–33. For the political role of Muslim leaders in the Guided Democracy period, see Howard M. Federspiel, 'Sukarno and his Muslim Apologists: Accommodation between Traditional Islam and an Ultra-nationalist Ideology', in Donald P. Little (ed.), *Essays on Islamic Civilization presented to Niyazi Berkes* (Leiden, Brill, 1976), pp. 89–102; and Federspiel, 'The Military and Islam in Sukarno's Indonesia', *Pacific Affairs*, 46 (1973), 407–20.

7. Ricklefs, 'Six Centuries', pp. 124–7; Boland, *Struggle*, pp. 231–3. See also W. F. Wertheim, 'Indonesia before and after the Untung Coup', *Pacific Affairs*, 29 (1966), 115–27; and Basuki Gunawan and O. D. van den Muizenberg, 'Verzuilingstendenties en sociale stratificatie in Indonesië', *Sociologische Gids*, 14 (1967), 145–58, for discussions of the relationship of religious differences to the 1965–6 events. As a lack of religious affiliation was taken to be a sign of communist sympathies under the New Order, it was impractical to declare no formal attachment, and this undoubtedly increased the number of proclaimed adherents of non-Islamic religions.

8. Hassan, *Muslim Intellectual Responses*, pp. 143–6. *Kebatinan* was included under the rather ironic title 'Belief in the One God' (*Kepercayaan terhadap Tuhan Yang Maha Esa*), it having been conceded to the Muslims that only monotheistic sects would be included. However, monotheism has been interpreted very broadly. For a good discussion of the religious basis of *kebatinan* groups, see Harun Hadiwijono, *Man in the Present Javanese Mysticism* (Baarn, Bosch & Keuning, 1967).

9. Hildred Geertz, 'Indonesian Cultures and Communities', in Ruth McVey (ed.), *Indonesia* (New Haven, HRAF Press, 1963), pp. 33–8.

10. For the background to the Muslim reaction, see Margo Lyon, *Bases of Conflict in Rural Java* (Berkeley, University of California Center for South and Southeast Asia Studies, 1971); Rex Mortimer, *Indonesian Communism under Sukarno* (Ithaca and London, Cornell University Press, 1974), pp. 276–328; W. F. Wertheim, 'From Aliran towards Class Struggle in the Countryside of Java', *Pacific Viewpoint*, 10 (1969), 1–17.

11. The usual Indonesian terms are no more helpful – *santri moderen* and *santri kolot*, *kolot* meaning 'old-fashioned', with the implication of backwardness. Needless to say, their use reflects the influence of secularist and modernist perceptions.

12. Ken Ward, *The 1971 Election in Indonesia: An East Java Case Study* (Clayton, Monash University Centre of Southeast Asian Studies, 1974), pp. 90–133, provides an excellent account of the role of the Muslim parties in the election and is almost the only serious political analysis of the Nahdatul Ulama. See also W. F. Wertheim, 'Islam before and after the Elections', in Oey Hong Lee (ed.), *Indonesia After the 1971 Elections* (London, Oxford University Press, 1974), pp. 88–96.

13. For a description of Dutch policy towards Islam, see Harry J. Benda, *The Crescent and the Rising Sun* (The Hague and Bandung, W. van Hoeve, 1958), pp. 9–99.

14. See Daniel S. Lev, *Islamic Courts in Indonesia* (Berkeley and London, University of California Press, 1972), pp. 8–30. This work is important not only for its treatment of the Muslim judicial system but for understanding the general socio-political role of Islam in post-colonial Indonesia.

15. See the denunciation of the 'McGill Mafia' in Nurcholish Madjid, 'Al-Qur'an, Kaum Intelektual dan Kebangkitan Kembali Islam', in Rusydi Hamka and Iqbal Ensyarip ARF Saimima (eds.), *Kebangkitan Islam dalam Pembahasan* (Jakarta, Yayasan Nurul Islam, n.d. [1980], p. 117. In addition, the government has encouraged the 'up-

grading' of staff of the state-sponsored Muslim tertiary educational institutes (IAIN) at Western academic centres by using the Netherlands–Indonesian cultural exchange to provide opportunities for their study at Dutch universities.

16. I am indebted to Daniel Lev for this point, as well as for criticisms of great value in revising the draft of this essay.

17. Umar Hasyim, *Mencari Ulama Pewaris Nabi* (Surabaya, Bina Ilmu, 1980), pp. 316–38, provides an account of earlier efforts as well as the establishment of the Majlis Ulama Islam Indonesia under the New Order. See also Hassan, *Muslim Intellectual Responses*, pp. 176–9. For the *fatwa* effort, see K. A. Steenbrink, *Pesantren, Madrasah, Sekolah* (Meppel, Krips Repro, 1974), pp. 129–31. For the evolution of the Ministry of Religion, see Deliar Noer, *Administration of Islam in Indonesia* (Ithaca, Cornell Modern Indonesia Project, 1978).

18. Steenbrink, *Pesantren*, gives an excellent description of the types of Muslim schools and their evolution. See also S. Soebardi, 'The Place of Islam,' in Elaine McKay (ed.), *Studies in Indonesian History* (Carlton, Pitman, 1976), pp. 42–53; Kenneth Orr, M. M. Billah, and Budi Lazarusli, 'Education for this Life or for the Life to Come: Observations on the Javanese Village Madrasah', *Indonesia*, no. 23 (1977), pp. 129–73; Lance Castles, 'Notes on the Islamic School at Gontor', *Indonesia*, no. 1 (1966), pp. 30–45; M. Dawam Rahardjo, 'The Kyai, the Pesantren, and the Village: A Preliminary Sketch', *Prisma* (English-language edition), 1 (1975), 32–43; Clifford Geertz, 'The Javanese Kijaji: the Changing Role of a Cultural Broker', *Comparative Studies in Society and History*, 2 (1960), 228–50; Zamakhysari Dhofier, 'Kinship and Marriage among the Javanese Kyai', *Indonesia*, no. 29 (1980), pp. 47–58; Hiroko Horikoshi, 'A Traditional Leader in a Time of Change: the Kijaji and Ulama in West Java' (Ph.D. dissertation, University of Illinois at Urbana, 1976).

19. Lev, *Islamic Courts*, pp. 215–17.

20. It is probably for this reason that younger-generation Muslim intellectuals have paid most attention to the role of the *pesantren* in present-day Indonesia, even though many more *santri* study in the *madrasah* system: as of 1978 there were 663,184 students in 3,745 *pesantren* in Java, as compared to 2,179,062 pupils in 26,465 *madrasah* and religious teacher training schools (PGA). See Zamakhsyari Dhofier, 'Tradisi Pesantren: Suatu Studi tentang Peranan Kiyai dalam Memelihara dan Mengembangkan Ideologi Islam Tradisionil', *Prisma*, 10 (1981), 84. For an example of the debate on the *pesantren*, see the essays in M. Dawam Rahardjo (ed.), *Pesantren dan Pembangunan* (Jakarta, LP3ES, 1974). For a general discussion of problems facing both types of religious school system, see Steenbrink, *Pesantren*, pp. 201–33.

21. For the background to the rise of modernism in Java, see Mitsuo Nakamura, 'The Crescent Arises over the Banyan Tree: A Study of the Muhammadijah Movement in a Central Javanese Town' (Ph.D. dissertation, Cornell University, 1976), pp. 58–105; for Sumatra, Taufik Abdullah, 'Modernization in the Minangkabau World: West Sumatra in the Early Decades of the Twentieth Century', in Claire Holt (ed.), *Culture and Politics in Indonesia* (Ithaca and London, Cornell University Press, 1972), pp. 129–45. For the development of modernist Islamic organizations, see Deliar Noer, *The Modernist Muslim Movement in Indonesia, 1900–1942* (Singapore, Oxford University Press, 1973); Howard Federspiel, 'The Muhammadijah: A Study of an Orthodox Islamic Movement', *Indonesia*, no. 10 (1970), pp. 57–80.

22. Some radically idealist Muslim modernists argued for Islamic internationalism, pointing out that to accept the independence struggle as the central political goal meant ceding ideological hegemony to the secularists; but this was always a minority position and virtually ceased to exist as a political factor after the 1930s. For a

translation and comment on the major statement of this approach, see Howard
Federspiel, 'Islam and Nationalism', *Indonesia*, no. 24 (1977), pp. 39–85.

23. Clifford Geertz, *Islam Observed* (New Haven and London, Yale University Press,
1968), pp. 103–67.

24. An excellent discussion of the problems of modernist Islam in coming to terms
with nationalism and the state may be found in Hassan, *Muslim Intellectual Responses*,
esp. pp. 44–77; see also Boland, *The Struggle of Islam*, pp. 7–84; Harry J. Benda,
'Continuity and Change in Indonesian Islam', *Asian and African Studies*, 1 (1965),
123–38; Allan A. Samson, 'Conceptions of Politics, Power, and Ideology in
Contemporary Islam', in Karl Jackson and Lucian Pye (eds.), *Political Power and
Communication in Indonesia* (Berkeley and London, University of California Press,
1978), pp. 196–226. For modernist efforts to define an Islamic state with institutions
suitable for Indonesia, see Z. A. Ahmad, *Konsepsi Negara Islam* (Bandung, Alma'-
arif, 1952), and Oemar Amin Hoesin, *Menudju Republik Islam* (Djakarta, Tintamas,
1953).

25. The major 'social revolutions' with strong Muslim involvement were in Aceh,
various Sumatran sultanates, and Banten. The Bantenese case, in many ways the
most interesting, has not yet been described. For Sumatra, see A. S. Reid, *The
Blood of the People* (Kuala Lumpur, Oxford University Press, 1980); also Henri
J. H. Alers, *Om een rode of groene merdeka* (n.p., De Pelgrim, 1956), pp. 74–93.

26. For the Darul Islam revolt in West Java, see especially Hiroko Horikoshi, 'The Dar
Ul-Islam Movement in West Java (1948–1962): An Experience in the Historical
Process', *Indonesia*, no. 20 (1975), pp. 58–86; also C. A. O. van Nieuwenhuize, 'The
Dar ul-Islam Movement in West Java', *Pacific Affairs*, 23 (1950), 169–83; Karl
D. Jackson and Johannes Moeljono, 'Participation in Rebellion: The Dar'ul Islam
in West Java', in R. William Liddle (ed.), *Political Participation in Modern Indonesia*
(New Haven, Yale University Southeast Asia Studies, 1973), pp. 1–57.

27. Ali Moertopo, *Akselerasi Modernisasi Pembangunan 25 Tahun* (Jakarta, Yayasan
Proklamasi/Centre for Strategic and International Studies, 1972), pp. 20–21.

28. Steenbrink, *Pesantren*, provides an illuminating discussion of this; see esp. pp. 156–7,
201–17.

29. Hassan, *Muslim Intellectual Responses*, is largely devoted to a discussion of
Nurcholish Madjid's ideas and includes translations of some of his most
important statements; see also B. J. Boland, 'Discussion on Islam in Indonesia
Today', in *Studies on Islam* (Amsterdam, North-Holland, 1974), pp. 37–50. For
Nurcholish Madjid's account of the origin of his movement, see his 'The Issue of
Modernization among Muslims in Indonesia: From a Participant's Point of View',
in Gloria Davis (ed.), *What is Modern Indonesian Culture?* (Athens, Ohio, University
of Ohio Southeast Asia Studies, 1979), pp. 143–55.

30. For the social and psychological dimensions of the Muhammadiyah, see James L.
Peacock, *Muslim Puritans* (Berkeley and London, University of California Press,
1978), and Mitsuo Nakamura, 'The Crescent Arises'; the latter deals (pp. 58–105)
with the role of the association in comforting a population experiencing economic
decline.

31. The screws were tightened further when, in preparation for the 1982 general
elections, the government accepted a list of candidates which placed NU spokesmen
very low on the PPP list and thus guaranteed that grouping much smaller representation than before. This humiliation added weight to the arguments of Muslims
who were urging withdrawal from formal politics on the grounds that participation
merely legitimated a regime hostile to Islam. The NU leadership being too
divided to respond strongly, victory went to the accommodationists; however, soon
afterwards Muslim prominence in pre-election riots in Jakarta demonstrated that

concessions forced upon Muslim leaders did not necessarily increase the malleability of their clientele.

32. Sartono Kartodirdjo, *The Peasants' Revolt of Banten in 1888* (The Hague, Martinus Nijhoff, 1966); and more generally his *Protest Movements in Rural Java* (Singapore, Oxford University Press, 1973), which treats rebellions in the late nineteenth and early twentieth centuries.

33. Harry J. Benda and Ruth McVey (eds.), *The Communist Uprisings of 1926–1927 in Indonesia: Key Documents* (Ithaca, Cornell Modern Indonesia Project, 1960); B. J. O. Schrieke, 'The Causes and Effects of Communism on the West Coast of Sumatra', in *Indonesian Sociological Studies*, vol. 1 (The Hague and Bandung, W. van Hoeve, 1955), pp. 85–166. For the PKI relationship with the Sarekat Islam, see Ruth McVey, *The Rise of Indonesian Communism* (Ithaca, Cornell University Press, 1965), pp. 19ff., and, for Islamic communist movements, pp. 170–7.

34. Benda, 'Continuity and Change in Indonesian Islam', p. 132.

35. Reporting on the Iranian revolution was sparse owing to the regime's clampdown on information. None the less, accounts did appear, which tended to stress the struggle against American-backed despotism; for an example see Baron Pudjiantoro, *Mengapa Pahlevi Tumbang Khomeini Menang?* (Surabaya, Pelita Bahasa, 1979/1980). For reactions to the broader Islamic revival, most of which comment on the Iranian revolution, see the essays by Muslim intellectuals collected in Rusydi Hamka, *Kebangkitan Islam*; also Umar Hasyim, *Mencari Ulama*, pp. 152–62. For a comment stressing the difficulties in applying the Iranian example to Indonesia, see Sidney R. Jones, '"It Can't Happen Here": a Post-Khomeini Look at Indonesian Islam', *Asian Survey*, 20 (1980), 311–23.

36. In 1974 the government announced the discovery of a secret Holy War Command (Komando Jihad) aimed at overthrowing the New Order. There followed the arrest of a substantial number of Muslim militants, particularly among East Java NU adherents. The Komando Jihad scare served to justify harassment of Muslim activists; the problem was declared to be 'solved' in early 1981, but shortly thereafter a spectacular airplane hijacking attempt, in which the perpetrators demanded the liberation of Muslim militants still held in prison, returned attention to Islam as a subversive force. It is hard to judge the substance of the groups involved, especially as Muslims claimed (and regime practice made credible) that they were largely the work of provocateurs.

12   Conclusion

ALBERT HOURANI

Each chapter of this book deals with an individual country where Islam is the inherited faith and culture of the majority. This arrangement reflects a decision by those who organized the conference from which the book sprang, that what is usually called 'the resurgence of Islam' is a phenomenon which varies greatly from one country to another and can best be understood within the context of individual political societies. Nevertheless some common themes have emerged, and it may be useful in conclusion to suggest what they are.

In virtually all the countries which have been discussed, there seems to have taken place during the last years something which may be called an Islamic revival. To some extent this may be an illusion: what has happened is not so much that sentiments and beliefs have changed, but that the scope of political discourse and activity has widened. Many of those who take an active part in the political process have been drawn, by way of the army or political parties, from a wider social range than before; young men and women who study in universities and enter government service or the professions also come from a larger area of society; the mass media make it possible to appeal to a wider audience. The new actors in the political process bring into it sentiments and ways of behaviour which they have always had, but which for the first time have become of political significance. There is more to it than this, however; there does seem to have taken place in the past few years some increase in the strength of religious consciousness, or at least of self-identification in religious terms.

This can partly be explained by the need (not felt only in Muslim countries) to give meaning and direction to the process of rapid and irreversible change in which we are all involved. In such a situation, men and women look for beliefs and symbols which will give them the possibility of behaving rationally, and the assurance that what they are doing, or what is being done to them, is somehow intelligible and in accordance with the nature of the universe. Some may find this assurance in a philosophy of history which holds out the hope that, in spite of appearances, the world can move forward and good can overcome evil; others fall back on inherited beliefs and loyalties which carry with them the conviction that there is some kind of eternal order which controls or judges the chances of natural life.

This may be particularly true of the inhabitants of the great swollen cities of the present-day world, and especially the capital cities of countries at a certain stage of development. For rural immigrants, seeking security, employment, or wealth in the city, cut off from the ties of kinship or neighbourliness which made life in the village bearable, victims of urban processes that they can neither understand nor control and living in a society of which the external signs are strange to them – for these, the religious community may provide the only kind of world to which they can belong. Its spokesmen use a language which is known and appeals to moral values deeply rooted in their hearts, its rituals and ceremonies are familiar, its shrines are already known to rural visitors as places where prayer has been valid: Sayyida Zaynab in Cairo, Muhyi al-Din Ibn al-'Arabi in Damascus, Mawlay Idris in Fez. If they do not find what they need in the city, they bring it with them from the country-side; if rural migrants have become city-dwellers, the cities, or at least the immigrant quarters, have been 'ruralized'.

These changes are taking place in many countries, and what is happening in one can be communicated and known in others more quickly than ever before. In spite of national and regional differences, there is some sense in which the *umma*, the community of all who accept the Qur'an as the word of God mediated through the Prophet Muhammad, is more of a reality than ever before. More than a million Muslims make the Pilgrimage every year, stand together in the plain of 'Arafa, and bring back news of it to all quarters of the world. Information and ideas travel freely and quickly and are communicated vividly by means of newspapers, television, and cassettes. It was possible for the Iranian revolution to be directed by remote control from Paris, and equally possible for images of it to spread far beyond Iran, and far beyond the Shi'i world, so that just for a moment it seemed that what was happening in Iran was really the 'revolt of Islam' which haunted the imagination of imperial Europe in the late nineteenth century. Financial aid from Sa'udi Arabia and other states of the Gulf serves not only to spread mosques, schools, and Islamic organizations wherever Muslims live (including western Europe), but also to support a certain 'fundamentalist' or 'traditionalist' view of what Islam truly is. Just as important, although less often mentioned, has been the spread of ideas – by way of books, newspapers, the cinema, and emigrants – from Egypt throughout the western part of the Muslim world, and to some extent in the eastern part as well; in a previous generation, the ideas of the periodical *al-Manar* aroused echoes as far away as south-east Asia, and in the present one the ideas and example of the Egyptian Muslim Brothers are widespread. The various Islamic international organizations based in Sa'udi Arabia are also becoming important for the spreading of information and attitudes throughout the believing world.

For these reasons and others, there has taken place in the last decade or so a change in the language of politics; a more explicitly Islamic element has come into the political discourse even of what may seem to be the most radically secularizing of regimes, those of the Ba'th in Syria and Iraq, and of South Yemen. (To some extent Indonesia appears to be an exception: Islam spread there in a society which already had its long-established ideas and symbols of authority and patterns of political behaviour, and the proportion of those who are no more than nominally Muslims is large.) Language is never a neutral medium through which to express the world, and wherever the political language of Islam is used it brings with it certain attitudes and tendencies: a heightened sense of the difference between Muslims and non-Muslims; a certain alienation from Western power, and suspicion of imported ideas; an increased respect for the great ritual observances of the faith, the annual Pilgrimage and the annual fast; a tendency to hold on to what is left of the *shari'a*, not as a rigorous system of laws but at least as a repository of moral values regarded as typically Muslim; and an emphasis on certain symbolic acts. Of these acts, the strict application of the *hudud*, the specific Islamic punishments, is not perhaps so important as it may seem: it may be doubted whether thieves have their hands cut off anywhere except in Sa'udi Arabia, where, if it occurs at all these days, it is not as a conscious reassertion of Islamic identity but as a survival of the rigorist movement which first created the kingdom in the eighteenth century. What are more important, as conscious gestures of identity and loyalty, are the wearing of traditional dress by women, the abstention from alcohol or prohibition of it, and the attempts to establish a banking system not based on the taking of interest.

For most regimes and in most countries, however, Islam does not provide the exclusive language of politics. To be effective, it needs to be combined with two other languages: that of nationalism, with its appeal to the unity, strength, and honour of the nation, however defined, and that of social justice, and specifically an equitable distribution of wealth. All kinds of combination of these three languages are possible, and all that can be said in general terms is that any government which wishes to claim legitimate authority, and any movement which wants to mobilize support in order to obtain power, will try to produce a convincing blend of all three. (Once again, there are exceptions: at one extreme, the present regime in Indonesia seems to avoid the use of religious language; at the other, a purely religious movement like the Takfīr wa'l-Hijra in Egypt takes as its aim a society ruled by the precepts of the Qur'an, and not needing to justify itself in any other terms.)

There is more than one possible view of what Islam really is and what it imposes upon believers, and therefore there can be more than one political language of Islam. It can be used both to justify an existing order and to condemn it, and in a polarized society it will be used for both purposes. It is a commonplace that in countries in process of rapid development the gap between different social groups grows wider and becomes more obvious than before. A small group of officials, land-owners, industrialists, and businessmen profit most and most immediately; at the same time, the cultural gap grows and becomes more apparent between those who have had a modern education and are able to adapt themselves to a new way of life and those who have not.

As a consequence of this, there tends to be a vast difference between the Islam to which rulers and dominant elites appeal, and the Islam of the masses, and potentially of revolution. Apart from revolutionary Iran, in all the countries considered in this book the ruling elite consists of some kind of more or less uneasy combination between two elements: on the one hand, the men of power, those who ultimately control the organized power of the government, whether by being members of long-established ruling families, or leaders of political parties, or military politicians who have seized power by means of the armed forces; on the other, the 'technocrats', that part of the educated elite which is willing to help the men of power, and without whose help modern government cannot be carried on – engineers, economists, and so on. Again with the exception of Iran, all regimes, having first acquired legitimacy by creating the state (as in Sa'udi Arabia) or leading the struggle for independence (as in Algeria), now try to claim it in new terms, those of development, of a concerted national effort, directed and led by the government, in order to create a modern society, one which is directly administered, literate, and predominantly urban and industrial. To the extent to which such a regime appeals to Islam for justification, it will

mean by it an Islam which is compatible with modern development and which can even be said to demand it. The kind of Islam which
is most fully in alignment with the interests and policy of such
governments is what may be called a modernizing puritanism: that is to
say, the version of Islam which first appeared in Egypt in the second
half of the nineteenth century, and which holds that there is an
unchanging nucleus of beliefs and moral values, embodied in the Qur'an
and the traditions of the Prophet but defensible by reason; accepts the
necessity of reinterpreting the social morality and laws derived from
these beliefs in the light of unchanging circumstances; and advocates
positive and communal effort, within the bounds of that morality, in
order to improve conditions in the world.

Such a version of Islam is particularly suited to the needs of a
'modernizing' society. Its insistence on the need to reinterpret the
social teaching of the faith makes it possible to accept and legitimate
whatever living in the modern world demands; it imposes no effective
limit on a government's freedom of action. It is compatible with a *de
facto* secularism in policy, law, constitution, and foreign relations, and so
does not disturb the vested interests which grow up around the secular
state – that is, those of administrators, lawyers, and teachers. By
placing the individual in direct submission to the will of God, it denies
the authority of those who, in former times, acted as intermediaries with
God, in particular the guardians of shrines and masters of Sufi
orders, and in so doing it prepares the way for the extension of direct
and uniform control by the government over all members of society.

There is a danger to regimes, however, in the use of this version of
religion as a legitimating agent. The danger exists even when, as in
Sa'udi Arabia, the rulers use it with what seems to be some strength
and depth of belief, and take care to carry the official spokesmen of
religion along with them; it is all the greater when Islam is little more
than a form of words. The claim to legitimacy can rebound. There is
always a tension between the principles in terms of which rulers claim
to be acting and the imperatives and temptations of power; the ruler
easily lays himself open to charges of hypocrisy and the illegitimate
use of his power. At another level, there may be contradictions between
the idea of independence which is implicit in that of an Islamic or a
national state, and the socio-economic dependence on outside powers
(whether of East or of West) which is almost inevitable in the early
stages of development; here too the government runs the risk of being
condemned in the terms it uses to justify itself. Movements of opposition
too can use the language of Islam, but since they are not involved in the

necessary compromises of power, it is likely to be a different language; either that of a revolutionary Islam which goes back to the Qur'an and interprets it in a new way, or that of a 'traditional' Islam which can act as a positive guide for the institutions of society and the state.

Movements condemning the secularism and tyranny of governments, and calling for a return to acceptance of Islam in its traditional sense as the supreme law of society, are to be found in almost all Muslim countries today: the Muslim Brothers in Egypt, the Sudan, Syria, and elsewhere, the Jama'at-i Islami in Pakistan, the Da'wa in Iraq. Their activities can certainly cause political disturbances, as is shown by the attack on the Great Mosque at Mecca in 1979, and the assassination of President Sadat in 1981. But can they provide a serious alternative to existing kinds of regime?

The consensus of opinion seems to be that 'the state will always win': in modern circumstances, whoever controls the machinery of government has such a vast power of coercion in his hands that he can always suppress opposition. This does not mean that he who has power will have it forever; although on the whole there has been stability, at least in the Arab countries, during the 1970s, most regimes have no deep root in popular sentiment and loyalties; they rest in the end on armed force and the solidarity of the men at the top, and are likely to be upset from time to time by splits within themselves – by palace revolutions or army coups. It is probable that those who come to power in this way will continue to rule within the same broad framework of 'national development' as those whom they have replaced.

Is this all that is likely to happen, however? Is there no likelihood of movements of another kind, the seizure of power by groups outside the ruling elite and committed to a radically different policy? If so, is it likely that these groups will be led and organized by men and women whose claim to rule is in some sense a religious one, and who will use power, once they have obtained it, for the creation of a social and political order which can be regarded as more authentically Islamic?

In answer to such questions, one can merely put forward a number of tentative suggestions. What matters politically in most countries is the city, and in particular the capital city, and the potentially important opposition to existing regimes will come from those elements in the city which lie outside the dominant elite, consider themselves alien to it, and believe themselves to be excluded from the main profits of power and development: those educated groups who have not been drawn into the technocratic elite; the petty bourgeoisie who do not possess the skills, education, or access to rise in the developing sectors of society; the industrial workers, particularly in countries where they have been able to organize themselves; the students; and, in some circumstances, the floating population of the migrant quarters.

Such groups can be susceptible to movements of protest and opposition which use religious words and symbols to condemn the tyranny of rulers and the imported style of life of the elite, and to depict an ideal order of Islamic justice. These movements can play a double role. First, they can impose certain limits on what a government can do and lead it to make those symbolic concessions to religious beliefs of which we have spoken; secondly, they can isolate regimes from the people they rule, so that when they are challenged not a finger will be lifted to save them. Can they do more than that, and provide the matrix for a new ruling group with fundamentally different ideas of what society should be?

There are some circumstances in which those who advocate an ideal Islamic order may be able to obtain power and use it – at least for a time – in order to impose such an order. This may happen if religious institutions are still strong: if there exist coherent and recognized groups of religious 'specialists', having some kind of solidarity among themselves and some deeply rooted claim to popular leadership, as arbiters in disputes and spokesmen for public grievances and the public conscience in the courts of authority.

The events of the past few years have shown that some of these conditions existed in one country, Iran. Certain special features of Iranian history and of the Shi'i form of Islam gave the religious specialists the opportunity to act as the only recognized spokesmen of public opinion: the long tradition of distance between men of religion and men of power, and the popular expectation that this should be so; and the system of religious endowments and voluntary alms which gave the *mullas* both a certain independence of action and popular respect when they acted justly. The dramatic collapse in 1978–9 of a whole political order, and of the forces of coercion on which it rested, left a vacuum in which they not only were able to influence the rulers, as they had done before, but themselves became rulers, and used their power to try to carry out their vision of an alternative Islamic order, conceived in broadly traditional terms. They do not seem able, however, to establish that solid alliance between power and modern technology without which a government can scarcely survive.

In some other countries, too, religious institutions have some independence of action and popular appeal. In Sa'udi Arabia, the absence until recently of strong bureaucratic control, and the dominant ideology of the Wahhabi movement, give the *qadis* a certain position of moral leadership. In Indonesia, the traditional religious schools, the *pesantren*, based on a strong link between master and pupil, can provide some kind of leadership for that minority of the population who are more than nominal Muslims. In the Sudan, a movement of religious purification oriented towards the creation of a virtuous state, the Ansar, is deeply rooted in the historical consciousness of the northern regions, and in modern times has been able to provide the framework for a mass political party. Its leading family has added to its religious prestige a considerable economic and political power, and seems able to produce a version of the ideal Islamic order which can legitimate social and political change. But its scope is limited by the existence of other Islamic movements and the fact that the southern part of the country is non-Muslim and largely autonomous.

Another kind of institution, that of the Sufi orders (*tariqas*), is likely to play a national political role only in unusual circumstances. Their main socio-political role in the past was in the uncontrolled countryside, where families connected with a shrine were able not only to act as arbiters of local disputes and links between different social groups, but also to acquire power of their own, either by alliance with secular leaders or by themselves becoming wealthy lords of the valleys. They were only able to play more than a local role in regions where cities were small and did not dominate the greater part of the countryside, and where the tradition of urban legal learning, counterbalancing that of rural sainthood, was weak: for example, in western Algeria in the time of 'Abd al-Qadir, in Cyrenaica, in eastern Turkey and northern Iraq. In such circumstances, families of Sufi origin could serve as intermediaries between government and rural areas, and could even found dynasties, as in Libya. Such a situation is not likely to recur. In Morocco, for example, the independent state inherited from the French protectorate a direct control over the contryside which it had not previously enjoyed, and political parties took over the role of leadership and mediation during the period of struggle against France. In Algeria too the position of families of Sufi origin was largely destroyed by the French after the revolt of 1871, the war of independence created new forms of leadership and organization, and the process of development since independence has made the countryside more dependent upon the growing cities. Similarly in Turkey, the extension of the power of government into the eastern provinces makes it unlikely that movements of opposition will ever again take the form of movements led by Sufi *shaykhs*; there is a high degree of participation in national political processes, and political parties committed to a great degree of secularization have become the brokers between local needs and central government. Only in Senegal does the socio-economic power of the Sufi leaders seem to have survived. During the period of imperial rule, the French used them in order to control the countryside, and in a situation of weak bureaucratic control and limited spread of new forms of political consciousness and organization, they have so far succeeded in preserving their influence with the government and their power not only in the countryside but over the rural migrants to the capital.

It does not seem likely that similar events will occur in most of the countries where the position of the Sunni *'ulama* was formerly strong, and which were parts of the Ottoman, French, or British Empires: the tradition of the Sunni *'ulama* was one of acceptance of power, or at least of a rather ambivalent acquiescence in it, and the tradition of the empires was one of a strong executive power exercised directly and bureaucratically. In such countries, where effective leadership by religious specialists does not exist, the movements of return to 'traditional' Islam must find their leadership elsewhere, among politicians of a modern kind using new methods of organization and publicity, and such movements seem more likely to cause disturbances than to be able to seize and use the power of the state. They suffer in general from two deficiencies. First, it is easy to speak of a just Islamic economic and social order, but difficult in practice to spell out what it means; a blueprint for such an order may have less appeal to the weak and disinherited than those socialist programmes which contain precise suggestions about the control of the means of production, the incidence of taxation, and the redistribution of wealth. Second, in countries where firm control by the government or the official party makes it difficult for those standing outside them to organize open parties as a means of achieving power, they almost inevitably resort to the methods of clandestine organization and urban violence, and such methods are likely to arouse a hostile reaction among those who have something to lose or who prefer any kind of order to anarchy.

In most circumstances, then, the effective movements for the overthrow of a regime are likely to be those whose ideologies combine some kind of modernist Islam which does not hinder development (based perhaps on a claim to reinterpret the Qur'an in a radical way) with a programme of social equality. Such movements can bring together alienated sections of the educated class (including army officers) and popular urban forces, in particular the growing number of industrial workers.

Index